Mark My Words!

Mark Goulden

W. H. ALLEN · LONDON
A Howard & Wyndham Company
1978

*Printed and bound in Great Britain by
The Garden City Press Limited
Letchworth, Hertfordshire SG6 1JS
for the Publishers, W. H. Allen & Co. Ltd,
44 Hill Street, London W1X 8LB*

ISBN 0 491 02144 5

Contents

List of Illustrations

The endpapers show a random selection from the hundreds of books acquired personally by the author and include some early examples of pioneer mass-market paperbacks.

Between pages 144 and 145

1

Introductory Interlude

All of life is a series of interludes. Some are protracted; some brief; some trivial; some vital and by turn they can be happy, sad, tragic, heartwarming and heartrending, disappointing, ecstatic or overwhelming and only in retrospect can it be seen how a definite pattern emerges. I believe that in each case the design is actually preordained—which has nothing to do with so-called fatalism. The sequence of events accurately reflects the person concerned—the shape is as individual as a fingerprint. Show me your life-graph and I will tell you what you are!

If, indeed, the ups and downs of life could be recorded diagrammatically, it would look something like the cardiogram of a mouse about to be consumed by a cat! The peaks and highlights of an active lifetime become vividly apparent when you call back yesterday for the purpose, say, of preparing notes for an autobiography, a task on which I have been engaged during the past year or so.

It is a chastening and rather deflationary exercise because if you possess even a modicum of discrimination, a touch of humility and the desire to be truthful, you begin to realise, with a jarring shock of recognition, how very little of what you have achieved is of any real consequence or deep significance in the stupendous panorama of humanity.

To you, personally, much of it may well have been of immense importance, sometimes pregnant with destiny—your destiny, of course! But to imagine that the written record of all this will necessarily interest, advantage or benefit some potential future reader is possibly to harbour a vainglorious delusion. Regrettably, the stream of literature—particularly contemporary literature—overflows with the outpourings of people harbouring just such delusions and, (heaven forgive me) as a publisher, I plead guilty (without mitigating

1

circumstances) to having, during the past fifty years, helped to swell the Niagara of biographical material (mostly rubbish) that has been foisted upon a complacent and largely undiscerning public. (Cue here for smart-alec critic: 'He's still doing it!')

Although by definition a straight biography or autobiography is regarded by most publishers as a 'one off'—and thereby inherently transient—it is nevertheless true that books of this kind can prove successful commercially, especially if the subject is immensely famous. It is a defensible assumption that forty per cent of all books published today come within this category and if you take into account that a great deal of fiction is vicariously autobiographical, then the percentage increases dramatically.

In earlier times, beginning with the Renaissance, biography—and its sibling the Memoir—produced some of the world's best literature. It was in the truest sense belles-lettres and it enriched language and intellect alike. Then, by a kind of Gresham's Law, the currency of fine biographical writing became debased by the intrusion and proliferation of what has become known as 'popular autobiography'. Everybody began writing their 'life-stories' and reminiscences and although it is a far cry from the self-narrations of St Augustine, Benvenuto Cellini, Saint Simon, Jean Jacques Rousseau and John Bunyan to the 'confessions' of Loretta the Manhattan hooker or the sexual gymnastics of Daisy Bedworthy the Hollywood *femme fatale*, they all qualify for inclusion in the genre of biography, mainly for the reason that there is no book-trade category by which the classic can be differentiated from the crap.

And if biography has dominated the publishing scene so intensely in present times, the category itself has in turn been dominated just as intensely by a specific type of publication flourishing under the generic title of show business books.

The spectacular début of books by or about notables of stage, cinema, television, radio, opera, ballet, music or the entertainment world in general, is without parallel in the annals of publishing the world over.

I am tempted later on to elaborate a little on this subject because it is, I believe, generally conceded that I was the pioneer in developing this particular kind of biographical literature and in the 'Show

2

Business Interlude' I tell, for the first time, the genesis of this quite remarkable evolution in publishing.

Mention of the word interlude leads me back to the theme of this introduction. Since I maintain that life is a series of interludes, I have chosen to structure this present book in similar fashion by presenting it as a sequence of interludes rather than as the usual parade of chronological chapters. This has called for a lapidary effort as well as some ruthless cutting—I have been constrained to take my own medicine.

My author and old friend Edmund Wilson refused to allow even a comma to be altered in anything he wrote. He also specified the actual format and type areas of his books. Perhaps this was a privilege which only the greatest living critic of his day—a writer with an enviable audibility—could command. It is axiomatic in the publishing craft that any book is improved by cutting and that, I may say, also goes for films, speeches, concertos, plays and pronouncements of all kinds. Brevity is the soul of readability.

What I have been at pains to do in these memoirs is to eradicate all guff and padding simply by excluding that which would be of interest to me *alone*. For the life of me I can't see why any reader should care a damn about how I began my career in journalism at the lowest level as a copy-boy or show any enthusiasm for details of the acropetal process whereby I rose to become the youngest editor in the British Empire and ultimately the second highest paid editor in Fleet Street. My personal experiences as a publisher—in Britain and America—abound in minutiae, trivia and insignificant detail which you will find pads out ninety per cent of all biographical material. You won't find it here. I have extirpated all triviality except where it is germane to the narrative or makes for readability.

The function of autobiography is not merely an exercise in narcissism. In the show business book and such-like the reader expects to be entertained by gossipy chit-chat and to be titillated by spicy peeps behind the tinsel curtain but I believe that the aim of a seriously-intended personal narrative should, above all else, be a distillation of the writer's own wisdom, judgements, opinions and philosophy garnered from wide and exceptional experiences in his

3

particular milieu. If he can pass on to the reader some sound advice, some cogent deductions from such experiences; if he can offer some controversial views for the reader's assent or dissent; if he has some formulae for success, or for making assessments, then, provided he keeps the telling lively and undidactic, he may contribute something worth while to the sum of human endeavour.

For myself, I am not intrigued by what goes on in Cabinet meetings or who Cecil King had to lunch. I can ignore Evelyn Waugh's sousings, his chasing of boys and his anti-semitism but I like to read his opinions about contemporaries, particularly the flotsam who floated through the portals of Rosa Lewis's Cavendish Hotel in Jermyn Street, where, as a young man, I used to live. It was this rendezvous that provided Waugh with material for his *Vile Bodies*.

I leave to the evaluative critics to discuss literary merit and to dish out that high-minded pabulum about the 'movements' in literature which they write mainly for each other's edification! My concern in this book is chiefly with the practice and ethos of publishing.

Having known Waugh personally I can put him under my own microscope and assess his personality—not his literary ability—in the only way that matters for me, and having done so, I conclude he was an unlikeable character, which was a pity because he was a gifted novelist. I have assessed and judged persons all my working life and I can state as a demonstrable fact, that I am a perceptive delineator of character, whose judgements have seldom gone wildly astray, even on first appearances, which can be notoriously unreliable.

With me it is a combination of intuition, psychic power (common to many Pisceans) and an extra-sensory perception of which I was aware long before the first book on ESP was ever written. Nobody fools me in an eyeball to eyeball confrontation and I can usually pre-determine the ultimate outcome half-way through any formal discussion, negotiation, interview or board meeting. I possess an uncanny facility for knowing when someone is lying to me. I cite a concrete example of this in the chapter, Radio Interlude.

I can spot a 'goniff' or a con-man a mile away—and in my time I have spotted a great many!

You will find in this Memoir—I am reluctant to call it an auto-biography—recurrent themes on such imponderables as moral

4

courage, integrity, gratitude, generosity, justice and what used to be known as principles. I once set much store by these qualities and in my early manhood they were my guidelines. But now, at the end of a vast and varied experience of life and people, I am prepared to say that if you try to keep up a standard of civilised living or to maintain principles in these times the dice are loaded heavily against you. Indeed, I regret to confess that, over the years, I have witnessed the steady erosion of most human decencies, the qualities of moral courage and the last vestiges of honest dealing. I have seen the triumph of wickedness, the denial of justice and the victory of villainy. I have often wondered in these maleficent times, how is it possible for an individual to try to behave well; to be a worthwhile human being, to play the game (in the best sense of the cliché) when all around him—domestically, politically, locally, nationally and internationally—he finds massive examples of cupidity, intolerance, bribery, cheating, treachery, duplicity, corruption, injustice, obsequious arse-licking and naked, unashamed dishonesty. What has become of the dignity of man? From whence can the upright ambitious young man these days derive inspiration, strength and encouragement to make his way in life without sacrificing his manhood or his rectitude?

From the moment I first set foot in a newspaper office, as copyboy, I knew that 'writing' was to be my career. I had a truly enquiring mind and I became a voracious consumer of the printed word in all its multitudinous forms, even the family Bible which I went through verbatim as part of my practice as a shorthand writer —a minor newspaper skill that I have sustained all my life.

As one's literary tastes develop, it is inevitable that one begins to favour a particular cult, or genre or a period and I well recall how, as a young man 'reading English', I quickly found an affinity with Jewish authors and poets. I literally devoured the works of Zangwill, Peretz, Bagelson, David Pinski, Sholem Asch, Bialik, M. M. Sephorim, Sholem Aleichem, Shenour and even the lesser known writers who were active in Russia, Poland and America at the time of the flowering of Yiddish literature.

I adored the simple schmaltzy tales of life in the pogrom-ridden Pale and the 'gemutlich' legends of joy and sorrow in the nostalgic lower East sides of New York and London and of the 'shtetl'.

5

Something within me responded to the heart-searing mixture of devout piety and brutal hardships; to the pervasive aura of Sabbath candles, grinding poverty, divine patience in the face of oppression; even down to the sad melodies of Jewish cantors which echo that unmistakable 'sob of Israel' ever-present in the songs, the poems, the music and the voices of Jewish people all over the world.

The pathetic submissiveness of a 'Bontsie the Silent' and the despairing resignation of a 'Teveye' would bring tears to my eyes. How unfair, how unjust that such harmless, kindly, undemanding people should be marked out for life-long penury, deprivation and unending toil, awhile they clung desperately to Messianic hope.

At that time, of course, I had dipped only one big toe into the murky waters of commercial life but it wasn't long before I learned to swim. And it was then that I began to take a different view of some of these non-heroes of my youthful reading. Gradually it infiltrated to me that the martyrolatry of these underprivileged people was not at all a heroic stance. I came to regard it as a form of cowardly evasion. It was ignoble and I felt contempt not only for the characters but also for the authors who created them. What these writers were doing was to romanticise the miasma of Ghettoism which I now recognised as a noxious disease that ought to be rooted out of Jewish life and philosophy.

In 1978 I still think so!

We praise the statesmanship and 'vision' of rulers who have waded through rivers of blood to reach their thrones. We abase ourselves before the power of money, influence and rank and when it comes to self-interest and the sheer struggle for survival our morals, principles and loyalties fly out of the window! Not even the discipline of religion can any longer impose restraints powerful enough to prevent racial strife, fratricide, organised brutality, massacre on the grand scale, torturings, terrorism, burnings and devastation. For years the world has watched brother killing brother in Northern Ireland until the slayings and the maimings have become commonplace and routine happenings, mere statistics on a 'score-sheet'! In cold blood, Catholic murders Protestant and vice versa, but neither the Pope in his Vatican nor the Archbishop in his Palace dares to threaten their blood-lusting flocks with excommunication if they don't stop the butchery! The pagan Romans may have crucified Christ but the enlightened Christians have crucified Christianity.

If the Princes of the Church are moral cowards, how can they command or deserve the respect of their congregants?

I never found any problem in making money, either for myself or for other people. Parenthetically I may mention I am the only publisher alive who actually sold his own business three times! Without deliberately seeking any such 'distinction' I have known (some intimately) many millionaires, including Isidore Ostrer, Paul Getty, Nate Cummings, Gulbenkian, Michael Sobell, Simon Marks, Irving Mansfield, Armand Hammer, Joseph Rank, John Ellerman, Armand Erpf, Ira Guilden and quite a few others who I believed were worth millions, although I couldn't prove it.

Fitzgerald is alleged to be the originator of the witticism: 'Of course the rich are different from us; they have more money!' Up to a point, that sarcasm may be true but it would be truer to say they are different simply because they have more 'power'. The gaggle of millionaires I have personally known were all endowed with most of the virtues and vices of ordinary mortals; there was little to distinguish them from the commonality except that unmistakable air of slightly patronising aloofness and evasive arrogance that only the possession of wealth (real or imaginary) manages to induce. When a man is rich or becomes rich, he acquires a mien that is uniquely the prerogative of the 'man of property'. He retains it even when he is down to his very last corniche or yacht, and if one day his fortunes should crash, the 'aura' of wealth still doesn't completely desert him. Lie down with gold and you must come up gilded!

The possession of wealth and the worship of mammon are, of course, two entirely different things. Much as I admire and like the Americans—with whom I have lived and worked for years—much as I revere American achievement and, in general, the American way of life, I am bound to record as part of my empirical experiences that worship of money (and its concomitant, material success) is the besetting sin of most Americans between the ages of nine and ninety.

Once upon a time I used to think that any American—like any

Frenchman—would sell his grandmother for money, but since Watergate and Lockheed, etc, I realise that this may be an underestimate. Let me hasten to add, for the sake of international good relations, that when it comes to hospitality and personal generosity the American (male and female) has few equals. But in business matters, commercial transactions—indeed in any activity where the cash-nexus is paramount—your generous American tends suddenly to metamorphose into a 'horse-trader' of implacable obduracy, unwilling to compromise, prepared to sacrifice long-standing friendships and associations rather than cut his dollar margin. In many a negotiation of this kind over the years I have seen friendship wither and die on the altar of money or moneysworth.

Some years ago I dined at the New York home of my friend Ilya Lopert, a big man in the film industry. He was obviously agitated about something and frequently left the table to make telephone calls, from which he returned even more disturbed than before. Pacing up and down his dining room, unable to contain himself, he finally told me the cause of his perturbation. For the past few hours his lawyer had been locked in battle with some property tycoons over the selling of a New York cinema. Ilya badly wanted this location and apparently he had a pretty strong case for getting it, seeing that the real estate men concerned were ostensibly his friends. But there was a rival bidder with a larger purse in the field, so the knives were out! Suddenly the telephone rang and, snatching the receiver, Ilya, the colour drained from his face, listened to his lawyer obviously telling him he had lost the deal. 'The dirty bastards' was all he could utter and he repeated the imprecation ever more vehemently. He was exhausted and depleted as any man might be after seeing half a million bucks slip through his trembling fingers. I tried to placate him by suggesting that he must have some legal redress. 'Can't you sue them?' I queried. A sardonic smile crept over his deeply-lined face. 'Nah,' he exclaimed, 'You don't sue such bastards. I'd have done exactly the same if I had been in their shoes!'

That little situation-comedy seemed to epitomise for me the entire American commercial ethos.

And if the cult of toughness has become the dogma of American business, let me add that it is by no means exclusive to the males of the species. The nation's business women have not lagged behind: with typical female abreaction the liberated woman has shed her feminine graces and in many cases the pupil is now tougher than the teacher. Heaven protect me from those Charles Addams' harpies who control so large a portion of the American literary scene, especially 'book rights'. I have known the worst of them and you couldn't find a more rapacious bunch of sexless, po-faced amazons in all the souks of Smyrna or the bazaars of Beirut. When they have a 'big property' to offer they will squeeze the potential buyer until the pips burst, and if they can create a bidding situation by what is now called 'simultaneous submissions' you can bet that only the sky is the limit. Hell hath no fury like a woman 'dealer' bidding up the ante.

God knows that commercial integrity in Britain doesn't always come up smelling of roses but I don't think it has the soulless crudity of American big business methods nor do I think we have created in Britain a breed of depersonalised valkyries like those who are now in the top ranks of American corporate life.

So with this slightly astringent interlude for openers I will proceed to set down some of the noteworthy episodes of my career—a collection of remembered moments that illuminate a whole life.

2

Interlude With Wings

Had the phrase been invented in the heyday of my journalistic career, I might no doubt have qualified as a 'whiz kid'. I was a prolific writer for the various trade journals of the newspaper industry; much in demand as a speaker at press gatherings; and very closely associated with advertising (I was official British delegate to the Philadelphia Advertising Convention in 1935). I also had a reputation as a typographer and lay-out man.

My watch was always set one hour ahead, and as a result I can claim a fair number of firsts. Newspapermen have always attached importance to being first, which is probably a throw-back to the times when the aim was to be first with the news. That was long before the high-speed telegraph, radio and television. The public then had to depend entirely on the newspaper for its hard news and in my earliest days a special edition was run off for every important event, every big race result and all major disasters. By means of the fudge-box or stop press column, a paper could be on the street with the result, say, of the Derby within minutes of the winner passing the post. A smart journalist could often pull off a scoop, but nowadays the chances of being 'first' with anything, or even exclusive, are getting more and more remote. So highly geared are the means of communication now that the media seem to get the news almost before it happens!

But I suppose every journalist can take pride in some scoop or other with which he made history for his paper. I recollect only one instance that deserves mention here, and purely on the grounds that my paper had it all to themselves—in other words the perfect scoop.

It was about the close of a hot summer's day (24 August 1921) when, as late-duty sub, I gave the word to the chief machine-minder that the last edition need not be held up. It was my job to watch the incoming news telegrams ('flimsies' they were then called) for anything important that might justify a stop press paragraph in the Final Edition. A lino-operator stood by to insert the lines in the 'fudge-box' if a last-minute item did turn up, but normally at five-thirty p.m. the day was over and very quickly the office would be deserted.

As I left the building on the day we are recalling, I saw that all heads were turned skywards. People were watching the graceful flight of the giant airship R38, as it passed over the City of Hull. Suddenly, the huge dirigible began to shudder and then to my amazement and horror, I saw it virtually break in half, bodies being hurled from the enormous gap in the fuselage.

Within seconds I rushed back into the office, shouted to the machine-room foreman to hold the last edition, and then I grabbed the stand-by lino-operator. Pushing him into his chair in front of the keyboard, I yelled: 'Set this. R38 passing over Hull this evening broke in two and crashed into the River Humber. Many casualties feared. See later editions'.

Three lines of sheer drama.

The operator was astounded, but he tapped out the lines, fixed them in the fudge-box and sent it down the chute straight to the printing press platform. And no sooner was it locked into position than the press roared into action. The newsvendors crowded around and, virtually grabbing the papers as they came off the folder, they rushed into the streets with news of the disaster—literally within minutes of it happening. The staff of the opposition paper had all gone home, so we had the field absolutely to ourselves.

Fortunately, we had a morning paper (the *Eastern Morning News*) and the staff of this journal—complete with reporters, photographers and process engravers—began to arrive as I telephoned the Managing Editor (who lived out of town) to get his permission to use the morning paper's personnel to bring out a special edition of the *Evening News*.

'You are in complete charge,' he ordered. 'Go right ahead.' Within three hours we had plated up an 'extra' edition, complete with a full story of the tragedy and a whole page of graphic pictures. We printed continuously far into the night until we physically ran

11

out of newsprint. Copies of the paper were despatched to London on the night mail train.

It was by any standard a classic scoop and my initiative was promptly rewarded; I was elevated from the newsdesk to chief sub-editor and my salary increased from five pounds a week to ten!

A few years later, when I was installed in the editorial chair, I became involved in another air epic, but a much happier one this time.

Hull had proudly boasted for many years that it was the Third Port of Britain because of its huge shipping trade, but times were changing and it occurred to me that Hull ought to be thinking about becoming a leading airport as well as a seaport. Croydon was the National airport but no similar facility existed in the provinces. It would be my task to convince the Hull Corporation that the City's future was in the 'air' as well as on the high seas. I had learned to fly and I had already organised a flying club with a handsome donation that I squeezed out of Joseph Rank, the rich flour-miller and father of the film Ranks. We leased a disused racecourse as our aerodrome and we had a substantial membership.

As editor of the local newspaper, I was of course *persona grata* with most members of the City Council, and particularly with the Lord Mayor (Councillor Benno Pearlman), a true progressive who was one of my closest friends. He, like so many people in those days, had never been off the ground and at first he thought flying was simply a sport for young men addicted to fast cars and frivolous girls. He was only partly right!

After we had got him into the air and given him a bird's eye view of his civic domain, he changed his tune and proceeded to back me to the hilt in advocating the airport scheme. The outcome was that the Corporation bought the racecourse aerodrome and Hull thus became the first municipal airport, even though it possessed no air traffic facilities other than a good runway, a well-constructed tarmac, some useful hangars and an attractive clubhouse.

I was Honorary Secretary of the venture and to celebrate the take-over, we planned a grand opening ceremony by HRH Prince Albert (later King George VI), and an air pageant such as had never been seen before outside of London. There would be a display by the famous 29 Squadron of the RAF and exhibitions of all known forms of aerobatics, most of which few people had ever seen. We had the full RAF band under its conductor Flt. Lt. John Amers. It was an exciting day and a landmark in the civic history of Hull.

During the morning I got a call from a girl named Amy Johnson (then almost unknown) who said she planned to fly up to her native Hull to be present at the pageant. I closed the air to all traffic after lunch in order to give Amy clearance—but she didn't appear.

Then, shortly before the show was due to begin with a fly-past of aircraft, a spot appeared on the horizon which soon blossomed into the outline of Amy's hired Moth, which she then proceeded to put down on the flying ground in a series of bounces that had us all squirming on our toes. She emerged wreathed in smiles and I greeted her along with her parents and sisters.

Amy confided to me that she was secretly planning a solo flight to Australia (she had not then qualified as a ground engineer nor did she possess a 'B' licence). Up to that time her longest flight was the journey from Hendon to Hull.

She asked if I could get her an introduction to the Air Minister (Lord Thomson), Sir Charles Wakefield (an oil magnate who might subsidise such a venture) and also to Sir Sefton Brancker (Minister of Civil Aviation), all of whom were to be present at the air pageant and later at the civic banquet in Guildhall.

After Amy's kangaroo landing earlier in the day, her chances of convincing anyone that she could fly solo to Australia didn't seem too promising, but believe it or not I introduced her to the people she wished to meet. They were only mildly interested, but we had broken the ice. In the ensuing months, Amy's projected solo flight to Australia (previous record-holder Bert Hinkler) became an obsession and she proceeded to get her engineer's licence and the navigational 'B'. Then she renewed contact with Brancker and later on to Wakefield and the *Daily Mail*. Wakefield agreed to finance the venture. Finally her father bought her an aeroplane for £600 to take her on the historic flight. The Moth was to be named Jason after the brand name of her father's famous kippers! She was all set to go and she plotted her own route, surprising all the experts by planning her first stop at Vienna (seven and a half hours) and then on to Constantinople.

She took off on her historic journey at seven forty-five a.m. on 5 May 1930.

Her flight was far more hazardous than any of the reports ever indicated. She told me that, crossing the Timor Sea, her altimeter went dis and she was at times only a few feet above the waves. At one departure point, some flying personnel tried physically to prevent her taking off because the weather reports indicated she could never survive in her frail craft. But she eluded her restrainers and, aided by her primitive maps, she got to her destination, not however without mishap.

I think she was one of the bravest women I ever met.

One night she telephoned our aerodrome to say she had crash-landed her plane on a mud flat in the Humber estuary and could we send out a rescue party? We soon found her and later she told me that she had completely lost her bearings over the water, and she was almost out of gas. 'I kicked off my flying boots,' she said, 'and I prepared to ditch as near to the coastline as I could. Suddenly I saw the mudbank and I landed on it.' It was all said in a matter-of-fact manner which gave no hint of alarm or sense of peril. But had she ditched 'near the coastline', she would certainly have perished almost without trace. And that, unhappily, was Amy's ultimate fate. Ferrying aircraft during the war, she failed to return from a mission and no clue as to her fate was ever found.

A strange family, these Johnsons. Her sister, a very beautiful and talented girl, was my secretary.

She had a real flair for writing and she could have become a first-rate woman journalist—they were rare in those days—and found an interesting and profitable career. But her life was cut short. One Saturday afternoon she left the office as usual, apparently went straight home and put her head in the gas oven. She was dead when neighbours broke in because of the leaking gas fumes. I attended the inquest and a verdict of suicide was returned. But there wasn't a clue as to why she had so tragically ended her life; the mystery was never solved.

The rest of Amy Johnson's story is now part of British aviation history.

The attempt to make Hull the first provincial airport fizzled out rather ignominiously.

The train journey from Hull to King's Cross in those days took about four and a half hours and to show that flying could annihilate time and distance, I decided to put on a striking public demonstration. A train and an aeroplane would leave simultaneously from Hull, bound for London, and the country and the city would thus be able to judge for itself how the speed of air travel eclipsed the fastest train time!

I and one of the Club's instructors were at the controls of the challenging aircraft and 'flying by Baedeker'—that is following the Great North Road from Yorkshire to London—we would zero in on the gas container at Hanworth and glide into the nearby aerodrome, usually under three hours and well ahead of the express train.

We had no navigational aids, weather reports or ground control, and we took off slap bang into a sixty-mile-an-hour head-wind. Our cruising speed being about ninety mph, we were almost stationary in mid-air! About half-way on the trip our petrol gauge was flashing ominously and, as we were nearing the Wittering RAF depot, we decided to go down and refuel. As we taxied towards the hangars, the car of the commanding officer rushed to intercept us. 'Get that bloody crate off my aerodrome at once,' roared the OC. 'Don't you know this is an RAF station?'

Full of apologies, I explained to the irate officer (one Douglas-Hamilton) that, in the interests of civil aviation, we were competing in a time race from Hull to London against a passenger train and we were already an hour overdue because of the head-wind. He burst into laughter. 'You couldn't beat a steam-roller with that awful kite,' he jeered. But he nevertheless filled us up, gave us a quick beer and we rumbled into the sky again to resume what was now a hopeless task. We eventually arrived at our destination exactly one and three-quarter hours after the train had reached King's Cross, and so, parking our slow-motion flying machine, we silently crept away.

England was not yet ready for internal air traffic! But it was bound to come and, in due course, it did. But Manchester stole our thunder and became Britain's first provincial airport.

3

Interlude on Gratitude

In or about the year 1929—as the affidavits say—I found myself managing editor of three newspapers, the *Eastern Morning News,* the *Hull Evening News* and the *Hull Weekly News.*

It was an important provincial group owned by the Wilson family—a famous shipping company (later the Ellerman Wilson Line), the founder of which was of course involved in the notorious scandal which took place at Tranby Croft, the Yorkshire home of the Wilsons (later Nunburnholmes).

The newspapers were liberal in politics and indeed Hull, as the Third Port of England, owed its prosperity to the Liberal tradition and the doctrine of Free Trade. It returned two Liberal members to Parliament.

It is well recorded in the annals of the British provincial press that the *Eastern Morning News* group was a famous nursery for rearing young journalists and not least among the great editors who emerged from this stable were J. L. Garvin, whose political polemics in the *Observer* profoundly affected the nation's affairs. Sir Robert Donald was also associated with the Hull group and both J. A. Spender and Sir W. Linton Andrews in turn edited the *Eastern Morning News.*

At one time I was able to enumerate scores of pressmen who, after serving under me, had subsequently made good on various national newspapers. Some are still alive, like Simon Kline, who worked for me and in due course became one of the best art-editors in Fleet Street. One man to whom I gave a start in journalism is well known in political circles today as Lord Peddie. Another is Lord Lyons of Brighton.

Because of my own early and unaided struggles to progress in journalism, I always had a soft spot in my heart for young people anxious to 'get on' and I never refused a request for help.

Which brings me to the tricky topic of gratitude—the keynote of this interlude. I can say with complete honesty that I never looked for thanks or gratitude when I gave a 'leg-up' to some aspiring and ambitious young journalist.

In my early days, journalism was a peripatetic profession. It was normal practice to gather experience in a variety of newspaper offices and consequently it was easy for an editor to recommend a promising youngster to fellow editors, especially in the provinces. The fact that a man had held posts on several local newspapers didn't mean he was incapable of holding down a steady job; on the contrary, it was indeed an asset since such a man's broader experience was always considered useful by an editor.

A provincial newspaper editor is a big fish in a small pond and during my editorship in Yorkshire, I was 'in' with what used to be called the exclusive 'county people', in whose lovely homes I spent many a happy visit. I throw in this snob-line merely to give me a cue to contrast the style of living in those days with what it is at the present time. These people lived graciously. Their country mansions were beautiful and beautifully maintained. A dinner invitation automatically meant black tie and the meal was usually served with elegance and culinary perfection, and a total absence of ostentation.

They lived well and among other useful aids to civilised living which I picked up from my association with these cultivated people was an appreciation of wine—something that has stood me in good stead over the years. At least I know the multitude of gradations between a 'plonk' and a Romanée Conti, which a lot of people think they do—but don't. Of course the county folk had servants—some had retinues—but the idea that these domestic retainers were a species of 'below stairs' menials is merely the clap-trap of our present day disgruntled Socialist tub-thumpers who are concerned only with 'levelling down' the community to a uniform crass mediocrity. The cult of the 'common man' knows nothing of grace, refinement, manners or style. The conforming masses today are fobbed off with labels like 'Marxist' or 'Trotskyist' to disguise the fact that they are sheep in sheep's clothing.

Domestic staff in stately homes knew the dignity of service—we all serve somebody—and they were very definitely part of the household from the butler to the under-gardener. The relationship between the two sides was always friendly, respectful (to each other) and based solidly on that element which is so sadly lacking in the world today—good manners.

I wasn't born into that milieu but I am thankful to the destiny which gave me an introduction to it. It was one of the most rewarding interludes in my whole life.

One day, the chairman of my newspaper group—a distinguished soldier and landed gentleman—asked me to dine with him at the Bath Club in London. I used to go up to London every week. I possessed a first-class 'pass' on the old London and North Eastern Line by which I could make unlimited journeys. At dinner, my chairman, Col. James Walker, DSO, introduced me to a very presentable young man who he suggested might be a useful asset to the advertising staff of our papers. His credentials were excellent and I recognised at once that this was much more a prospective son-in-law for the gallant colonel than a possible acquisition to the strength of our advertising department! Nevertheless George had charm and style and a pleasing personality, but it soon became clear after he joined us that his apprenticeship as an ad-man was going to be long and arduous.

But fate intervened as, in my reckoning, it always does. Out of the 'light blue' (actually it was a letter from the Cambridge University Appointments Board) George got an invitation to apply for a rather attractive job with an advertising and promotion organisation—the Gas Users Association (I think it was called), and after returning from the initial interview, George asked if he could see me very urgently.

'I can get this job,' he confided to me, 'only if you are prepared to give me the right kind of reference. I know I haven't been here long and I'm not much damned good,' he added disarmingly, 'but I would dearly like to get this post and I know it's mine if you will support me. I promise I won't let you down if you will do this for me.'

At the time I was a very young editor (twenty-seven to be exact) and still guided by my youthful 'principles', ideals and values. This was a problem that called for a judgement of Solomon. But what influenced me most was George's promise 'not to let me down'. I liked that. So rather against my better judgement, I wrote a letter to his prospective employers which left no doubt that the applicant was a cross between Lord Northcliffe and Sir Charles Higham. He got the job.

Some time later the advertising 'account' of this Gas Association was passed over to the leading advertising agency, the London Press Exchange, and George went with it. He must have impressed his new employers because within no time at all they appointed him 'space buyer' for all provincial papers—a most powerful position which virtually gave him control of huge advertising appropriations to papers outside of London. When I heard about this, I sent our London advertisement manager—the well-known Matt Blythe—hot foot to the LPE to convey my congratulations personally to George on his big appointment. This of course gave Matt a heaven-sent chance to make direct contact with a man who could be vital to his task of getting advertisements for our group of papers. The London Press Exchange was already one of his biggest clients and the *Eastern Morning News* was always on the list for those juicy full-page prospectuses which the issuing houses used to launch so frequently and lavishly in those days.

Well, it looked as though the 'risk' I had taken in recommending George was going to pay off handsomely. We could be reasonably sure of getting a fair slice of the 'space' largesse that George now had it in his power to distribute.

Then one afternoon the 'bomb' fell. A heart-broken Blythe telephoned from London to say that our entire group of papers had been peremptorily 'axed' from the list of the London Press Exchange's advertising appropriations. At one fell blow we had lost one of our richest sources of advertising revenue.

Dismayed, disappointed and incredulous, I hastily wrote to George asking why he had cancelled all space bookings in my papers? Surely there must be a mistake. It was, as he well knew, a fine group of papers, and after all (I hinted obliquely) it had been the stepping stone to George's own career in advertising!

I got a formal reply in which George said his company had instructed him to cut down on their provincial advertising schedules and it was unfortunate and regrettable that 'his old paper' should have to be one of the victims of the economy axe.

19

'Blow, Blow, thou winter wind', etc. But was that the end of the little saga of ingratitude? Not quite. Once again the fickle finger of fate points the way.

It is the lounge of the Mount Royal Hotel in Montreal and I am introduced to a fellow newspaper-director—a Colonel Thomas of the South Wales group of papers, belonging then to the Berrys. 'Your name seems to ring a bell with me,' Col. Thomas confides to me. 'Just before I left Cardiff we were considering applicants for the post of advertising manager to the group. We particularly liked one candidate and we were influenced by a reference which you seem to have given to him while he was in your employ. We shall confirm the appointment when I return. But this appears to be a wonderful opportunity for you to tell me more about this man. It's a plum job and we want to pick the best we can.'

Shades of divine justice! Echoes of retribution! Flutterings of chickens coming to roost! Frantic wavings of the long arm of coincidence! Or other clichés of the crime writers' vocabulary. So what now, ungrateful George? Here's your come-uppance! Do I now 'put the squeak' in for you as once you did for me?

Well, as Col. Thomas ordered another round of cocktails, I put his mind at rest by saying I stood by every word I had written about George's qualifications. 'He's a man who will go far and he is efficient to the point of ruthlessness!' I added as memory prodded me. 'First-rate material; you couldn't make a better choice, etc.'

Thomas was deeply grateful. 'I think you've solved the problem for us. I'm going to cable Cardiff right away to confirm the appointment.'

So George got the job and it turned out that once again he did well. So well, in fact, that the Berrys brought him to London with them and in due time when Lord Camrose acquired the *Daily Telegraph* George was made advertisement manager. And he was to do even better still for within a few years, George G. Simon became general manager of the paper—one of the great prizes of Fleet Street.

I never saw George again until one evening many years later, when fate placed us side by side at a Newspaper Guild banquet at Stationers Hall. He was 'overwhelmed' to see me, even a little excited I thought. The time lapse must have been well over twenty years and George hadn't altered much except that he had acquired poise and confidence, and he played the top executive role *par excellence*. He seemed to know everybody and as he introduced me to some of his friends, he added (rather ambiguously I thought), 'Mark was once my editor in Hull.' From the way he inflected those words, it really sounded as if he had been the boss and I was one of his editors.

Perhaps nuances can also be ungrateful!

To say that I helped a great many aspiring young journalists to win their spurs in the newspaper world and quite a few talented writers to achieve some measure of success in literature is to chronicle a simple statement of recorded fact. And as I have mentioned earlier, I never looked for thanks—which may have been just as well since I rarely got any! This has to be said twice if I am going to keep this narrative truthful.

It may therefore be understandable why I should remember after all these years a solitary instance of entirely unsolicited thanks. Nothing monumental, but heart-warmingly sincere. It came about one day when a young man walked into my office in Essex Street (a very famous 'publishing' street which used to house Methuens, Sampson Low, Secker & Warburg, Quality Press, two bookshops, etc.). My visitor presented his card which, as I recall, read 'Jack Fishman, Editor, *Empire News*'. I knew the paper along with the *Sunday Chronicle* which was in the Hulton stable when I worked in Withy Grove, Manchester, but I didn't recollect the bearer. Anticipating my thoughts, he said, 'You won't remember me but you happen to be the man who gave me my first job on a newspaper. I haven't done too badly since then and I have often thought about you. It would be a token of my gratitude to you for what you did for me if you would accept for publication a book I have just written, and which I think you will like.' Whereupon he plonked a hefty typescript and pictures on to my desk. The approach was sincere, if a little ingenuous, since he wasn't to know that we were getting, on average, forty manuscripts per week—and refusing most of them!

The book he had written was about the Nazi prisoners still held in Spandau prison,* and when I had read it I had no hesitation in putting it into the list.

* *Seven Men of Spandau* by Jack Fishman, W. H. Allen, 1966

It proved to be the first of many other books on the same subject, but this pioneer publication did very well indeed. Subsequently Jack wrote another book for me about Winston Churchill's wife.*

This one did even better than his first book and I sold the rights in America for a very substantial sum.

It's nice to be thanked; even nicer still to have the thanks doubled!

Sometimes kindness can be misunderstood or even unrecognised. In the early days of the war a bomb fell on my offices in Essex Street, destroying all my records, the wonderful collection of W. H. Allen books published since 1801, together with twenty copies of Dylan Thomas' first-ever book of poems, which I published in 1934. Today they would fetch about £300 each.

After the bombing I moved up the street to new premises opposite the famous Essex Hall, a glass-roofed building that was destroyed when a second bomb fell later on the same street. Hitler obviously didn't like publishers, because still another of his souvenirs hit the street and this time it shattered the building in which Secker & Warburg were located. Luckily nobody was hurt but the street was a shambles, and scrabbling among the debris trying to rescue valuable papers and documents were Fred Warburg, his partners and members of his staff. They were knee-deep in the detritus and to add to their woes it began to rain heavily and soon the area was a wasteland of mud, papers, broken furniture, etc.

It was a pathetic sight, but one all too familiar in the general devastation of the 'blitz'. Consequently no one paid much heed to the spectacle of bombed-out tenants trying to salvage their property and chattels. There was little any outsider could do anyway. It was happening to businesses, shops and offices all over London and the victims had largely to fend for themselves, the biggest problem being where to start up business again.

I went up to the rain-soaked, exhausted Warburg and told him I had a couple of spare rooms at the top of my office just up the street which he could temporarily use while he was finding a new place to re-start. Then, for the next two hours there was a procession of people tramping their muddied feet up my office stairs, dumping the sodden remnants of a bombed-out office on to my office floors. But

* *My Darling Clementine* by Jack Fishman, W. H. Allen, 1970

22

by nightfall the evacuees were safely installed, with a roof over their heads until they could be re-housed.

The next day Warburg's secretary came to see me bearing a message: Mr Warburg presented his compliments (not thanks, mark you!) and would like to know how much rent I proposed to charge him and how long could he stay on in the rooms! I was speechless; I was livid; I was hopping mad. I felt like Scarpia must have felt when Tosca cried, 'Quanto Costo?'

It had never crossed my mind when I offered temporary shelter to victims of the blitz that they should pay for the accommodation. Does an ambulance charge a casualty the taxi-fare? When my anger had subsided a little, I said quietly to the distressed girl, 'In offering him refuge in my offices, I thought I was merely doing your boss a neighbourly kindness. I wasn't trying to make money out of his misery. Now go and tell the ungrateful idiot to get out of my premises as quickly as he can!'

And the next day the mud-stained procession went into reverse and the evicted 'refugees' quitted my offices, but not before Mr Warburg had sent down to me a huge box of cigars, which I promptly returned!

In retrospect I am prepared to believe that Warburg's rather condescending response to my disinterested rescue act was the result of his traumatic experience in being 'bombed out'. It's certainly an explanation, but in no way an exculpation. Many years later when Warburg wrote his memoirs, I found no reference to this incident in the somewhat turgid pages of *A Profession For Gentlemen*. Perhaps being 'bombed out' and being rescued is all in the day's work when 'there's a war on'.

One day, walking along the Embankment to the House of Commons—it was in the days when trams ran from Blackfriars to Westminster—I saw a girl fall off her bicycle and plummet half-way across the road. Her tyre had skidded on the tram lines. I rushed to pick her up, retrieved her bike—and her hat—and inquired solicitously if she was all right. 'Bugger off,' she replied. This rude ingratitude was no doubt induced by the traumatic experience of being de-biked in a public street!

The two supreme examples of monumental ingratitude are both within living memory. One concerns Sir Winston Churchill, who with his stupendous courage and his inspired leadership brought Britain safely through to victory and thereby deserved the gratitude of the entire nation. And how did they show their thanks to this wonderful man? By kicking him out of office at the very first opportunity!

During the war years we provided a base from which General de Gaulle could rally the remnants of his defeated (and collaborating) France. And on D-Day we invaded Europe, drenched the beaches with the blood of our finest young men in order that de Gaulle one day could head the victory procession glorifying his country's liberation. And how did Le General express his gratitude? By twice vetoing Britain's entry into the European Common Market!

Sometimes in the little things of life you may discern the core of a great truth. A simple sentence can hold the essence of all philosophy or touch the hem of immortality.

Tucked away at the foot of a news column in the paper I was reading the other day, I came across the brief report of an inquest on a farm labourer who had shot himself when he learned his sweetheart had jilted him. By his side was a note. 'I loved her, but she didn't love me', he had written in his untutored but ineffably sad farewell. In those eight words did he not epitomise all the heartache, all the tragedy and all the pity of unrequited love that has ever been recorded in poetry, song, drama, literature or art since man first found the means of saying what goes on within his deepest heart? A farm labourer, unknown, unlettered, unremarked had, with 'broken heart and a contrite spirit' surrendered his soul to God and penned a valediction, the exquisite pathos of which is like a grace note among the immortal melodies sung of Romeo and Juliet, Paolo and Francesca, Abelard and Heloise, David and Bathsheba, Dante and Beatrice, Tristan and Isolde and all other lovers.

Here was no inspired village muse writing for effect. A simple son of the soil was bidding the world goodbye with a tender avowal and confession that encapsulates the anguish of the human situation—'I loved her, but she didn't love me', was all he wrote.

4

Front Page Interlude

Because newspaper production was my hobby as well as my work, I enjoyed inventing new 'layouts' and new styles in headlines and 'splash' features.

Very early in my career I realised how close was the interaction of 'editorial policy' and 'advertising' in the welfare of a newspaper, and I took a very active interest in all matters connected with the advertising profession.

It is the traditional editorial shibboleth that the editorial policy of a journal 'has nothing whatever to do with advertising'. The two elements are poles apart! No advertiser, even though he may spend vast sums in patronising the advertisement columns of a paper (or any other kind of publication) is able to exercise the slightest influence on the 'editorial people!' Any such suggestion brings forth howls of anguished indignation and frenetic denials from those concerned with the 'contents' of the paper. The power and the status of the editor are absolute, inviolable, sacrosanct and any interference by an advertiser—no matter how oblique—would be resisted to the death!

It is a beautiful myth but it has no basis in fact. The most powerful executive in the whole newspaper hierarchy is, without question, the advertising manager. On his efforts alone depends the viability of the paper and the jobs of all who work on it. The man who can 'get the advertising' is worth his weight in rubies and unlike editors—brilliant or otherwise—successful 'ad men' are very rare birds. Journalists' unions and 'fathers of the Chapel' can tell an editor what to print or whom to employ but they dare not utter a word of criticism against, or attempt to dictate policy to, an advertisement manager.

Once upon a time there were a few independent, incorruptible, courageous editors, particularly on the smaller provincial news-papers, but they have long since gone to where all the flowers have presumably gone. And gone also are the writers with 'punch' and 'thrust'. I can't name more than half a dozen: Paul Johnson, George Gale, Colin Coote, Auberon Waugh, Frank Johnson, Bernard Levin (occasionally)—but who else?

The editorial *coup de grâce* was administered by—of all people—an ex-editor, the egregious Michael Foot, who very much in the tradition of another ex-journalist (one Benito Mussolini) dealt a mortal blow to the independence of the British press in general with his so-called 'Closed Shop' Act. If Michael Foot could have got enough advertising for his *Tribune*, he might have still been the editor today.

No paper—or periodical—can succeed or even exist for long without a minimum of paid advertising and any so-called editor who does not understand or accept this elementary truth is wasting his time and his proprietor's money. A paper declines *pro rata* to the decline of its advertising volume. A few try to defy the economic law by keeping alive on sales and subscription revenue, but this is merely throwing the baby out of the sleigh in order to delay the wolves' attack!

A case in point is the satirical paper *Private Eye*. If I controlled it, I would guarantee to make it one of the most powerful and prosperous periodicals in the country. It has its particular field almost to itself, which is a priceless asset, but its direction and its publishing 'philosophy' are, in my view, depressingly amateurish. There is obviously a lot of talent in this ocular enterprise but there is over-much fifth-form 'humour' and a general lack of professionalism which must preclude it from becoming a tempting medium for advertising's big spenders. Yet it could be a money-spinner in the right hands. Some of the 'legal actions' it has been involved in need never have occurred. The 'story' concerned could have been put over with a subtlety which would have avoided libel and yet made its point. That is the secret of being satirical without the danger of a subsequent 'belly-crawl'.

A successful managing editor is one who combines in proper pro-portion the editorial and commercial elements of his job which, incidentally, seems to be the recipe for a successful publisher—the good 'bookman' plus the good businessman. As managing editor with Provincial Newspapers Ltd, I had many opportunities to exercise these synthesist abilities and I managed to build up a bit of a reputation as a 'newspaper-doctor', to be called in whenever an ailing property was in need of a little therapy. I received such a 'call' in the early thirties when I was asked to take over the *Yorkshire Evening News* in Leeds. It was a challenging assignment since the local newspaper situation was, to say the least, unique. Both the evening papers (the *Post* and the *News*) were printed on a sickly buff-coloured newsprint, both carried 'small' advertisements exclusively on their front pages and both seemed hide-bound by antique tradition. My terms of reference were to 'revolutionise' the *Evening News* and to maximise its profits!

As soon as I was nicely installed in my role of managing editor—with plenary powers—I seemed to sense a general atmosphere of hostility to my actual presence. By a few old stagers I was regarded as some sort of interloper. The subtle attitude of amiable non-co-operation from the long-serving top executives looked formidable at first, but I beat it by ignoring it! The 'revolution' was something else. After all, a newspaper is a newspaper and provided it gives the reader 'all the news fit to print', it ought to be discharging its duty pretty adequately and therefore prospering accordingly. In this particular case the balance sheets reflected no such cosy state of affairs.

So, in the best manner of Napoleon, I decided to find a way—or make one. The situation called for a 'clean sweep'. First, we would change the buff newsprint to the normal white and, secondly, we would put news on the front page—two revolutionary changes. So I went into active 'hibernation' for a few weeks during which time I experimented with every possible form of 'make-up' and typographical combination in order to produce a front-page 'layout' that would justify the 'change-over'.

When I was satisfied with my formula, I had 'dummy' copies run off and these I duly presented to a specially convened meeting of all the executives to whom I then disclosed my strategy. At the outset, the reception of my ideas was a good deal less than enthusiastic. The general manager—a very crabby Yorkshireman belonging to the

27

well known Crabtree family—told me that successive editors of the paper during the last twenty-five years had all put forward ideas similar to mine but no one had dared to implement them. The danger was that the stolid Yorkshire reader didn't welcome drastic changes of this kind and if we carried out the plan, we would probably lose a lot of circulation—and a great deal of advertising revenue. It would be prudent therefore to 'stay as we are'.

The advertising manager, Fred Cook, a famous figure in advertising circles, grudgingly admitted that my front page was 'great' but the danger of losing all those permanent and profitable 'small ads' by putting them 'inside the paper' was enough to veto the experiment out of hand.

We argued and debated for over three hours but in the end I wore them all down, and the 'revolutionary' plans were unanimously endorsed. It was something of a victory for the 'interloper', but any rejoicing—it turned out—would have been premature. I hadn't reckoned with that tricky old devil—human duplicity.

I conveyed the news of the agreed plans to the directors of Provincial Newspapers and we (the general manager, the advertising manager and I) were summoned to a board meeting in Fleet Street. We had a cordial meal on the night train from Leeds to Kings Cross and my two colleagues went off to the Waldorf Hotel while I, as usual, chose the Savoy. We arranged to meet next day at Salisbury House for the fateful board meeting.

Having circulated the 'dummy papers' to the directors, I immediately gave them a quick run-down on the whole project and I took the precaution of pointing out that the two 'solus' advertising spaces, which I had allocated on the front page, would set off any potential loss of revenue from the re-positioning of the 'small ads'. All the directors made nice noises of approval and the chairman (Sir Herbert Grotrian, MP) particularly praised the page one lay-out, so it looked as though the board would agree to the transmogrification of its provincial evening newspaper, and we'd be up and away.

I could hardly believe my ears when I listened to a sudden interjection by the general manager. 'It is only right for me to say,' he began, 'that Cook and I stayed up half the night debating this matter and we decided to revert to our original view that the proposed changes in the paper are untimely and unwarranted and if carried out will prove disastrous. We would like this opinion to be put on record.'

Flabbergasted—that expressive colloquialism—is the only word to describe my reaction to this utterly unexpected and deliberate *volte face*. I was also angry. This was a classic double-cross; a last-minute attempt at sabotage. And as such it stank to high heaven. The fact that forty years ago this was 'boardroom tactics' only goes to show that today's standards of business, chicanery, deception and venality stem from a long tradition of double-dealing.

I am happy to relate that on this occasion Judas got his 'come-uppance', as the Americans say. Without consulting his colleagues, J. A. Akerman, the managing director, took the initiative and routed the dissidents. He said it was the desire of the board that the changes, proposed by the managing editor, should be carried out completely. A strong character this Akerman. He had once sailed before the mast and at one time was assistant manager of *The Times*. He was a newspaper boss and he behaved like one. He closed the meeting with this command from the quarter-deck: 'Now all of you, get back to Leeds and produce the paper which we have agreed to.'

And we did just that, and the new paper prospered. We didn't lose a single 'small ad' and the display advertisers fought to get on to the re-modelled front page. It wasn't long before the rival sheet took similar action.

Sometimes success can be a handicap. The Provincial Newspapers board were so pleased with the new-style paper I had created that they gave me a handsome bonus and ordered me to stay on in Leeds—indefinitely! Nice work in normal circumstances but it so happened that I had received an invitation to become managing editor of a national newspaper—the *Sunday Referee*—which meant Fleet Street at last. I submitted my resignation and it was promptly rejected. The board decreed that I must remain until they could find a 'suitable successor'. So I asked the spirit of Napoleon to show me how to 'make a way', and he led my steps to one W. L. Andrews, a former editor of the *Eastern Morning News* and presently editor of the *Leeds Mercury*, mainly a racing journal owned by the *Yorkshire Post* group. I asked him if he would like my job! It carried a salary of

£3,000 a year plus a bonus based on results, which was top money in those days and probably double what Andrews was then earning himself. I expected he would leap at the chance, especially as the word was out in Leeds that the days of the *Mercury* were numbered. (They were as it turned out.)

Andrews asked for time to think it over and a week later, to my astonishment, and disappointment, he told me that he had decided to turn the offer down. It seemed crazy and crazier still seemed Andrews' reason for rejecting the job: 'I propose to stick it out here,' he confided, 'because I have a feeling that one day I will edit the *Yorkshire Post*!' (The private with the general's baton in his knapsack!) The editorship of the *Post* was one of the plum jobs in provincial journalism and it was currently held by Arthur Mann, a renowned journalist and obviously a 'fixture'. Nevertheless, Andrews, defying all the odds, turned down a 'certainty' for an outside chance—and he proved to be right! He must have received guidance from one of those Yorkshire spiritualist groups which we all knew about, because he did stay on in Leeds and he did become editor of the *Yorkshire Post*! He also finished up with a knighthood, all of which grosses up into another little saga of a 'provincial lad' who backed his own hunch and made good.

Eventually, Provincial Newspapers promoted one of their local editors to my job in Leeds and after a very enjoyable spell in Yorkshire, I left the city to fulfil my destiny in Fleet Street.

It had been a rewarding experience because I met so many interesting people and visited a lot of interesting homes in the West Riding. Among many others, I made friends with a little man who had started work in Leeds by selling cloth caps in what was then called 'door-to-door salesmanship'. He got the orders and his partner made up the caps on a hand-operated sewing machine. Those were the humble origins of Sir Montague Burton and his friend Sol Hurwitz who built up the great multiple tailoring concern. I remember, too, a remarkably foresighted man named Cope who gave up a prosperous couturiere business because he had faith in a new craze called 'football pools' and into which he invested his money. His prescience was amply rewarded.

When I left Leeds for London one of my editors decided the moment was ripe for him to come to the metropolis too. He was my radio editor, Leslie Baily, and I am sure his appointment was the first of its kind ever made in British newspaperdom, since radio at that time was merely an emergent art. I gave him a job on my Sunday newspaper in the same capacity and very soon he made some good contacts with the BBC, an organisation which he later joined permanently. He developed the famous Scrapbook programmes with much success and later with equal success he wrote several books, by which time I had become a book publisher. But he never offered one of his books to me!

I can't resist mentioning occasionally these gratuitous kicks in the teeth because they have seemed to come up with alarming frequency.

Ingratitude is wrought by want of thought as well as by want of heart. We often excuse these omissions by a homely cliché (aren't all clichés homely?)which reminds us that 'people are just forgetful'. It's all nicely epitomised in the story of the lower East Side of New York in which two cops have rescued a small boy from the canal. 'This your kid?' asks the soaking policemen as they hand over the half-drowned brat to his Jewish mother. 'Oi veh!' she shrieks as she grabs the child, 'And V'er is his god-damned cap?'

And how's this for virtue being its own reward? One day I had a visit from two Bow Street policemen who said they had information to the effect that one of my warehouse employees was stealing the company's books. They therefore proposed to search his home. Later the same night they phoned to say they had found a 'great many' of the firm's books in the man's home and they had arrested him. Would I go to Bow Street to sign the charge?

Jumping into my car, I rushed to the police station and there in the charge room was my warehouse foreman; scared stiff and terrified about his wife and children who had seen him 'taken away' in a police van.

I asked the station inspector to show me the books they had found. They turned out to be mostly single copies of a variety of books. What I had expected to see were piles of unopened cartons and packages obviously filched straight from the warehouse! At worst these assorted books were 'specimen copies' which most foremen (and other senior employees) might take away and, accumulated over a long period, they would look like a substantial quantity. I explained this to the inspector, thanked him for his vigilance, and requested the instant release of the 'prisoner' since I was prepared to say the books were taken with my knowledge and consent. The policeman was furious. He maintained it was a clear case of theft—pilfering, if you like.

'Let him go,' I insisted, 'or you will find yourself on the wrong end of a charge for wrongful arrest.' Police court procedures were all too familiar to me as an ex-crime reporter. Sometimes it's useful to know the ropes!

The inspector became placatory. 'Tell you what we do,' he confided. 'You sign the charge, the man will make a brief appearance in court in the morning and I will tell the magistrate the circumstances. The charge will either be dismissed or the man will be put on probation, and it'll all be over in minutes,' he beamed.

'No way,' I answered. 'Either you drop the charge and let him out, or I will wait here until the morning and when the court opens, I will then tell the story my way. And heaven help you.'

After which bit of explosive rhetoric, I put my feet on the bench and prepared to 'sit it out'.

The infuriated officer retired to the charge room from whence I discerned high-pitched voices in heated debate. Suddenly the inspector reappeared, this time leading the bemused and bewildered foreman by the arm.

'OK, take him away,' he blurted out, and I moved towards the door with the 'released' man. They had decided to 'drop the charge', which was wise because they had no case at all. Had it been 'flagrant theft' I would have given my full support to the police.

Suddenly the officer shouted: 'Hold on a minute, what shall we do with the books?' It was clearly a trap question, and my think-computer whizzed into action instantly. Turning to the inspector, I said very quietly and calmly, 'You must return the books to the foreman's home. They are his legal property.' The cute cop had been outwitted. I had trumped his ace.

'You're a clever bastard, aren't you?' he said to me with the nearest thing to a smile he could conjure up. Then, calling a driver-cop, he said, 'Put these books in your car and drive that fellow to his home in Islington.' It was now after midnight.

I said goodnight to the foreman. He was in tears and chokingly told me how he had feared spending Christmas (it was two days off) in jail and being away from his wife and kids.

But for my intervention, the theft charge could easily have been made to stick and a good workman would have had a black mark on his career.

So a right merry Christmas was had by all!

Two weeks later the foreman was offered a better-paid post in the Maxwell organisation and without a moment's hesitation, and to the disgust of his fellow workers—who knew about his narrow escape—he took the job. Thanks for the memory, Tom!

5

Interlude Sycophantic

The world is full of 'arse-lickers'.

A bit crude and inelegant? Yes, but so wonderfully descriptive of the vermicular creatures I am about to dissect in this chapter. After all, I have been dealing in words most of my life and like all word-smiths I know there is always the exact locution to fit the subject in hand; the trick is to find it, seize it and apply it. I therefore have no hesitation in using the coarse term to nominate a genus which I have always despised but which flourishes exceedingly in all walks of life today.

By a strange circumstance, certain professions and trades seem to attract to their ranks a disproportionate number of sycophants, but if you exclude such vocations as the law, medicine, nursing and religion, I think it is true to say there is hardly a calling which does not have its fair share of them. Mind you, of course, no such character really exists at all! He is always the creation of other people since nobody would admit personally to being an 'arse-licker' just as no ordinary German ever confessed to being a Nazi. Nobody goes home at night and in the silence of his lonely room reproaches himself for having sucked up to the boss or to the big boys during the day. Neither the congenital 'arse-licker' nor the unmistakable Uriah Heep condemns himself for his contemptible behaviour. He will rationalise his conduct (if indeed he even examines it) and conclude that in life's rat race the means justify the end. Nor is he always the little man; too often he is a big cog among the big wheels. It's a universal commodity. Check mentally on a few you can identify!

I realise I may be offending lots of people engaged in film and show business, certain areas of journalism, all politics, most corporate enterprises, the civil and armed services, when I say that these are among the callings which offer the lick-spittle a congenial milieu wherein he can thrive and prosper.

It has been a long-held theory of mine that 'Yes-manism' actually started in the movie-making business—a business which virtually began in the gutter and which from its inception was dominated by a peculiar breed of opportunist entrepreneur. They quickly established an all-powerful oligarchy and then proceeded to surround themselves with hordes of obsequious adherents all of whom were determined to muscle-in on a bonanza the like of which hadn't been seen since the Gold Rush days.

Money cascaded into the coffers of this nascent industry and the founding fathers—the czars, the moghuls, the tycoons—speedily became multi-millionaires. Mostly illiterate, but obviously men of vision, these Midases were tyrannical and like all tyrants and dictators they were a law unto themselves, demanding instant, unconditional obedience to their desires and whims, and there was no lack of 'arse-lickers' ready to do their bidding, ready to say 'yes' to all their edicts, for it was mandatory that these egocentrics must never be wrong and never be contradicted! 'Yes, Mr Goldrocks' wasn't a joke. It was the passport to promotion and a share in the pickings of which there seemed no end. These parasites remind me of those jungle birds which travel on the backs of wild beasts, picking off the insects and bacteria from the festering sores, the eyes, the nostrils and the anuses of those mighty but complacent monsters who roam the African forests.

I hate to say it, but this tradition of toadying to the big shots has survived to this day, and contaminates an industry which has given wonderful entertainment to all the world, the while it has wallowed in wealth and spent money with a profligacy that no other trade has ever matched. Good faith and sincere friendship have lost all meaning for the movie Fat Cats with the commercial integrity of Bedouins. Their favourites may be riding high on Monday and out on their ear by Wednesday. And to grab the ensuing vacant job, fifty erstwhile bosom pals of the fallen angel will trample on each other in the mad scramble to take over. It's all part of the phoney philosophy which pervades show business in general. They make jokes about it. 'So where are you these days?'—'I don't know, I haven't opened my post yet.'

You may remember that mordant cartoon which is captioned: 'I love that guy'. It depicts a gross, grinning fat-belly cordially shaking the hand of a smiling friend at the same time poising a dagger at his friend's back. That lampoon could find an appropriate place on the walls of a thousand boardrooms these days—and not only in Hollywood or New York. There is a sizeable quota operating in every city in the world.

From time to time—so the books about the tinsel city remind us—a few independent souls have had the courage to tell the domineering power-drunk bosses to 'fuck-off'—in precisely those endearing but invariably fatal words. These martyrs may rate a plaque in the Hollywood pantheon but never get one. The brutal truth is that defiant heroism of this sort is neither admired nor condemned by the conformers. 'A live dog is better than a dead lion' is the axiom of the arse-licker.

Anyone who has had much to do with what is generally called 'financial circles' knows that it is riddled with duplicity, cheating, bribery, corruption, double dealing, swindling, fraud, deception and artifice, and it is only when some scandal suddenly makes the headlines that the general public gets an inkling of what goes on all the time below the surface in the 'City' or in the purlieus of Wall Street.

The whiz-kids of London's notorious money-making manors such as property, fringe-banking, asset-stripping operations, gambling joints, non-dividend paying public companies (milked at source by directors), inter-office financial manipulations, loans to directors, tax evasion, tax havens in foreign countries—these wide boys never had it so good. For every published failure or crash there are ten thousand successes which go unrecorded. They laugh at the Company Acts, the Department of Trade, and the law-enforcement authorities, because they manage to keep just within—occasionally just a fraction without—the Law.

These city slickers and big-spenders get away with it because they carry on their backs jungle birds (like those mentioned earlier) to comfort and protect them. These particular raptorial birds are known as company lawyers ('shysters' in America), tax accountants and financial advisers. They know every trick in the book and some

36

companies support a whole aviary of such feathered predators. In their spare time they haunt the casinos, the expensive night-spots and the expense account clip joints along with their well dressed bosses. In summer they migrate to the Riviera and in winter to the ski resorts. To the money-grubbers—from the mighty to the minuscule—these 'back-room' sharpsters are indispensable. In America they are the highest paid operators in the legal and notarial professions. Their tax-wangling is now almost an exact science. These manipulators have added a new dimension to business and finance.

It may be asked what has this diversion into the realms of big business skulduggery got to do with the reminiscences of an editor and publisher? I will tell you. The excesses of the City cry aloud to be exposed. But the journalists and the publishers—who believe they have a mission to protect the public weal and unmask roguery and villainy—are almost powerless to do so. The financial journalists know all too well the inside stories of boardroom malfeasance and many a publisher has been handed a manuscript—utterly unpublishable—containing sensational revelations about chicanery in high places and flagrant corruption in parochial and national affairs. But the miscreants have an ever-present and powerful safeguard behind which they can hide. The egregious libel laws of Britain shield the evil-doer. They effectively curb the enthusiasm and activities of the investigative newspaperman, and woe betide the publisher who dares to put out a book lifting the lid on the misdeeds of a public figure or his business associates. It would be to invite a writ for libel and the probable award of punitive damages.

First, he would have to defy his own libel-insurance lawyers who have the right to vet any book that may contain anything even slightly defamatory. The libel insurance cover—which most publishers carry—insists that the publisher shall submit to them any part of a manuscript that may be considered contentious or about which the publisher has received prior warning from an interested party. Failure to get the lawyers' clearance could vitiate the terms of the insurance policy in the event of legal proceedings. Consequently, writers and publishers rarely take a risk with anything remotely accusative or revelatory concerning living persons, even though the truth of the allegations may be beyond a doubt. 'Is it capable of proof?' is the formidable litmus by which lawyers test a derogatory statement.

It is true to say that editors and publishers live in constant fear of libel threats and most newspapers actually operate an in-house legal department to ward off the dangers of possible libel. It is not always effectual as can be seen from the frequent publications of retractions, public apologies and sometimes the payment of agreed damages. I am certain that the general public does not appreciate how warily a writer, an editor or a publisher has to tread in trying to uphold the freedom of the press and the right to publish, hobbled as they are by legal restrictions. An injunction to restrain publication of a book or an article is never difficult to obtain in the courts, and the delay in waiting for the case to be heard can involve the newspaper or the publishing house in huge expense. A whole edition of an important book could be held up or ultimately scrapped. 'When in doubt, leave out' is all the support, encouragement and back-up the courageous editor is likely to get from his so-called legal advisors.

When my company published the autobiography of the Duchess of Argyll, there were countless sessions with lawyers before the contents were rendered innocuous in terms of defamation. As a result, readers who might have been expecting some juicy passages were disappointed. On almost every paragraph which the lawyers queried, we had to give way although the Duchess herself was prepared to guarantee a personal indemnity. Naturally this book didn't earn out its big advance but the lawyers did well out of it, as did the bookseller who still got his forty per cent discount on every copy that he sold in his bookstore.

In fifty years of editing and publishing, I have been literally deluged by threats, writs and demands 'that all further publication shall cease and all copies of the book recalled forthwith'.

Some have given me sleepless nights and some have had the firm's insurance lawyers near to apoplexy, but I am happy to record that I was never taken into court to defend a case.

In time one becomes expert in coping with voracious lawyers and outraged complainants. Sometimes a little bluff is called for. I once got a lawyer's letter which concluded with these words: 'We have therefore advised our client that he should institute proceedings for libel.'

It didn't seem to me that the substance of the complaint was very heinous so I replied quite succinctly as follows: 'You say you have advised your client to institute proceedings for libel. I think you have given your client a piece of very bad advice.'

I never heard another word.

Rarely is there anything funny about libel matters. They are always tiresome, too often unnecessary and really time-wasters for all concerned. The editor who tries to justify an obvious libel is a damned fool and ought to know better. Unless it be a subject of vital national importance from which the editor or publisher could emerge with some honour and much valuable publicity, the finest advice is stay out of court. You simply can't win. If you get a favourable verdict the costs and the wasted effort will show you a debit balance at the end of the day.

I can recall only one humorous episode connected with libel and defamation. A titled lady—editor of an illustrated news-paper—spotted a picture on the front page of her journal just as it was about to go to press. It was a photo of the prize bull at a Christmas cattle show and it displayed in all its glory the bull's paramount asset as a bull—its testicles, which almost touched the ground. The outraged lady editor stopped the press while the dis-gusting picture was substituted by one from which the sexual mag-nificence of the prize-winning bull had been 'touched-out'.

The very next day the furious owner of the emasculated bull demanded that the true picture of his valuable livestock should be promptly reinstated. 'You have castrated my bull,' he complained, 'and the photo you have printed is simply a bad joke. My bull has been turned into a worthless eunuch.'

Whether this came under the tort of 'slander of goods' I don't remember, but I do know that the original photograph, correctly testiculated, was subsequently printed and the proud owner monetarily recompensed.

Clearly even a lot of bull must sometimes be respected!

The primary theme of this interlude is sycophancy, so I must get back on course. I have had a lot to do with show business people in my journalistic and publishing experience and I have always been fascinated and amused by the blatant insincerity of such folk, especially the false adulation and patent hypocrisy of first night congratulations. It may all be rather harmless and inconsequential and at worst it is perhaps only an extension of the exhibitionism which all actors (by the very nature of their calling) must either possess, *ab initio,* or must cultivate as they go along.

Nothing depresses me more than the back-stage spectacle of some star performer holding court in a usually unkempt dressing room, and I find few things more nauseating than witnessing almost profane adoration being lavished on a performer by bewitched or entranced worshippers. I am allergic to gush or sentimental affectation in any form and you see it at its worst in the social lives of theatre people.

Some years ago I was having lunch in the Savoy with Ivor Novello and my author 'Popie' (W. MacQueen Pope, the stage historian) when a singularly attractive girl approached Ivor and in a torrent of 'my dears', 'darlings' and other false felicitations, they exchanged greetings like long-lost lovers, which for certain reasons they couldn't have been. Presently this gave way to a flurry of endearing farewells and 'must-meet-again-soons' whereupon the men resumed their seats at the table. Then the sloe-eyed Ivor laconically turned to Popie and whispered: 'Who on earth was that?'

The passing years have not erased the memory of an episode of cowardly abasement (arse-licking) which I once witnessed and which troubled me for a long time, because it so offended my own canon about human behaviour and dignity.

When I edited the *Sunday Referee* it was my custom to have a weekly meeting with the proprietor (Isidore Ostrer) at the offices of the Gaumont-British Film Corporation in Wardour Street, at which we talked about the progress of the newspaper. We usually met just at the end of the normal GB film conference presided over by the chairman, C. M. Wolff, whose tough and humble origins were reflected in his accent and his aggressive manner. I recall one particular meeting that had just ended and I was mixing with the three Ostrer brothers, Michael Balcon, Arthur Jarratt and other GB big-wigs. I heard Wolff shout to the publicity director (Jeffrey

Bernard), 'Come back 'ere a minute.' Waving a sheaf of papers in his hand, the formidable Wolff (nicknamed the Big Bad Wolff) glowered at Bernard and exclaimed, 'These grosses (box office figures) you have given me are all wrong. You have tried to deceive me.' Trembling with anger, he flung the papers at his surprised underling and literally screamed, 'You are nothing but a fucking liar.' It was an ugly scene and most of the other directors discreetly began to inch their way out of the boardroom as though they had not heard the offensive outburst.

I expected that Bernard would have immediately picked up a heavy object from Wolff's desk and clobbered him with it; instead of which he smiled broadly, shrugged his shoulders, spread his hands in a supinate gesture, and smirked, 'So I'm a liar, C.M.' This cowardly counter-blast to a humiliating attack so astounded me that I was speechless—and so was Wolff. It was all over in minutes but the incident has stayed with me a lifetime because of its sequel.

An hour after the episode we were all having the usual after-conference lunch at the Kit Kat Club (which the company owned), when the still smiling and imperturbable Bernard came over to speak to me. My reputation as something of a forthright and independently-minded editor was not unknown to the GB chiefs, whose films were vigorously and consistently criticised in my paper whenever they deserved such treatment, in spite of the fact that the chairman 'owned the paper'.

'What did you think of that little scenario in Film House this morning,' Bernard blurted out, and before I could answer he went on, 'I suppose you would have busted his jaw? Well, you see, I'm not that kind of bloody fool.' Leaning over me he continued confidentially, 'Do you know that I get £10,000 a year (in those days a princely salary); that they give me a Rolls; that I get a kick-back on every tub of ice-cream we sell (they had over 100 cinemas). I also get a rake-off on everything, even on the batteries in the usherettes' torches. Do you think I would give up all that just for the satisfaction of slapping "big mouth" for calling me "a fucking liar". I'll have the last laugh yet.' And he did. He continued to enjoy his salary, his Rolls and his perks for many years before he went out to Hollywood to live—and die.

I often used to ask myself was Bernard, with his survival

philosophy, smarter than me with my so-called principles? Had a man spoken to me like the coarse Wolff had spoken to Bernard, I would have thrashed hell out of him without a moment's hesitation. But is discretion the better part of valour? Can you, reader, name offhand anybody who you believe would sooner sacrifice his job rather than his pride and principles? If you do, treasure his friendship. He's ONE IN A MILLION

I once knew a man, in my Fleet Street days, who really developed the art of arse-licking into something you couldn't help marvelling at; he did it so superbly and camouflaged it with such subtle skill.

He was a journalist-politician named Beverley Baxter, former editor of the *Daily Express* and a Member of Parliament. He possessed a soft and pleasing Canadian drawl and he achieved some eminence in life by exercising and exploiting the smooth approach, ably abetted by an ever-smiling chubby babyface. His suave manner disguised his innate servility but he never appeared to be fawning or cringing. His deferential attitude passed for tact and diplomacy but I knew—as indeed he knew—that he was putting on an act. He believed you caught more flies with honey than with vinegar—and he was a great flycatcher.

One night 'Bax' and I were dining *Chez* Charles Graves (who wrote a gossip column for my paper) when in the middle of the meal a telephone call came for 'Bax' summoning him to go to Lord Beaverbrook's town mansion in St James's Park.

There was no question of his disobeying the command or even delaying it so with suitable apologies to the host, he left.

A couple of days later I saw him in Fleet Street and asked him what had been so important that he had to leave our dinner party so abruptly the other night. With his cherubic smile, he told me it was nothing serious. Just one of Max's sudden whims. And although it wasn't urgent, he was nevertheless instructed on arrival at Stornaway House to go straight upstairs to Beaverbrook's bedroom. This is how Baxter related the interview to me. 'Max was apparently in his bathroom and when I reached it he called out, "Come in here Bax". I entered the bathroom and to my surprise found the Beaver almost naked, sitting on the lavatory seat. "All right, Bax," he said, noticing my startled look. "You must have seen a man taking a shit before. Sit down on that bathstool and I'll tell you what I called you for."

'He then brought up some trivial matter concerning the previous day's editorial page and we discussed it while the Beaver concluded his eliminatory formalities.'

As he told me all this, Baxter evinced no sense of disgust at being cross-examined while his eccentric boss was moving his bowels. With his beguiling smile, Bax added quite complacently, 'He often does this to his people.'

My comment to Bax was: 'Had I been in your shoes I would have pushed the little bastard down the bowl and pulled the chain on him!'

But Baxter maintained his condescending Mona Lisa smile, and certainly didn't indicate that he endorsed my remedy for terminating lavatory auditions. Indeed, a few weeks after this bathroom comedy, Baxter and I found ourselves guest speakers at a public luncheon, when lo and behold I listened incredulously to the irrepressible Bax enlivening an otherwise dull speech by recounting this very incident, in all its unsavoury detail.

When it was my turn to speak, I couldn't resist getting in a dig. 'Mr Chairman and Gentlemen,' I began, 'You have just heard Mr Beverley Baxter, MP for Wood Green, telling you how he became a Privy Councillor.' It got the expected laugh from everybody except Bax. He couldn't stand ridicule.

While I despise any sycophant for being an affront to God and to man—surely God didn't make *him* in His image—I despise his very existence on the grounds that he helps to debase and destroy all business and social ethics. He is, in my view, a greater malefactor than the common criminal.

When the last yes-man has licked the arse of the last boss, maybe the world will be a better place to live in.

And while we're on the subject, it would be quite wrong to assume that your typical sycophant is always the male of the species. Women can be just as obsequious, but they will usually camouflage it with what pulp-writers call feminine wiles. The end result (intentional pun) is the same!

All my life I have admired courage in its varied manifestations just as ardently as I have loathed moral and physical cowardice in their myriad expressions. In my professional careers I tried hard and often to take, when possible, a courageous stand and I want to say here and now in the clearest possible terms that it is a pursuit for which you get no medals and seldom any thanks. I am, of course, not talking about spontaneous acts of bravery, which often are inspired by the meanest motives.

I remember, for instance, in the first war watching a 'swaddy' knock back half a petrol-can of issue-rum just before going over the top on a night-sortie. In minutes he was mad drunk and in half an hour he was back at the forward trench, shepherding a dozen 'Jerries' whom he had rounded up single-handed! For this he got the DCM and years later he got 'life' for killing his wife in a drunken frenzy!

Bravery of that kind has little to do with the quiet courage and fortitude of terminal invalids or those dedicated souls who look after them.

I am, by nature (and there are perhaps genetic reasons for this) an inveterate lover of justice and I could rarely forgo the right or the desire to strike a blow for liberty even in small mundane matters. Whenever I witnessed something unfair, unjust, unnecessarily cruel, I felt the urge to intervene.

Once I was on a crowded bus. At the next stop the conductor allowed a few persons to get on but peremptorily rejected a mother whose little boy had managed to scramble aboard. The conductor signalled the bus to go, whereupon the small boy, seeing his mother left behind, howled in terror. I pressed the bell vigorously, which stopped the bus, and round came the driver who, however, ignored the screaming boy—and my protest—and drove off again. And again I pushed the bell and stopped the bus. Did all the other passengers rally round and support me in the attempt to get a terrified boy restored to his probably terrified mother? They did not; shouts of 'Lets get on wiv' it', 'The kids'orl right', 'Oo the hell are you to interfere', assailed me. So I got off the bus with the boy and walked him back to his distressed parent. *'Viva la bagatelle!'*

This incident ought to come within my embargo on trivia but I include it because it seems a typical if homely example of the futility of trying to do the right thing (even in small matters); of standing up for simple justice; of intervening instead of evading, and I could easily multiply a thousandfold such episodes, often so much bigger and more menacing. But not once can I recall ever getting a shred of support from the lookers-on. Indeed I well remember the time when I actually got the bird from the victim herself! Late one night as I was walking with a friend along a dark and rather shabby street leading to the railway station in Hull—a seaport notorious in those days for its tough dock-workers, we caught up with a couple who seemed to be having a violent and ugly quarrel. Both were drunk and every few strides the man would turn to his woman and punch her savagely in the face. She was in a horrible state, blood streaming down her cheeks. 'Fuck off,' said the brute when we told him to desist—'she's my wife' he added, emphasising the matrimonial imperative by landing another blow on her swollen face.

'How about the old one-two,' whispered my friend to me. 'OK,' I replied, whereupon he side-stepped the bully and whipped in a left to the wife-basher's belly. As he doubled up, I let go the uppercut, which of course took him clean out cold. But to our horror, the woman began shrieking hysterically. 'They've killed my husband.' 'They've murdered him.' 'He's dead,' she wailed, even though the drunken lout sprawled on the pavement was already beginning to come round. But before the inevitable crowd could collect in strength, we beat it to the station.

'Really doesn't pay to interfere, does it?' my friend casually remarked as we downed a welcome double whisky in the station-hotel bar. '*Vae Victis!*'

Because I could, in the Yorkshire phrase, 'use my knuckles' as a young man, I used to get into many a scrap but I never deliberately sought a fight. There was always a good reason and usually it was either to redress a wrong or to protect someone.

I recall one 'punch-up gig' that is the paradigm for so many others. The scene is a crowded Manchester dance hall in the late twenties.

I was seated with two young ladies at a table alongside the balustrade which enclosed the dance floor. There was a sudden scuffle around the entrance doors where a couple of bouncers were trying in vain to keep out a bunch of apparently drunken

45

gate-crashers. 'It's the rugger crowd', screamed my two lady companions—and promptly fled.

Apparently it was a common Saturday night diversion of the 'county' rugby-players to get half stoned after the game and then invade the 'palais de danse' to rough up the Jew Boys. One hefty scrum-half leapt over the balustrade on to the dance floor and in a flying tackle seized an obvious 'Yid' whose dance partner—with others—had panicked and fled. The companions of the muddied oaf cheered as he grabbed his victim's necktie and proceeded to pull it so tight that 'Ikey' began to go blue in the face. His eyes were bulging; he was slowly being strangled in the sight of hundreds of unprotesting onlookers.

Leaping over the balcony I crashed a punch straight to the sportive bully's unprotected jaw. It sent him sliding on his arse right across the smooth, shining dance floor where he came to rest in an inert heap. Minutes later the police arrived and bundled the whole gang out into the street. The dance went on.

Many a time I asked myself why should I intervene in episodes like this? I am a 'professional' man; not a street brawler. It is undignified, and in any case no one else seems to bother. Surely one day I will get 'done' myself. (Thankfully I never did.)

It must not be thought that in those days I was some sort of glorified boy scout or a crusading knight rescuing distressed damsels. No doubt I distressed a few damsels myself! There was no sense of mission on my part and I certainly wasn't bellicose by nature. Nevertheless I simply couldn't stand idly by when somebody was being 'mugged', any more than I could in later years, either by silence or consent, condone a business deal which I considered to be improper or crooked, or a manifest injustice.

But as the years went by my zeal as a rectifier of abuses and malfeasance ran out of steam. I tended more and more to do what most people did—and still do—look the other way.

A classic example of this *laissez-faire* happened in New York a few years ago. In a lonely residential street in the heart of Queens (a New York suburb) the night-time stillness was suddenly rent by the shrieks of a woman. From a hundred bedroom windows which were flung wide open, heads looked down on the spectacle of a young woman being repeatedly stabbed by an assailant. Her cries for help momentarily scared the attacker off, which gave her a chance to crawl into a doorway. But the marauder returned and with several more stabs, finished his victim off.

Did any of the window-watchers utter a shout of protest; did anyone hurl an object at the murderer; did anyone go to the women's rescue; did anyone even telephone the police? The answer to all these questions is 'No'. Nobody did a thing but watch—from a safe distance. There was, of course, a tremendous outcry in the papers during the next few days. Questions were asked in the State Assembly; sermons were preached denouncing the inhumanity and indifference of those who had looked down upon the sight of a woman being publicly murdered.

But was 'fun-city' New York stunned into shame and remorse by the brutal and disgraceful behaviour of its citizens in their suburban dormitory? If it was, I saw no evidence of it. On the contrary, many of my friends seemed stolidly to accept the situation and mitigate it on the grounds that it was inadvisable and imprudent for outsiders to get mixed up in other people's calamities since it involves all sorts of inconveniences and there is even the danger of subsequent retribution by the culprits concerned. 'Just walk away from it' is the standard advice. Consequently you can rarely get a witness to come forward—even in a street accident. 'Not me; I didn't see nothing!'

What a commentary on the decline of courage, civic conscience and moral duty in the human situation. And don't imagine the foregoing episode is something peculiar to the American way of life. It happens in all civilised countries, even law-abiding London—and it simply reflects the couldn't-care-less syndrome which seems to affect the larger part of mankind today. 'I'm all right Jack—fuck you.'

6

Dartmoor Interlude

'A gentleman to see you, sir,' called my secretary on the intercom. 'He says he's a journalist, but he hasn't an appointment and asks if you can spare him a few minutes.'

It wasn't unusual in those days for itinerant newsmen to call directly on provincial editors in the hope that there might be a vacancy. Journalism was a peripatetic profession and the turnover in staff was such that an opening could occur at very short notice.

'Tell him to come in,' I answered and as the door opened, there appeared a man in his middle years, soberly dressed and full of apologies for having barged in on me without any introduction. He had a nicely modulated speaking voice, tinged with a slight Scots accent, and very quickly he disclosed the purpose of his visit—yes, he wanted an editorial job.

'So, tell me something about yourself,' I invited, having offered him a cigarette which he declined. He then proceeded to give me a quick run-down of his career, which I must say was impressive.

'You're holding out on me', I announced after he finished detailing his newspaper experience. 'There's something you haven't told me,' I added.

It didn't really need any intuition on my part to deduce that there must be a reason why a journalist with this man's record should be out of work. What was the missing link?

Rather wearily he replied: 'I suppose if I tell you the truth, you'll show me the door like everybody else has so far.'

'Let me decide that,' I advised, trying to inject a note of hopefulness into the curt words.

His lips trembled as he then blurted out, 'I've just finished a prison sentence. I left Dartmoor four weeks ago and I have tramped the country looking in vain for work. As soon as they discover I'm a jail-bird they don't want to hear any more.'

He looked anything but a jail-bird to me, even in his dejection.

I encouraged him to tell me the whole story and it came out that at one time he was city editor of a Scots journal and in his editorial capacity he had boosted and helped to promote a financial operation that turned out to be a swindle. He had obviously been the patsy for a bunch of share-pushers, and his subsequent sentence of four years' penal servitude seemed unduly harsh on a man with a previously unblemished record.

In the early 1930s there was a surplus of manpower and no employer needed to take on an ex-convict in order to fill a vacancy. So this man's chance of getting back to journalism—or any other profession—could be rated as nil. He knew it, and so did I. But there was no doubt he was a first rate newspaperman and it so happened that there was an editorial vacancy on my morning paper which, under normal conditions, he was eminently qualified to fill.

Having unburdened himself of his tragic tale, he was half ready to depart, but I motioned him to sit down and I said, 'This shall be a matter between you and me alone. I will regard what you have just told me as top secret and no word of it will ever come from me. If that goes for you too, I am prepared to offer you a job as senior sub-editor on the *Eastern Morning News*. You can start, if you like, on Sunday night. Just keep your own counsel and go to work normally.'

The shock of acceptance overwhelmed him. For some moments he couldn't speak and when at last he began to stammer his thanks, I cut him short and tried to let him understand that signing on Dartmoor alumni was all part of the day's work for me!

From almost the very first moment, he proved his worth as a good journalist; his conduct was impeccable and he settled down into the job with professional ease.

At the end of a fortnight he came to see me. With some diffidence he asked if he might introduce his wife who wanted to say thank you to me. Then he ushered her in, together with two very presentable teenage daughters.

The wife was what the Scots so perciently call a nice little body. It would sound a bit maudlin if I attempted to describe that little scene in the editor's room. All they wanted to say was already in their lambent eyes. Words were quite superfluous. Truly the eyes are the windows of the soul.

All my life I have been appalled by man's inhumanity to man. So many times I have tried to fathom the motivation for wanton and senseless acts perpetuated—for no discernible reason—by one person against another. Why do they do it? Is there within all of us an inherent principle of evil that must come out at certain times, no matter how we try to suppress it either by the disciplines of convention or the restraints of one's conscience? Do we all carry about with us a dirty tricks department which sometimes gets out of control? I am not thinking now of the criminal type who stands to gain from his wickedness, or those who get a sexual thrill out of mayhem. To a certain extent the motive here may be comprehensible but in so many other cases people turn swiftly to do evil without cause or motive. It is one of the many mysteries of life and I have sensed no diminution as I have grown older. How many cases have come within your orbit?

Typical, therefore, is the case of my convicted journalist's redemption. The episode might well have ended happily with his new-found lease on life.

But it didn't.

One day I was horrified to see, scrawled in soap across the mirror of the men's room of the office this despicable message: 'Keep your hands in your pockets; there are crooks about.'

Clearly it was aimed at the new sub-editor. Somebody had nosed into his past—it's called investigative reporting today—and had dug up his solitary misdemeanour. It didn't take me long to confirm that the guilty secret of the man from Dartmoor was now out in the open and very quickly it took on a most ominous turn. Some other members of the staff made no attempt to disguise the fact that they not only objected to the man's presence, but they would refuse to work with him.

Returning one Sunday evening after a day's golf, I stopped off at the office for the usual station identification and to my surprise I found that a crowded meeting was just ending in our spacious reporters' room. The convenor informed me that the entire East Riding Branch of the National Union of Journalists had held an emergency meeting at which it was unanimously decided that the 'ex-convict' must be dismissed or strike action would be taken forthwith. This was a drastic and entirely improper ultimatum, and after reminding the meeting that it had been held on my premises without permission, I requested everybody who was not a member of my staff to quit the building at once.

Addressing my own colleagues, I then said their action was as contemptible as it was inhuman and quite unworthy of enlightened people like journalists. I made it absolutely plain that I had no intention of dismissing the person concerned. I therefore accepted the challenge in the ultimatum. And this was my answer: I would immediately draw up a timetable stating clearly the exact time each individual staff member would report for duty the next day. I would post two tellers at the door and any listed member who did not turn up on time would thereby have signified that he had forfeited his job in accordance with the instant-strike threat. The 'clocking-on' process was both unprecedented and drastic but it was expedient.

I went home, scared stiff that a strike might take place. There was no legal validity for my retaliation and in those days there were no such things as industrial courts and conciliation bodies. And above all else I was a very young editor who couldn't afford the luxury of an office strike which would be a bonus to the opposition paper!

The next morning, without exception, the entire staff turned up; my man of sorrows remained in his job and I thought I had heard the last of this mean and despicable episode—until a couple of weeks later when the top NUJ officials came up from London. They tried to pretend that 'they were not against the man himself', but his presence was objected to on the grounds that he was not a member of the union.

'Then make him one,' I retorted, but this they couldn't do since he was ineligible. 'Ineligible because of his one fall from grace!' I queried. 'He has paid the penalty, why persecute him? Is this how the noble brotherhood of trade unionists operates?'

I tend to use bad language when I am angry. I refused to debate the matter further. The man would remain in his job and I told the whole delegation to 'piss off'.

As a result of this imbroglio, several local members of the NUJ resigned, but I heard no more about it—at least not for nearly twenty years when the long arm of coincidence reached out to me!

It came about when I was commissioned to do a new typographical lay-out for the *Daily Herald*, which entailed my working in the Odhams office in Long Acre. It was strictly a union house (the *Daily Herald* was the organ of the Labour Party) and before I could work in the office, it was necessary to get a union card.

So I trotted off personally to the NUJ headquarters in Fleet Street with my request for a card and the officials there told me they must look up my record as a journalist. I was (and still am) a member of the Institute of Journalists, which should have been enough. But it wasn't, and very soon one of the officials was back with a bulging folder. 'We seem to have had a bit of trouble with you some years ago,' he remarked as he leafed through the documents in the file. He had unearthed the record of the episode in which I had defied—and beaten—the National Union of Journalists.

'Well, it was a long time ago,' he mused, 'perhaps we're all a bit wiser now.'

I came away with my card.

7

Royal Interlude

The power of the principal media—the Press, television, radio and the cinema—is a highly debatable subject and any conclusions must always remain purely personal and individualistic. Statistics are no help, and there has never been—nor is there ever likely to be—any unanimous opinion on such broad-based topics as the influence of the media on violence and public morality or the power of the press in moulding public opinion.

Numerically, the balance of power must always lie with the broadcast, for the obvious reason that its captive audiences are immeasurably greater than that of any other form of mass appeal. Nobody knows this better than the politicians and many people aver that elections can be won or lost solely on the strength of television performances.

The newspapers like to think that their editorial policy exerts a tremendous influence on the thinking of their readers. As an old newspaper editor, I do not wholly subscribe to this view. A widely-read journal can certainly initiate or stimulate a public outcry on some given subject; it can spark off a nationwide controversy, it can campaign for the removal of somebody or something, it can, by constant reiteration, demand that a certain course of action be taken, and there is little doubt that if several papers united on some topical issue—which they rarely do—then they would positively influence that amorphous but formidable element called 'public opinion'. I say influence which is not the same thing as deciding.

For the life of me I cannot think of a single big national campaign initiated by a newspaper that ever got off the ground. Beaverbrook's gallant advocacy of Empire Free Trade (a really worthwhile concept) regrettably came to nothing; Northcliffe's many famous

53

gimmicks (from National bread to square bowler hats and the slogan 'These Junkers will cheat you yet'); the *Daily Mail's* brief flirtation with Mosleyism; all these and many more just faded away without a sliver of success to record. Therefore the so-called 'power of the press' is to that extent illusory but it undeniably possesses a terrifying power when used perniciously. A scandalous gossip paragraph can do fearful damage to reputation and character. By giving undeserved publicity to an obscure privileged statement, untold misery can be caused (as it did in the case of Jeremy Thorpe); a report by a vicious critic can ruin a play or a player, a hint of financial difficulty can jeopardise the welfare of a great business.

Examples—pro and con—are countless. Every editor—and all press barons—recognise the power and the sense of power which ownership or control of a reputable journal confers, and when the chance comes along for an editor to exercise his power, say by launching an appeal, making an original proposal, putting up a monetary reward, advocating a cause or denouncing a scandal, he usually grabs it with both hands provided the risks aren't too great and that the prospects of success are at least reasonable.

I chanced my arm many times during my innings but there is only one episode which I can recall with a frisson of pride, possibly for the reason that it really succeeded handsomely. The story has never been recorded before so, for what it is worth, here it is.

In the period when I was the editorial director of the Argus Press (newspaper owners and press printers) I had charge, among other things, of a weekly journal called *Cavalcade* which I ran on the lines of a news-magazine. It had a circulation of 100,000 copies and each week I wrote the front-page editorial, a platform which achieved some renown and a chore which I immensely enjoyed because I was at liberty to say precisely what I pleased—a privilege few editors enjoy.

The events which I am about to relate happened in the very tense and anxious days of 1939. Europe was seething; Nazism in Germany was at its peak; Mussolini was triumphing in Italy; the international situation was disturbing, with Civil War in Spain, and over everything there brooded the sombre and dire menace of an impending outbreak of war—with Germany.

One happy interlude in the doleful European panorama was the

54

recent State visit of the King and Queen to France, which at least had cemented the ancient bonds of the *entente cordiale* in a Europe riven by enmity, strife and fear.

Pondering over this very successful act of international amity by the monarchy, I got to thinking that a State visit to America might have the effect of making our ties with the United States stronger and friendlier especially at a time when I, and many others, believed fervently that America would be our only hope if ever a second world war did break out.

I turned the subject over in my mind for a long time because I knew only too well that nothing could be more damaging to a journal such as mine than to commit a public gaffe. Ridicule can be a killer.

No reigning British monarch had ever set foot on American soil; protocol would frown on any attempt by an outsider to suggest what the Crown ought to do and there was always the daunting possibility that America itself would veto the whole idea if indeed it were promulgated.

I was friendly at the time with the US Ambassador to the Court of St James's, Joseph P. Kennedy, and as a first step I hastened to tell him what I had in mind. I could see at once that he was intrigued but, diplomatically, he wouldn't commit himself. Anyway, after more heart-searching, I decided to take the plunge and publish my proposal, and on the front page of the issue of *Cavalcade* 26 July 1938 I launched the brash suggestion with as bold a splash as the limitations of page size would permit.

The editorial (as can be seen from the reproductions elsewhere in this book) read:

> . . . *Cavalcade* makes the suggestion that in the interest of Anglo-American relations—in the interests of democracy—plans for a Royal visit to the United States of America next year ought to be submitted now for the gracious approval of Their Majesties.

It was added that such a journey—taking in also a visit to the great World Fair in New York—could be included in the itinerary of a visit to Canada. At that time no visit to Canada was contemplated.

Immediately the announcement appeared, the news agencies flashed the suggestion to the American Press and overnight it became front-page news throughout Canada and the United States.

Grover Whalen, President of the New York World Fair, cabled his endorsement of my proposal and he promised his wholehearted welcome and co-operation.

I seemed to have started something. Newspaper cuttings poured in showing that over three hundred USA and Canadian papers were backing up the idea of a Royal visit to America.

The following memo from Joe Kennedy was a diplomatic non-committal ploy.

London, September 8, 1939

Dear Mr. Goulden,

I am always intrigued by your suggestions, but I doubt very much if it would be possible to get the President to take any action at this time on the one outlined in your letter to me of September 7th. As you know, conditions in the United States are rather hectic at the moment - due somewhat to the sinking of the "Athenia" - and my own impression is that the President will look everything over very carefully before he makes any move at all.

If it is possible to pass your suggestion along in my own way, I will be glad to try to do so.

Yours sincerely,

Joseph P. Kennedy

Mark Goulden, Esq.,
  Managing Editor, CAVALCADE,
    8-10 Temple Avenue,
      London, E.C. 4.

It indicated to me that if my proposal began to attract even more favourable public reaction the Ambassador would get behind it. Later on, he said that is exactly what he did and looking back on the sequence of events I am positive that my suggestion for a Royal visit to America reached the eyes of the President with the blessing and the support of his London Ambassador.

One cable which I particularly liked came from Barry Bingham, son of a former US Ambassador and now editor of a famous Kentucky newspaper. Here it is:

> I note in your issue of 30 July your excellent suggestion that their Majesties King George and Queen Elizabeth visit the United States next year.
>
> The success of the Royal visit to France would be eclipsed, I believe, by the tremendous enthusiasm that would mark the appearance of your King and Queen in this country. At this juncture in world affairs, it would surely be desirable to signalise in this way the strong bonds of friendship between the two great English speaking nations. I am sure my late father, Robert W. Bingham, who served as Ambassador to the Court of St James's, would have endorsed your plan with enthusiasm. I hope the suggestion you have made will be adopted.
>
> Barry Bingham
> The Louisville Times
> Kentucky

Although the first reaction was startlingly good, it wasn't going to be plain sailing from there on. My company in those days was very 'establishment'. In our premises in Tudor Street we printed the *Observer* and the *Financial Times* and we owned important newspapers in the provinces.

I encountered some unexpected opposition in my own office. The chairman of the company (Sir Herbert Grotrian, MP, a power in the Tory Party made it quite clear that a newspaper shouldn't advise the Court to 'seek invitations from foreigners'.

The deputy chairman, 'Jack' Akerman (a former assistant

manager of *The Times*) thought I had backed a loser since the proposal had, in his view, little hope of acceptance.

I got a bit of encouragement, however, from chums at the Press Club (of which I have been a member since 1929) who congratulated me on an 'enterprising stunt', but another colleague—actually the diplomatic correspondent of the *Morning Post*—was a little less enthusiastic. 'I think you're up the bloody creek with your Royal visit caper,' he admonished me with nice diplomatic indirection. 'You'll probably get a rocket from Buck House into the bargain,' he warned.

This alarmed me more than a bit because I well remembered once meeting my old friend Tom Clarke (editor of the *News Chronicle*) after he had been summoned to Buckingham Palace following the publication in his newspaper of some alleged indiscretion. He had just come from the Palace audience when we met and he looked completely deflated and shattered. He never told me what had taken place and I haven't the slightest inkling as to why he looked so bemused and bushed. It seemed as though he had, amongst other things, been induced to take a vow of silence. His lips were sealed. He never let on, even years later when the Press had become considerably more 'liberated' and vastly less inhibited. But somebody or something had scared the hell out of him when I met him coming from his Palace audition.

I was nevertheless undeterred by any obstacles, and in the next issue I plugged the proposal once again and reproduced a lot of the press and other reactions from America. And I kept it going as the front page lead for two subsequent issues, and on 27 August I was able, triumphantly, to announce on the highest authority that my suggestion had been offically adopted and that the Royal Visit to America would be announced in the King's Speech to Parliament three months hence! That in itself was another scoop.

I got a letter from Joe Kennedy saying he was glad to learn of the favourable response. He had just come back from a trip to America and I am quite sure he had paved the way for President Roosevelt to send the official invitation to King George and Queen Elizabeth.

It remains only to record that the visit duly took place and it was a glorious triumph for Anglo-American relations—so soon to be drawn together in the battle against Hitler.

I think Joe Kennedy's final letter to me is worth reprinting:

```
                                    London,
                                  June 14, 1939.
Personal

    Dear Mr. Goulden:
        I am glad to hear from you again.   I
    have thought of you frequently during the
    visit of Their Majesties to America.   I
    remember your early advocacy of the idea and
    the keen interest which you always took in
    the trip, an interest which I was glad to
    second.
        The visit was, as you say, one of the
    outstanding events of the war years.
    Anyone who was, in any way, responsible for
    it has every reason to feel proud.   He has
    done a service not only to his own country,
    and to mine, but to the larger cause of human
    understanding upon which, when all is said and
    done, our hopes for peace must rest.


        Yours sincerely,

        Joseph P Kennedy
```

And I replied as follows:

Dear Mr Kennedy,

Now that the Royal Visit to America is over, and passes into history as one of the epochal events of pre-war years, I feel I ought to conclude the correspondence we had over this matter by a formal letter of thanks for the courtesy and encouragement which you have extended to this journal since first the idea was mooted.

I recall that almost a year ago, when I advanced the suggestion for the Royal Visit to America, it was rather ridiculed by some of my fellow-editors, but you were courageous enough to endorse it wholeheartedly, even to say you would do your best to implement it—and in due course you did.

You may not know that it was an unprecedented thing, in this country, for a journal to make a direct suggestion to the Throne, the more so when a question of international policy was concerned.

But it so often happens that the impossible and unthinkable soon becomes a reality when someone takes the initiative and has the support of the bold in spirit.

In contra-distinction to the American and the Canadian press, the newspapers in Britain have never referred to the origin of the Royal Visit idea, with the possible exception of the Beaverbrook journals, which I am happy to note pay tribute to your own splendid efforts.

Yours sincerely,
Mark Goulden

It may seem to the reader a bit odd that no British newspaper printed a single word about the genesis of the Royal Visit idea, but there was good reason. It was traditional, in those days, for newspapers never to mention in their columns the name of a rival journal, except perhaps for the purpose of 'knocking' it. It was an unwritten (but extremely mean and rotten) law and vestigially it still persists today in some quarters.

Forty years ago I promoted the first ever professional golf tournament sponsored by a newspaper. My *Yorkshire Evening News* 1,000 Guineas Golf Tournament became internationally famous and drew entries by pros from all over the world. The course of the games each day in Leeds was fully reported in every paper throughout the land, but not a single paper ever called the event anything but 'The Thousand Guineas Golf Tournament'. The 'boycott' of the sponsor's name was total.

It was only after I had protested to the Newspaper Society (the trade organisation of the provincial press) about the matter that some of the papers relented and in future gave my paper credit for organising the event. It is very different today when the commercial backers of big sporting events (golf, racing, show-jumping, ocean yachting, grand prix, tennis, cricket, etc.) now get voluminous and unanimous acknowledgement from all sections of the media. There is of course one good reason for this. Most of these sponsors are also big advertisers and that alone guarantees they get top billing in every newspaper in the country.

8

Interlude
With Midas

When the man-with-the-Midas-touch, Jean Paul Getty, died amid the ancestral splendours of Sutton Place near Guildford, I mourned his passing as one who had known him since he first came to England—the country from which he never returned to his own native land.

He came to London from America via Rome in 1953, together with his then current girl-friend, a petite, attractive Jewish writer, Ethel le Vane, who was born in Manchester. She had met Getty on the Super Chief Express from Chicago to Los Angeles and he seduced her twice on the journey in his private compartment.

They were an odd pair but from a very close acquaintance with both of them I am reasonably sure he had a real affection for this garrulous, lively little woman who was so obsessed with Getty that she talked (interminably) about little else.

Between them they had written a book concerning Getty's art treasures, and how he had acquired them, and Paul asked me if I would like to publish it. We spent a lot of time in my office licking it into shape and I gave it a rather saleable title—*Collectors' Choice*—which was a spin-off from a widely popular radio programme of the time called 'Housewife's Choice'.

As in everything he did, Getty tried, while the book was gestating, to acquire a sort of expertise in publishing and production. He specified the quality of the paper to be used and the type-face, he supervised the illustrations and he read and corrected the galley proofs meticulously. He came often to the office in Essex Street and I frequently went to see him in his headquarters at the Ritz, consisting of two tiny rooms in what must originally have been the servants' garret of the hotel. He had similar quarters in Paris, his two small rooms in the George V being the cheapest accommodation that could be obtained in the entire hotel.

From these dens he conducted the affairs of his vast oil empire and each night he would post his mail personally, since he wouldn't trust anyone with his correspondence.

And to his sumptuous quarters in London his devoted girl-friend, known to all of us as 'Bunny', would also repair frequently in order, among other things, to wash out Getty's socks and underpants of which he, presumably, had few changes!

They both had a preoccupation with sickness and when Paul went into the clinic for a face lift, Bunny would stay in an adjoining room until he was discharged. And similarly when Bunny, who 'enjoyed' consistent ill-health, had to be hospital-ised, Paul would accompany her, having already made himself something of an expert in the etiology of whatever she was currently suffering from.

Their social life was minimal. They knew very few people in London and I supposed they dined and visited at my homes (in Hertford Street and later in Down Street) more than anywhere else at the time.

The newspapers first began to get on the trail of Getty soon after an article appeared in an American journal in which he was dubbed the 'richest man in the world'. But he shunned publicity and he refused to talk to journalists, referring all personal enquiries direct to me. At one point he wanted me to become his PR man (as a sideline to my publishing activities) but I had neither the time nor the desire. Besides, I already had much evidence of his pathological greediness and there were other sides to his character that didn't altogether commend themselves to me.

The bond between him and his 'Bunny' extended to the intro-duction of many a nubile girl until he began to suffer from impo-tence, to counter which he took pills that seriously affected his health. He provided, parsimoniously, for Bunny but she was happy to serve him. Between them they developed a code of 'baby talk' in which they could communicate with each other and it was regarded as hilarious by people in my household. Often from my home she would telephone Paul in Paris and it was impossible not to overhear parts of their extraordinary 'love language'. The cross-talk usually

opened with: 'This is ickle Bunnykins calling ickle Pauly. Is my
Pauly-Wauly happy in naughty-waughty Paris?'

Once, after dinner, a call to Paris had started up the 'nursery
dialogue' on a telephone that was within earshot of the other guests,
and when the beaming Bunny proceeded later to give everyone a
blow-by-blow account of her Pauly's adventures in the Gay City,
one member of the party (the film producer Raymond Stross, an
outspoken character) suddenly rose from his chair, strode across the
room and shouted at the loquacious Bunny, 'Do you know you are
the biggest bloody bore I have ever met? I'm sick of hearing about
you and your senile friend so I'm off.' And out he went into the
Piccadilly night!

In his autobiography, Getty writes: 'Mark and Jane [my wife]
became good and close friends and we have had many good times
together.' Living as I did in Mayfair—a stone's throw from the
Ritz—it was easy for Paul to dine with us and he enjoyed many
parties which I gave. He was easy to cater for. His invariable menu
was medium-rare steak, Idaho potato, ice-cream and coffee. He
didn't smoke, drank very little, and although my wife happens to be
a dedicated and knowledgeable cook with a reputation for keeping a
good table, nothing in the way of culinary exotica would tempt Paul
from his plebeian Texas food preferences.

One night we had for dinner (that sounds like one of those
'gastronomic cannibalisms' in Cecil King's memoirs) the Chicago
millionaire grocer Nate Cummings, Armand and Michaela Denis
(the jungle explorers), Ben Huebsch (doyen of American publishers) and Mitchell Samuels, perhaps the greatest antique dealer in
the world. Mitchell had advised Getty on many of his art purchases
and he knew everybody in the business from Duveen to Berenson
as, of course, did Paul. His warehouse in mid-town Manhattan was
an Aladdin's Cave of treasures, the like of which was not to be seen
outside the walls of a museum. There were panelled rooms which he
had brought in their entirety from stately homes in England and had
re-erected them piece by piece on his premises. It would have taken
weeks to see it all, so vast was the collection. Eventually it was taken
over by Parke-Bernet in New York.

Mitchell, crippled with arthritis, was a delightful person whose
stories of the art world would have filled a book. He was courteous,

kindly and generous—utterly unlike that repulsive breed of 'dealers' who infest salerooms and public auctions, picking over other people's 'household goods' like so many rapacious vultures eviscerating a cadaver.

I think it was Mitchell who first suggested that Getty should buy Sutton Place from the Duke of Sutherland (who was one of Mitchell's clients) and this, of course, is what Paul actually did in 1958, when he acquired the property as European headquarters for his oil empire.

At the particular dinner party I am chronicling—it was a really nice 'mix' which is something not always achieved even by meticulous table-planning—Getty, who was normally (at that period) morose and withdrawn in company, 'warmed up' to Armand Denis. They had a common interest in wild animals and while Armand was one of the greatest living authorities on anthropoids, Paul seemed to be able to hold his own in any discussion about the fauna of the jungle, especially lions. They also had something else in common: they were both as mean as hell!

They were cultivated men. Paul, who had studied political science and economics at Oxford, spoke five languages fluently and could write and speak learnedly about art, as well as commerce. Denis was a handsome aristocratic Belgian of considerable erudition and he was formerly married to one of the Roosevelt women. He made a lot of money from his jungle films and TV programmes but he stuck to his earnings like a limpet! I have just remembered another egregious affinity he shared with Getty—his impoverished wife and partner, Michaela, used regularly to wash his socks since he boasted only one pair on and one pair off! Perhaps there is a Freudian explanation of this sock-washing syndrome which seems to afflict men of wealth. Maybe it's what the psychiatrists call a 'feetish'—if you will forgive the pun?

The stories about Getty's frugality are legion and presumably most of them are true. I figured in some of these parsimonious incidents like the one about waiting twenty minutes for five o'clock to strike so that we could go into Crufts Dog Show for half price!

Round about the time I am recalling, it was very difficult for British visitors to America to get by on the meagre dollar allocations which the exchange control permitted. One had to get up to all sorts of 'tricks' in order to subsist and we, who were helping to restore the nation's export trade, were under a severe handicap. I remember Paul asking me one day how I and my wife managed, dollar-wise, when we visited New York twice a year on business. My ears quickly pricked up! I knew that he owned the palatial Pierre Hotel on upper Fifth Avenue and I felt reasonably sure he was about to offer me terms to stay at his hotel on our future trips. I truthfully replied that we had to conserve our funds by staying at rather inferior places and my wife chipped in with a timely cue-line: 'We have to stay wherever I am able to make breakfast so that we can save a few dollars on that alone.' This wifely regard for economy instantly appealed to Paul. He proceeded to commend it. 'That's a good girl, Jane,' he growled in his gravelly voice, 'always look after Mark's money.'

End of conversation.

We didn't stay at the Pierre!

Funnily enough, he did come to my aid once when it was necessary for me to overstay a trip in New York. I had tapped most of my friends including Gertie Lawrence, Jessie Royce Landis, Fanny Holtzman and Evelyn Kessel, and it looked very much as though I should have to book a bench in Central Park for the rest of my stay!

Then Paul came to the rescue by instructing one of his minions to advance me a thousand dollars. Tracking down this executive in a down-town Getty skyscraper (which, like the new Getty building on Madison Avenue, Paul never saw) was akin to looking for a marble in the Hampton Court Maze! And when at last I nobbled the cashier, I had to sign documents which seemed to include the Declaration of Independence and Magna Carta before I could get my eager hands on the green stuff!

Under the category of niggardly jokes, I should include the story of a small party which Paul once gave at the Savoy on my wife's birthday, a fact imparted to him at the last minute by Bunny. It opened on a rather disconcerting note because Paul was angry over a notice he had received that day from the Home Office telling him his visitor's permit had expired and he would have to leave the country! He was livid. 'I have brought great sums of money to this country since I came here,' he exclaimed, 'and this is the way your people show their appreciation. They need a lesson and they'll get one from me.'

66

I tried to placate him. 'It's a typical piece of Whitehall bureaucracy,' I said. 'I will get the notice cancelled at once. I have a friend at the Home Office who will deal with it personally and immediately.'

But he refused to be appeased. Waving the little green official card requesting his departure he said, 'This insult will cost your Government dearly. I have just placed an order on Clydeside for one of my super-tankers and tomorrow I will cancel it. The order will go to Japan.' And it did; even though Whitehall's error was subsequently expiated.

After a false start like this it is difficult to get conversation back on to an amiable level but the evening passed uneventfully and as I was paying the bill, Paul handed to my wife a small box of Fortnum & Mason chocolates as 'a little something for your birthday'.

It looked ostentatiously modest coming from one of the world's richest men and on our way home, after dropping Paul and Bunny at the Ritz, my wife said as she fondled the little gift box, 'A bit patronising, don't you think?' My reply is unprintable but she eased the tension by brightly remarking, 'Maybe it's a big fat joke; there's probably a diamond or a pearl in each of the chocolates.' An exciting thought! We garaged the car with dangerous haste, rushed into the apartment and with nervous glee decapitated the first of the chocs. But obviously they were *virgo intacta*. The autopsy revealed nothing; no diamonds! No pearls!! Not even a Ciro!!! We got a good laugh out of the mirthful incident and we got a lot of mileage out of it as a conversation piece for a long time afterwards.

I once tried to fathom the cause of Getty's studied, deliberate, unnecessary and calculated parsimony, and I came up with a startling conclusion; he really lived 'apart' from his wealth. Of course it existed, and he did everything he could to increase it, but it was in a way an abstract thing that didn't somehow belong to him; a kind of sacred, priceless orchid not to be touched and from which no petal must ever be plucked. He spent lavishly on the things that would escalate his riches or give him tax relief—like his California museum and his art treasures, and what after all can a millionaire spend his money on? But so far as money in his pocket was concerned, Paul was impecunious—in his own pet phrase he was 'cash poor'.

He was not above talking about it sometimes but he always trotted out a carefully contrived alibi for his greediness—he didn't need to give to charity since he gave employment to vast numbers of people and that was much better than giving money away uselessly!

I think he really believed in this subterfuge and I recall how upset he was when I once dubbed him a miser in public. It happened in 1958 when *Time* magazine in its issue of 24 July ran a cover story on 'oilman J. Paul Getty—the do-it-yourself tycoon'. It was written by the paper's Paris correspondent, Thomas Dozier, and he had no fewer than fifteen interviews with Getty who at the end of the ordeal said he wouldn't go through it again for $100,000. It must have been lacerating at that price!

Because I was Getty's publisher and one of his closest acquaintances, Dozier also interviewed me and printed my candid opinions about the subject of his cover story. He asked me to sum up in a sentence my impression of Getty as a human being and I promptly replied: 'He's just a bloody miser.' *Time* magazine, which in those days was rather more Nice Nelly than it is now, cut out the adjectival expletive although Dozier, at my request, had carefully underlined it in his original story as a must.

I don't think anyone else had ever publicly excoriated Getty for his congenital and contemptible meanness but it was high time someone did. That was eighteen years ago and my gratuitous character-reading never made any difference to our friendship; nor did it have, so far as I am aware, any effect on his incurable frugality.

We kept in touch over the years and I watched with amused interest his metamorphosis from a shy retiring wallflower into the glittering social butterfly he later became. Early in 1970 I met him in the lounge of the SS *United States* heading across the Channel for Le Havre. He wouldn't cross the strip of water on anything smaller than an ocean liner—nor would he ever travel by air—and as we reminisced a little, he pulled out a pocket diary, consulted it and said, 'Do you know how long we've known each other? It's over eighteen years.' I wonder what else was in that little book. At his home he kept a voluminous diary and I gather the contents of these notes are now up for grabs as a book.

Almost in the last year of his life he decided to write his autobiography and I undertook not only to publish it, but also to edit it.

It was actually written by an American/Hungarian author, Bela von Block, who spent long hours with Getty at Sutton Place assembling the material for the story. Every page of the manuscript was vetted and initialled by Getty's personal attorney, C. Lansing Hays, and I had to select the illustrations from twenty huge leather-bound volumes containing every photograph of Getty and his family and associates spanning nearly eighty years. It was a formidable task but as one reviewer remarked, the pictures were alone worth the price of the book.

They highlighted the hectic social activities in the later years of a man who had shunned any such human contacts or duties and they disclosed the 'harem' of devoted acolytes which he had gathered about him in his Surrey palace. This was apart altogether from a coterie of female friends whom he had cultivated since the time he had broken out of his anti-social stockade. Many others came within his ken and he held many of them in secret contempt. He had told Dozier that he received thousands of letters, 'all seeking a chunk of his fortune', and to me personally he confided one of the basic premises of his entire philosophy: 'I have to assume, Mark, that anyone who tries to approach me is primarily concerned with getting some of my money,' he pronounced, as though he was handing down a precept from Sinai!

Like all rich men, he couldn't escape the hordes of flatterers, sycophants and parasites—men and women alike—who milled around him or invited him to posh parties, first nights, press luncheons and such-like gatherings of free-loaders—all part of the social milieu in which he now revelled with zestful eagerness.

Few of these courtiers knew the real Getty—a sad, disillusioned man unfortunate in his many marriages, unlucky in his children with whom he never got close enough to communicate properly; an avowed womaniser; physically unprepossessing but inwardly a person desperately wanting to be loved yet incapable of being lovable. This didn't rule out the constant availability of a bevy of women eager and ready to jump into bed with a man who had lost count of the lays he had enjoyed with five robust wives and countless casuals on the side—a sexual marathon that must have lasted nearly seventy years!

Poor old Paul died a few weeks before his autobiography appeared. There was to have been a big launching party at Sutton

Place (for which the publishers were to pay) but it never took place.

He had written to me a little while before the end, saying: 'It was a source of considerable satisfaction' to him to learn I was personally editing his book, 'Indeed, I am flattered,' he added, and expressed the hope that it would live up to my expectations. He signed off 'My very best personal regards to you and Jane'.

That was the last I heard from the man I had known a great many years and much better than most people knew him. In my own fashion I liked him even though I abhorred his meanness and derided his lechery. His life story was in no sense an inspiring tale of a splendid life well lived to ripe old age. It was an infinitely sad story of a man who apparently had everything in life but in reality had nothing. As I said at the time in an article published in the *Sunday Express*: 'I doubt if he could have counted five faithful friends in all the world and I would question whether anyone, anywhere shed a tear of genuine grief when last month, among his earthly trappings, in Sutton Place he quietly closed his chronicle of wasted time.'

That was a tragic epitaph for a man who was powerful enough to conquer the business world, strong enough to have defeated those who sought to prey on him yet too weak to win for himself those priceless gifts, the love and affection of his fellow creatures.

I think his human frailties could have been vanquished had he found the kind of woman who could have loved him for himself alone instead of for his well-insulated wealth. He had a certain innate nobility of character that could have blossomed under the loving care of a selfless woman devoted to the task of humanising a man who, without such help, was destined to become a money-machine and little else. Perhaps he was seeking the mother whom he always adored. When he knew his days were numbered he pleaded with his ex-wife, the beautiful Teddy Lynch, to remarry him. He adored her, as indeed he adored the child she bore him. But she turned his offer down. With all his millions he was no bargain!

With a fine and dedicated woman by his side, J. Paul Getty—with his Midas touch—might have made a notable contribution to humanity.

But there aren't many women like that around these days any more. Most of them have emancipated themselves out of their womanhood!

70

9

Interlude Romantic

What's happened to Romance? That could very well be a good question coming from a publisher, but I don't ask it in the context of publishing, even though the romance I have in mind has much to do with our profession. Romance, of course, is a publishing genre.

But romance, in its normal usage, has departed almost entirely from the way of life in the western world and I often wonder if this hasn't been a contributory factor to the universal sickness that assails us.

Not so long ago, an aura of romance belonged to many things, to many places, and to many people. It was, one might say, an essential element in most of the activities concerned with the pleasurable side of living. Those who catered for people seeking a little surcease from the strains and stresses of modern existence deliberately cultivated the romantic atmosphere. Its subtle influence permeated a vast spectrum of things like eating, travel, poetry, the theatre, reading, dressing, painting, meditating, love, human relations, home-making, music, sculpture, the cinema, etc. etc. It was really a vital ingredient in the sweet cakes which most human beings—from babies to nonagenarians—crave for in life.

If you look into the very etymology of the word itself, you can see that it derives from a revolt against anything that was prosaic, stilted or pedantic and that in art particularly, romanticism was a protest against the dull classicism that had held sway for so long.

Many writers have tried to describe it variously as imaginative, dreamlike, magic, *sehnsucht* (nostalgia), lyricism, extravagance, fanciful, but one definition which seems to express it really accurately—if one can accurately define an intangible—says that it means building castles in the air. That is something people don't do any more in these hard, materialistic down to earth times—and more's the pity.

71

Many of us can remember how romantic in almost every respect was a journey across the Atlantic in one of the great liners. The boat train itself had a romantic atmosphere; the first glimpse of the mighty ship at its moorings was a romantic sight tingling with promise, excitement and a pervading happiness. The whole ambience of the preliminaries made the blood race. It was an occasion and everything about it was joyously romantic.

And how does that compare with a transatlantic flight today? What could be duller, uglier, more boring than the preliminaries here, where people are driven and herded like sheep in unlovely waiting rooms then corralled into a cramped metal container to sit for several hours without moving a limb, except perhaps to visit the loo? Some scratchy, nearly inaudible canned music vainly attempts to create a bit of atmosphere, but really it is a cold, unimaginative, graceless experience which everybody prays will end as quickly as possible. A long rail journey is worse, unless dirt, decrepitude and discomfort constitute romance! How desperately—and unsuccessfully—have some air carriers tried to inject a romantic touch into their advertising! You are virtually invited to have a slap and tickle with the hostess—the cheerful Americans or the bewitchingly modest Asiatics—all the way over. 'Fly Me' means whatever you think it means.

Is going to the theatre or a West End restaurant any longer a romantic, exciting event? On stage you will probably be entertained by a kitchen sink drama or scared stiff by a psychiatric thriller in which the romantic urge centres on the motivations of a young man with an obsession for blinding or disembowelling horses! And so far as dining out is concerned, if you think being jammed table-to-table in an overcrowded, noisy, smelly super-bistro (that happens to be the chi-chi in-joint of the moment) is romantic and glamorous, then you might as well have stayed at home glued to that most unromantic of machines—the telly—and its concomitant the instant telly supper!

Once upon a time you got all dressed up, well-bathed, refreshed, looking good and smelling good to enjoy a night out with friends who also took special care to look nice, feel nice and smell nice for the occasion. It was civilised.

And you went perhaps to a restaurant which played its part in making the evening romantic and memorable, with good food, good service, soft lighting and quiet music that all conduced to the building of a few castles in the air for an hour or two. Or you may have gone to see a romantic live musical such as Ivor Novello, Cole Porter or Noël Coward conjured up for the delectation of those who preferred a flight of fancy into the theatrical dream-world. Or you might have been beguiled by the romantic songs of 'Hutch' and listened to the nightingales in Berkeley Square! Today all you would get would be a North Country lout yowling and yammering in the current scouse fashion or be treated to a feast of minstrelsy, romantically called Punk Rock. The very nomenclature of our present day recreation is enough to kill romance!

Of course it's so much easier today for a young lady going out to leap into a pair of skin-tight denims—fragrant as only skin-tight garments can be—throw on an eye-catching plunging top and rush to meet her big romance (seventies style), no doubt clad also in hygienic crotch-squeezing denims (a little recognised cause of impotence), open-necked flowered shirt looking the essence of romantic maleness with his lank hair falling about his shoulders, aping the masculine mediocrities who abound today in all the best places.

The steatopygous effect of stretch denims may look sexy, but romantic 'it aint'!

It is my absolute conviction that the craze for marijuana started when young people, perhaps subconsciously, began to realise that all romance had gone from their drab lives. Miraculously, they had found a readily available substitute!

A tiny cigarette had the power to lift them out of their dull, unromantic environment and magically send them on a 'trip' to a dream world, to an unreal land where they could so easily build castles in the air, alone if necessary. This was ersatz romance but it caught on quicker than a virulent epidemic. Few people today realise just how widespread the addiction to pot has become—especially in America. There is hardly a school or college in the country where the grass problem hasn't become a major issue and I haven't the slightest doubt that it is already rampant in this country. It must inevitably become, in the near future, a matter of the utmost gravity to educationalists and others concerned with the welfare of our youth. We are, at present, shutting our eyes to it.

For many years now it has been self-evident that people of all ages and both sexes, starved of romance in their daily lives, have found refuge in a 'joint', and until life has something better to offer, the practice is bound to increase. And, as we know, the step from innocent pot to main-line drugs is all too short a stride.

For millions, pot has replaced booze as the escape route to a romantic other-world. I count this to be one of the ineluctable truths of modern civilisation and like so many basic issues, it is not fully comprehended. We have now got the measure of smoking (another romance-inducer) as a menace to health but it is easier to quit smoking than it is to give up pot, and that's something the health authorities ought seriously to heed.

When did romance go out of fashion? And why? Those are questions which others can grapple with. Let me here say that at least publishers—always leading purveyors of romance—have done something to keep it alive. The Love Story is still—disguised though it may be with gymnastic sex or orgasmic violence—the basis of the true novel.

The kitchen maid (even if such relics existed today) may no longer lose herself in *Peg's Paper* or soft-cover romances, but she seeks the equivalent in 'Coronation Street', 'The Liver Birds', or other broadcast programmes with which producers cater for the universal yearning for romance, but all the time pretend that sentimentality is a bad word.

The adult reader still loves a love story and from time to time, to the publisher's surprise, a novel will hit the bestseller lists for no other reason than that it is essentially a romance.

Some authors (and some publishers) have won fame and fortune by sticking rigidly to the love story formula, some unashamedly, like Rose Franken, Barbara Cartland, Winifred Scott, Faith Baldwin, etc., and others less directly like Jacqueline Susann, Georgette Heyer, Jackie Collins, Rona Jaffe, etc. The work of the old timers such as Elinor Glyn, Ethel M. Dell, etc., never went out of print.

Rose Franken is a remarkable instance of an author who created two romantic fictional characters (Claudia and her husband David), and in so doing touched the peaks of wealth, fame, recognition and the gratitude of millions of readers the world over. Left a widow with three children, Rose went out to Hollywood and, with no experience whatsoever, became, in an astonishingly short time, a professional script writer for the films.

A short story in a fiction magazine was the precursor of her Claudia saga which in the course of time ballooned into one of the most successful literary properties of the century. Her books sold by the million—they were turned into plays, movies, television and radio features; they were translated into dozens of languages and from the vast proceeds of it all, she brought up and educated her three sons and lived in sumptuous style in Connecticut and California. She is also a gifted playwright.

And what was the secret of Rose Franken's Claudia books? I will tell you because I published all of them and therefore I know the drill. They were *romances* and they appealed to people who needed some romance in their lives—which means at least half the adult population in the whole world.

It wasn't literature; it wasn't scintillating prose and it wasn't in any way intellectual. But it certainly wasn't sentimental slush. And it was much more than the simple love story—it was written and dedicated to the sanctity of marriage and it was addressed in the main to all those people who believed in the wonder, romance and nobility of home-making—now almost a forgotten art.

I blame women—the liberated legions—largely for the murdering of romance. They have deliberately taken away from their men-folk the romantic incentive of providing, of being the bread winner; they have robbed the male of the urge to go out and work for the little woman, to protect her and care for her. By sacrificing their womanliness, they have reversed the fundamental human roles.

In America I have watched, over the years, the women slowly and surely emasculating their men and the men (heaven forgive them) have willingly accepted the assault. The he-man, the gun-toting frontierman, the Tarzanine males, the virile cow-hands—these are the screaming myths of the century. The average American male is scared witless of his wife and (if he only understood what the word means) he would know that he is living in a matriarchy. The emancipated woman today does everything she can (consciously or unwittingly) to masculinise herself, and she regards natural femininity as a badge of servitude. The first sign of sanity returning to our mad world will be when women evince the desire to become women again!

Rose Franken believed in the things she wrote about. She married a handsome writer (who became her manager) and she herself was a most wonderful home-maker. Had she not been a gifted novelist, she could have been one of America's greatest interior decorators. She had a genius for converting any abode, no matter how decrepit, dilapidated or physically unsuitable, into a home of immense beauty, impeccable taste and faultless amenities, with no suggestion of ostentation nor taint of *nouveau riche*. She had an unerring instinct for proportion, elegance and decor and it was always accomplished with unbelievable economy. She could spot an antique bargain a mile off!

Once upon a time she actually moved an entire house, lock stock and barrel, from one site to another and she personally landscaped farmland into exquisite formal gardens complete with running stream and rustic bridges.

With her husband—he was quite a talented author—she virtually lived a Claudia and David existence—romantic, blissful, opulent and invariably successful. Romance and success—what a formula for a love story!

She used to get an enormous fan mail and I remember once mystifying her by sending on to her a letter which had come to my office. It briefly said, 'All of us here enjoy your books. They are the most frequently asked for in the library and I thought you should know what pleasure you have given to so many people.'

Rose replied saying that she got hundreds of similar letters. 'What was so special about this one on the blue notepaper?' When I told her it had come from an inmate of Dartmoor—then Britain's top security prison—she was intrigued and very touched.

One would have thought that with the decline of romance in the daily lives of people (which is really the subject of this interlude) and with the rejection of home-making as a feminine virtue (by the liberators) the success of the fabulous Claudia books would have diminished. But quite the contrary; they have never gone out of print in over twenty-five years and they have been paperbacked for succeeding generations of new—and entranced—romance seekers.

But romance in real life as well as in fiction can sometimes wither and fade, as indeed it did so ironically for the woman who had apotheosised marriage and had consecrated home-making.

Rose's romantic husband, whom she adored, and who really was a parasite battening on her wealth and fame, suddenly and for no reason 'turned against her'. He left her to go and live in a country cottage (which Rose had so wonderfully restored!) with a dull, dowdy female. He was surrounded by acres of sporting and game country and he lived like a phoney squire with his string of horses and his armoury of guns—a pair of which he would often buy from Purdeys or Churchills in London for anything up to a couple of thousand pounds. He drooled over them with a lover's ecstasy but I never heard him fire one!

He had made off with most of her money and so bitterly had his love turned to hatred that he even plotted to get his wife certified as insane!

Her marriage was in ruins; she gave up her lovely home in Riverdale and went to live in a tiny Fifth Avenue apartment which (typically) she quickly turned into a miniature mansion. But love had gone. Or had it? In spite of his atrocious behaviour, I never heard her utter a word of recrimination against her beloved 'Bill'. She made excuses for him and she never tried to recover the money he had misappropriated.

They say love dies hard. Before her husband died she forgave him all his misdeeds. He lived in the wrong century. He thought himself to be a Regency buck with a love of finery and an ability to hold his liquor. He didn't disguise a latent anti-semitism which is surprising because he was actually married to a Jewess, even though Claudia/Rose had fantasised herself out of her Jewish background and origins to the extent that she thought she was an Irish colleen!

I seem to have written most of the above in the past tense, implying that Rose Franken has retired from the literary scene. That is by no means the case. She resides now in a fashionable private hotel in Upper Manhattan and though well over eighty, she is at work on a new play—not about Claudia. 'The old girl has been very good to me,' Rose Franken says about her creation, 'and I won't do anything to tarnish her memory.'

Apart from anything else, the stage roles of Claudia brought fame to many actresses. The plays are always in demand for repertory and Rose still collects considerable royalties from them.

The direction, casting and production of her plays was always supervised by Rose, who is a demanding and strong-willed personality. She has an abrasive tongue and often a cutting manner, and in her private life she exemplifies the ineluctable truth of the Ovidian dictum that in order to be loved, you must be lovable.

It's strange how many successful women authors—from Colette downwards—have been meal-tickets for their spouses. I could name a dozen right off the bat within my own publishing experiences. In some other spheres of life there is a pejorative term for gentlemen who enjoy the fruits of their wives' labours!

10

Interlude with Good and Evil

It is wholly appropriate and even necessary in a book that records the outstanding events and experiences in my long career as journalist and publisher that I should devote a chapter to the subject of metaphysics, a subject which, with its cognates—parapsychology, extra-sensory perception, spiritualism and psychic phenomena—has not been without significance to me, especially in what may have been my formative years.

I spent much of my early life in the North of England and it was there that I first became acquainted with what is known colloquially as the unseen world and my interest gradually extended to various other aspects of the magical and esoteric arts—necromancy, precognition, the supernatural, thought-transference, divination, kabbalah, palmistry—the occult in general.

I dabbled in it all. That's probably the wrong word—dabbled; let's say I investigated all these phenomena, maybe not in great depth but with sufficient exploration to form a judgement and to reject anything that savoured of charlatanry or palpable deception.

The cult of spiritualism, and particularly the subject of life-after-death, flourishes exceedingly in the North and I early discovered that the seance was a highly organised affair which attracted devotees from, as the cliché says, all walks of life.

It wasn't very difficult for a newspaperman to nose out the ramifications of this underground movement, and to gain admission to its close-tiled circles.

Consequently, I saw at first hand a good deal of what goes on at these gatherings and while I do not propose to enter into any considerable detail about it, I am prepared to say quite categorically, as a trained and objective observer, that I experienced certain happenings for which I can give no rational explanation whatsoever.

Any confirmed spiritualist might say precisely this—and more—but I am not a spiritualist; yet I do say that I am totally mystified by and utterly unable to explicate certain events which I—over twenty-one and in my right mind—actually witnessed.

Let someone explain to me how a medium (in ordinary life a charlady) could go into a trance and recite abstruse Latin verse? Let someone tell me why a working-woman medium was able to transmit a message in song from Madame Melba in a pure soprano voice just like Melba's, or to conjure up the spirit of Harry Lauder and to give a life-like imitation of the famous comedian in all its Scottish nuances? This woman could have earned a fortune on the halls as a mimic or impersonator instead of transferring voices from the other side for a mere pittance.

By what means did a medium discover, without a moment's hesitation, a nickname which a friend of mine once bore and which he swore to me no living person other than himself could now possibly know? He had never seen the medium in his life. I could multiply such incidents almost indefinitely and all I am able to say by way of a summation is that they defy logical explanation.

During the war I once went to a seance arranged by Harry Ainsworth, a leading newspaper editor, and among others present were Gerald Kersh, the novelist, Hannen Swaffer, the 'Pope' of British spiritualists, and three other journalists whose names I forget—about ten persons in all. The meeting took place in an air-raid shelter which was actually a huge metal cupola taken from the deck of a scrapped naval vessel. There was only one small entrance door; there was one electric light bulb on a flex which was led in from a plug point in the main house. There was no window in the place, and ventilation was afforded by three large vents let into the metal walls. I mention these points to eliminate from the subsequent proceedings any possibility of mechanical or electrical interference from outside.

The medium was a lady from Brighton who didn't know the name of any one of the participants. She was not even formally introduced to us before the seance began and as soon as we were all seated she started to make contact with various persons who had passed over and who, apparently, knew some of those present. Lord Northcliffe, for instance, spoke to Swaffer; a magazine-editor had a dialogue with Kersh and suddenly a strangled voice materialised from a man whose name was unclear but who said he was in the First World War with me. 'You lied about your age,' whispered the hoarse voice. 'But I knew you were under seventeen because I was in the company records office at Dunstable.' The rest was undecipherable but what he had said was perfectly correct. And so it went on with messages coming through via the medium for everybody in the room. I confess that I was a little shaken by what I was hearing and Kersh, I recall, seemed to be trembling.

Then came an incident which literally made my hair stand on end. There had been a conversation between the Rev 'Dick' Sheppard and Hannen Swaffer when the latter said in a loud clear voice, 'Before you go, Dick, let's see your crucifix.' And then and there in the stygian darkness of the air-raid shelter a brightly illuminated crucifix appeared, moved slowly across the arc of the cupola and disappeared. We were all stunned and when the solitary electric bulb was switched on, we were able to see each other's pale and startled faces. I am absolutely certain nothing was attached to the crucifix—no electric cable to light it, no wire to suspend it; it wasn't handled by anyone in the room because it rose at one time to over twelve feet to the roof of the shelter—and to this day I haven't fathomed the mystery of the illuminated crucifix.

I was a close friend of Swaffer both in my newspaper period and in the early days of my publishing and one day he came to see me in my Essex Street office on a very urgent matter. 'Swaff's' appearance never changed; the tall Thespian figure with black homburg, black cravat and the inevitable cigarette dangling from the corner of his mouth, shedding a flurry of ash down his coat lapels.

'I have been urged by my friends in the spirit world,' he began, 'to write my autobiography, and they have advised me to come to you to publish it.'

Swaff was then at the height of his fame as a journalist and critic, but he had never attempted a book. I appreciated that he would be a welcome addition to my list, especially since I was then known as 'Publisher in ordinary to the Journalistic Profession'. This appellation had been conferred on my company by *The Bookseller* because I had specialised for some years in publishing the works of newspapermen and women, people who earned their living by writing. I had even put up a prize of £500 (a substantial sum in those days) for the best manuscript—fiction or non-fiction—written by anyone connected with the press, or advertising, or public relations. It was won by a Manchester press officer for his book on 'Dalys Theatre'.

I published a great many books by journalists and I was entrusted with the task of publishing the official history of the National Union of Journalists, an important work entitled *Gentlemen, The Press*.

But back to Swaff and his directive from the spirit world. He first told me how he became converted to spiritualism—how he had come to scoff and stayed to pray. He had been commissioned by a newspaper to do a series of articles exposing spiritualism as a sham and a deception and his job was to investigate the whole subject and particularly to shatter its claims to be able to communicate with the departed.

'It was the biggest story I had ever tackled,' Swaff told me, 'because I found the cult was deeply rooted throughout the length and breadth of the land, and I should have to travel far afield to dig out the facts and get "behind the scenes" .'

But Swaff had not been on the story many weeks before he began to change his entire approach to the subject. The more he investigated it, the more convinced he became that it wasn't a 'sham' at all. He interviewed all the famous spiritualists; he attended numberless seances and psychic demonstrations and before he had written a single word condemning the whole system, he had himself become a convert. From that moment he virtually devoted his life to all manifestations of spiritualism; he became not only its protagonist but its protector. Woe betide any journalist who wrote a derogatory word about spiritualists or their religion; Swaff was on his track instantly. In time he became known as the 'Pope' of spiritualism and he was revered by all who belonged to his 'Church'.

Having completed the publishing formalities—Swaffer set about writing his book in earnest, and when nearing the end of the task, he asked me to suggest a name for it, to which I responded with a very appropriate title. His investigation into spiritualism had been Swaff's biggest journalistic assignment—so what better title therefore than *My Greatest Story*. Swaff was intrigued by the title, but he said he must first ascertain if it would be 'acceptable'. 'I will be able to tell you tomorrow,' he added, and the next day he came to my office and in his usual solemn and emphatic manner (he loved to force home a point by digging you in the ribs or poking a finger into your chest) he declared, 'Yes, "they" like the title immensely and approve it.' And so it was that I published *My Greatest Story* by Hannen Swaffer in which the 'Pope' related many astonishing tales of spirit manifestations and psychic phenomena. He was proud of his authorship even though the reviewers (in the lay press) gave it scant attention. Curiously enough, the late Tom Driberg never mentioned the book in his biography of Swaffer.

Long after 'Swaff' passed over—spiritualists don't die—I continued my interest in the cult and in some of its practitioners and I published several other books on the subject, notably one by Ena Twigg, a very famous spiritualist whose advice is regularly sought and accepted by lots of eminent people.

Of my own list of inexplicable occurrences, I will here relate only one other that has defied the attempts of a great many people—including well known para-psychologists and ESP experts—to suggest a plausible or intelligent explanation.

In setting down the facts it is important for the reader to accept the absolute truth of all the details I give in order to rule out the easy solution of coincidence.

One night I had a dream which I vividly recalled on awakening. I had dreamed that two Rabbis had accosted me on a lonely, dark country road seeking my help. They had been in an aeroplane when the pilot had a sudden seizure. He managed to land the aircraft in a field and then collapsed and died. The two distressed Rabbis pleaded with me to aid them. 'We know you can fly an aeroplane. Will you please take over this machine and fly us to Israel where we have to deliver to Premier Ben Gurion by tomorrow some papers of the highest importance and urgency.'

I answered their strange request by confessing it was years since I had flown an aircraft and without the proper navigational and ground assistance I could never get them to Tel Aviv. They begged me at least to try and I therefore got the machine into the air and made a few circuits of the field. 'It's no use,' I told them, 'this is a Cessna equipped for international flying—which I'm not familiar with—and we'd never make it.' They renewed their appeal. 'The route is easy, we have done it before,' they urged. 'We fly south to Nice; then on to Cyprus and from there it's not far to Israel.'

I literally had to tear myself away and leave them, crestfallen and distraught.

All through the day the memory of the weird dream kept recurring. The same evening I was walking home along Jermyn Street when I stopped to look into one of those exclusive men's shops. Suddenly a hand tapped me on the shoulder and I recognised an old friend of mine named Grahame, who used to be my auditor. I hadn't seen him in years, and he was delighted to meet me again. Then he said something that startled me to the soles of my feet.

'I have thought about you a lot lately,' he said, 'because you, without knowing it, were instrumental in my taking a certain course which has been of great value to me. I remember in the old days how you used to tell me about your air experiences and this prompted me some time ago to take up flying myself. I got my licence and bought a Cessna which I now use for business purposes. I have made trips all over Europe and the Middle East. I often go down to Nice and Cyprus.'

Then came a bomb! 'As a matter of fact,' he confided, 'I am flying to Israel tomorrow. I have just completed an important survey and I am actually delivering the report personally to Ben Gurion in Tel Aviv. So you see what you did for me!'

Little could he guess what he had just done for me! The details of my dream the previous night flashed before me in all its stark detail so similar to what Grahame had told me about his impending air journey to Israel. My head swam. I thought I was about to faint—for the first time in my life. I made a hasty and confused apology to my friend and, on legs that didn't seem to belong to me any more, I staggered round the corner into Ryder Street where I lived.

Several brandies later I had recovered my shocked senses and finally persuaded myself that what had occurred in front of a shop window in Jermyn Street was for real and not simply an extension of my nightmare with the two Rabbis. I never had the chance to tell Grahame the crux of this interlude in Jermyn Street and so far as I know, he still flies about Europe and the Middle East on business, oblivious of any occult influences!

Nevertheless, what was the connection between my dream and its strange sequel? Over the years I have discussed this singular experience with a variety of knowledgeable people and I have received a variety of explanations—not one of which I have ever found acceptable—not the time theory, not pre-cognition, not transference and certainly not coincidence.

If any reader of this book would like to take the trouble to write to me with a reasonable or probable interpretation, I would be very grateful. It still mystifies and haunts me.

As a self-confessed cynic, and hard-bitten journalist/publisher, I suppose I should be expected to pour scorn on such arcane matters as those included in this interlude, but I do nothing of the kind. It's all too easy to dismiss the whole thing as specious, unrealistic and even nonsensical—just as it is easy—and convenient—to become an atheist or an agnostic . It saves a lot of time, trouble and heart-searching!

There are those who say one should not look too deeply into the occult. But that is an evasion which doesn't appeal to an enquiring mind. I, for one, like probing into things I don't understand. This is not meddling; this is the search for experiential truth and although the quest may prove inconclusive you can at least preserve an open mind. That is my stand on the incomprehensible and the inexplicable. I recognise the fullness of all creation, but also the finitude of the creature.

In the pre-war days of my editorial activities, I was ever on the alert to find new recruits to the distinguished team of staff-writers which I had put together on the *Sunday Referee*.

There was plenty of talent about and many writers were eager to join up, but my search always inclined towards the unusual. And it turned up one day in the person of Aleister Crowley who, at that time, had already achieved a certain notoriety but nothing like the aura of calumny which he attracted later on.

I knew and admired his work as a poet and I was not unfamiliar with his literary, artistic and esoteric background when he came to see me in Tudor Street about a job. He looked something like a cross between Sir Jasper, the melodrama villain, and a well-to-do mortician, but there was no mistaking that he possessed what today is called 'charisma'. He had a compelling presence and he spoke in an urbane, cultivated manner. Crowley was very much a personality, difficult to fathom but not beyond the scope of my psychic radar which soon picked up vibrations of evil that were alarming and disturbing.

At the end of a long talk, I engaged him to write a series of weekly articles on subjects drawn from his wide and weird experiences of life in many spheres. I planned to publish them under the generic—but quite meaningless—title of 'In Search of the Ultimate'.

Crowley's weekly visit with his copy was an occasion for a friendly chat on current affairs and I must say that I found his company congenial, whereas other people I knew simply couldn't stand the sight of him.

One day he turned up with an article which I put into my briefcase so that I could read it at home. It is an understatement to say that I couldn't understand it. The piece seemed to ramble on, inchoate, confusing, and incomprehensible. It was a two thousand-word mish-mash that would have made the paper ridiculous if I had published it, even though some tolerant readers may have considered it simply a bad joke! I therefore rejected it.

I wrote to Crowley saying his article was unacceptable and that he must replace it with something at least intelligible. He came hot foot to the office and I could see that he was blazing with anger and indignation. 'Who are you to reject the writing of a Master?' he demanded.

I coolly reminded him that I was actually the editor of the paper and it was for me to decide what went in. 'And this piece of unmitigated bloody tripe certainly isn't going into my paper this week, or ever,' I added.

He rose from his chair. 'You damned provincial nobody . . .' he blurted out, but he got no further because I literally threw him out of the room. All the way down the stairs he was shrieking, 'I'll sue you for all you've got; nobody treats Aleister Crowley like this.'

The doorman saw him safely off the premises and I thought that was the last I would see of this odious creature. But it wasn't. True to his word, he sued me and the paper for breach of contract and in due time the case came up before Mr Justice Hodson.

I called my literary editor, 'Ted' Hayter-Preston, as my chief witness to confirm that the article was worthless and I gave evidence

86

to the effect that I was justified in sacking the author on the spot because of his bad work and also on account of his atrocious behaviour.

When Crowley went in to the witness-box, an astonishing scene occurred. While he was giving evidence he began to make strange signs and gestures with his hands in the direction of the Bench. Everybody in court was astounded as he kept up these weird calisthenics. Was he trying to mesmerise the judge or to transmit some 'secret influence' on the court?

Suddenly his Lordship whipped round to face Crowley and in ice-cold tones, he said, 'Would you please desist from making those hand signals and other movements, and conduct yourself properly in the witness-box. Otherwise I will order you to stand down.'

That put an end to Crowley's astonishing tic-tacing but for some reason it alarmed Hayter-Preston, who began to look ill. I told him to leave the court and get some fresh air outside.

At the end of a very short hearing, the judge said it was simply a matter of credibility. Who was telling the truth? 'I have no hesitation in saying that I entirely accept Mr Goulden's version,' he announced, 'and I therefore find in favour of the defendants with costs.' We had soundly beaten the 'baddie' of the literary world.

I joined Hayter-Preston outside the court, and told him of the verdict, but instead of being justifiably pleased, he appeared disconsolate and deeply disturbed. Anxiously, I asked what was upsetting him.

In an agitated voice he exclaimed, 'I wish I had nothing to do with this ghastly case. Didn't you see that Crowley was trying to put a "hex" on the judge in court and now that he has lost the case he'll put a curse on us.' And he really meant it. He was scared witless and I took him into a nearby pub to calm him down with a drink or two. I tried to ridicule his fears and his insupportable assumption that Crowley possessed evil powers that could be transmitted to a third person, but I couldn't shake him out of it. He was under the spell of a witch doctor.

For the next few days at the office, Preston went about like a man carrying an incubus on his shoulders and it was clear to me that he truly believed that Crowley had pronounced a malediction on him. In the course of time, he seemed to slough off the effects of this supposed imprecation but it never quite left him until the day that we heard of Crowley's demise. I am prepared to swear that from that moment onwards, Preston became a different person. An unseen burden had been lifted from him. He was no longer obsessed with the fear of Crowley's malevolent powers. The devil had been defeated.

The 'worst man in the world' as one biographer called him; 'The human beast' as another writer tagged him, had at last gone to rejoin his nether-world companions whom he had long served on earth as their disciple in the arts of black magic.

11
Radio Interlude

No newspaper could survive very long if it dropped its radio and TV programmes. They take up a lot of space but today they are as essential to a paper as the newsprint on which it is printed.

But it wasn't always so. Indeed, not many years ago the press was scared stiff about radio (and later TV) as being the greatest potential enemy of the newspaper industry. The Press Barons refused to even acknowledge the existence of those continental radio stations that were pioneering commercial broadcasts and they did everything in their power to keep such programmes out of their papers, hoping that this boycott would ultimately destroy the various stations which were gradually stealing advertisers away from the papers.

I came back from an American trip in 1935 full of enthusiasm for something I had closely observed on the spot—the dramatic expansion of sponsored radio in the USA. It was estimated that 100,000,000 dollars was being spent on radio advertising (there was no TV of course) and the agencies were paying up to 5,000 dollars on putting together just a half-hour programme. In Britain there was no such service although it was calculated that over seven million radio sets were licensed—with perhaps another million pirates.

For some time my newspaper (the *Sunday Referee*) had been publishing the radio programmes of the two continental stations, Radio Normandy, which operated from the little town of Fecamp, and Poste Parisien, which was of course the chief French station.

The Fecamp outfit was owned by Captain Leonard Plugge, a former MP and father of the woman murdered in Jamaica by her coloured lover who was subsequently hanged. Plugge was on to a good thing in commercial radio because his station attracted many advertisers who had been quick to recognise the high value and consumer response of commercial broadcasting. I made a deal with Plugge whereby my paper would print his programmes in full and I would take a certain amount of advertising time on his Sunday broadcasts. We also published the Radio Paris programmes and the combined lists made a very popular feature because something like four million listeners preferred these programmes to the sober BBC offerings, and they had no other means of knowing what was on.

There was a sudden dramatic development in this commercial radio. A new station had come on the air—Radio Luxembourg—on 1300 metres with a peak period potential audience in Britain of over four million listeners. Taking a bow at venture I booked the whole of the English-speaking time on Sunday. Then we offered to all advertisers a package deal—advertising space in the newspaper plus time on Luxembourg's radio programmes. To sustain the continuity of the broadcasts was a headache I hadn't anticipated. I therefore engaged a very excellent producer (Stephen Williams)—he must have been the first British disc jockey—who kept the programmes going with the aid of records and the keyboard contributions of my brother Louis, a professional pianist. They both went each week to Luxembourg to provide the musical content of the programmes.

The advertiser was at first resistant. He wanted proof of the new station's coverage, which we couldn't provide. But fate once again came to the rescue. We made a deal with the Cow and Gate people whereby in a one hour programme they invited listeners to send up for a free sample of their product.

With records and piano music the programme went over well and that the response was sensational. For the next few days a procession of vans arrived at the company's factory in Norwich with mailbags full of applications for samples. The advertiser couldn't cope with it and we had to cancel the ensuing week's radio programme. But we had proved the value of commercial advertising and from that moment the whole concept gradually became big business.

Like all national papers my newspaper was affiliated to the Newspaper Proprietors Association and I had a seat on the council of that august all-powerful organisation—now called the Newspaper Publishers Association. And at practically every meeting one item on the agenda of the NPA was Radio Advertising, of which of course I was the maverick. The chairman was Lord Riddell, a wily Welshman and owner of the notorious *News of the World*—a paper which boasted the largest circulation in the world, built up largely on the reporting of scandalous court cases—rape, homosexuality, divorce, brothel-keeping, living on immoral earnings, etc. Leg-men in every big town fed in a weekly stream of such reports to the paper, thus providing a feast of pleasant Sabbath reading for one in five of the entire population!

Riddell was the self-appointed Nemesis of commercial radio. He saw in it a menace that would bring ruin to the newspaper industry. It must, he warned, inevitably take the big advertisers away from the papers and since advertising revenue is the very life blood of all journals, their doom was sealed!

He was backed up by all the members of the council and naturally I became the target of his condemnation and invective. It was richly ironic that the proprietor of a paper which prospered by purveying soft-core pornography should be the defender of newspaper ethics and conduct!

My case was quite simple. By publishing the commercial radio programmes we were doing nothing illegal or disreputable. We were indeed rendering a service to our readers and this method of attracting new readers was far less objectionable—and less costly—than the free gifts schemes which every member of the council was plaguing the public with at that time.

'I refuse to discontinue publishing these programmes and you can't stop me,' I shouted back at Riddell during one hectic dialogue in which he had hinted that if we didn't desist we might be expelled from the NPA—a dire threat.

The member sitting next to me was a little man called Elias (later Lord Southwood), proprietor of Odhams Press, one of the big combines. He rarely spoke at these meetings but he leaned towards me on this occasion and whispered: 'I'm on your side.'

'Then damn well say so,' I retorted loud enough for Riddell to hear.

There was apparently someone else who was on my side. Mr Esmond Harmsworth, owner of the *Daily Mail*, sent a message to me asking if I would meet him at his home, Warwick Lodge, in St James's. 'You really believe in this commercial radio, don't you?' he said to me and I replied, 'I think it is the medium of the future, and now is the time to get in on the ground floor. It is bigger than you imagine.'

Harmsworth, who obviously had been pre-sold on radio advertising, then said, 'Here's what we must do. At the next NPA meeting I will get up and say we are not sufficiently informed about the value or otherwise of commercial broadcasting. I will then suggest the whole subject be held in abeyance while it is being investigated by a sub-committee. By that means we can keep it open-ended indefinitely.'

It was an excellent ploy, and its conspiratorial nature highly intrigued me. Besides which, it now looked as though I had at least the moral support of a powerful newspaper group. This would be a breakthrough which would vindicate my stand.

And sure enough, at the next NPA meeting, Mr Harmsworth rose to his full six feet and informed the chairman of his proposal to postpone further discussion about commercial radio pending a full enquiry into the whole subject.

Riddell was aghast. Before Harmsworth had really finished speaking, the lean, irate Welshman jumped up and in icy tones said: 'Sit down, Mr Esmond; you are out of order. We are going to take a decision today on this matter and you would be better advised to give your attention to that dying old ladies' journal which you are interested in.'

I took this to be a sarcastic reference to *The Times*.

My crestfallen and deflated fellow conspirator resumed his seat and shortly afterwards Riddell moved a resolution (which was carried) that the *Sunday Referee* be expelled from membership of the NPA unless it discontinued publishing commercial radio programmes.

'You must let me have your decision by the next meeting,' said the chairman in magisterial tones, 'but I want you to understand that if we do take this drastic decision your paper will not be excluded from the newspaper trains.'

I thanked his lordship for this assurance about the trains and promised our decision by the next council meeting.

The newspaper trains, it should be here explained, were the exclusive transport of the NPA which hired them direct from the railway companies to carry, overnight, millions of Sunday newspapers to railheads in all parts of the country from whence they were collected for local delivery. No Sunday newspaper had ever been banned from using those special trains, since any such edict would be virtually a sentence of death on the paper concerned.

But, in spite of Riddell's assurance, I left this plenary session with a strange sense of defeat and depression which wasn't justified on a cold analysis of the meeting's decision.

After all, expulsion was a formality which entailed no real hardship and the chairman had explicitly stated that we would be able to use the newspaper special trains. It was, if anything, a victory. But, as explained elsewhere in these memoirs, I have extra-sensory perception of some depth and also a mental antenna which infallibly signals when someone is lying to me. I can't explain this sensation, nor its etiology; it just happens but the indicators are rarely wrong.

I was positive Riddell was lying about the trains and I told my circulation manager, the renowned Valentine Smith (first circulation man to notch a million net sale) to start organising our own distribution service—just in case we were banned from the trains after all. It was a formidable undertaking but the challenge was a trumpet call to the redoubtable Valentine. In his famous cockney twang he cried, 'I can do it', and for the next twenty days, with wall maps sprouting flags each time a new recruit was signed on, Valentine organised the independent distribution of a Sunday newspaper from Land's End to John o' Groat's. He had roped in every form of transport from motor cycles to light aeroplanes and this miracle of logistics now only awaited the all-systems-go signal. I hoped and prayed we should never need to press the button—but I still had a hunch!

We were duly expelled—the first newspaper ever to suffer such a fate—and in saying goodbye to me, Riddell congratulated me on my misguided advocacy but cordially reiterated his pledge about the trains. My radar whispered: 'Don't believe it!'

That was on the Thursday, and on the following Saturday morning, our early edition pages were going to press normally and there was no reason to think we wouldn't be using the special trains that night. So my intuition had (happily) failed me for once!

Then, just before lunch, the front office commissionaire announced the arrival of a gentleman named Sir Thomas McAra, secretary of the NPA. As he came in, I saw in his hand an envelope. There was no need for him to say a word. Nor did he. I knew what was inside the envelope and McAra, an ascetic little man—a cross between a urologist and an ageing family doctor—knew that I knew.

'I'm terribly sorry about this,' he stammered at last, and clearly there were tears in his eyes. I personally am not the weepy type, otherwise he might well have detected a tear in my eye, because this could easily have marked the end of my career as a young editor. It was a bitter moment. I turned to the bearer of the fateful news and asked him: 'Do you have a son, Sir Thomas?' 'Yes, indeed I do,' he replied, surprised by the apparently irrelevant question. He extended his hand towards me but I refused to shake it. Obviously he had been a party to the deceitful conspiracy and so far as he or his association knew, this would be the end of our paper and perhaps of my editorship and career. Clearly that must have been their intention. By holding back the notice until almost the last minute, they figured by then it would be too late for us to improvise even a partial distribution. It was a wickedly calculated double-cross.

'So you were dead right, after all,' Valentine exclaimed when he heard about the hangman's visit. 'Not to worry,' he shouted as he dashed away to his circulation headquarters, where for the next few hours he was burning up the telephone wires and the telegram services.

We went to press as usual and Valentine's distribution miracle was put to the test. It came through with flying colours. Literally, we hardly lost a copy and in some places we were actually ahead of the newspaper trains.

Of course we told the readers all about the plot to destroy their favourite Sunday newspaper and we got a heartening response, including tributes from other papers—outside the NPA of course.

The price of independence, however, comes high. As the circulation rose so did the cost of our independent distribution and for fifty-two weeks, the proprietor, Isidore Ostrer, met the heavy bills unflinchingly.

But not even a generous millionaire can be expected to dip into his pocket indefinitely, and so after a year of defiance, we had (against my wishes) to return to the fold. We dropped the contentious programmes, resumed our membership of the newspaper bosses' 'closed shop', and licked our wounds.

'Go fight City Hall' is the sardonic American expression for such misplaced valour.

But we had made newspaper history.

Consider the change which time has wrought. Forty years ago a national newspaper nearly committed suicide by publishing radio programmes—today a paper might indeed be committing suicide if it *didn't* publish them.

12

'Here Come the Brides' Interlude

I think I must have been the first British publisher to make the 'scouting trip' to America after the end of the Second World War.

I had undertaken many journeys to the States prior to the outbreak of hostilities in my capacity as a newspaper editor but this was my first foray as a publisher into the literary heartland of America. It was my view then—as indeed it is today—that America provides the richest lode of source material for British publishers. There is little doubt most books which achieve 'best sellerdom' in America will travel to Britain and win similar acclaim. And as for run-of-the-mill American books in all categories the British market will always remain an assured outlet. The reverse is not always the case. Many of our bestsellers do not automatically hit the jackpot in America and I attribute the cause of this to the simple fact that Americans are by no means as 'Anglicised' as we are 'Americanised'.

Without question the Americanisation of Britain was brought about in large measure by the post-war flood of Hollywood films and it was perpetuated by the later advent of American TV programmes.

In other words, the average Briton knows infinitely more about the life-style of Americans than the ordinary US citizen knows about British modes, manners—and speech. Today practically everybody in these islands speaks and understands the American idiom but to millions of Americans—and by no means merely that amorphous body known as 'the Middle West'—English everyday speech is virtually a foreign language. American vaudeville is notoriously a graveyard for British comedians simply because the audiences just don't know what the comics are talking about, apart from the fact that typical British humour, which is the funny-men's stock in trade, really doesn't register spontaneously. The average

American will laugh on Wednesday at the British joke he heard on Monday!

This marginal mental idiosyncrasy is nevertheless significant because it highlights and emphasises a basic view which I have long held as a result of my intimate and extensive acquaintance with the American people and country— there is a polar disparity in our respective ways of life, even though we share cultural origins. The popular belief that we are 'cousins' is a monumental myth; and any attempt to enumerate the ways in which we differ would be tantamount to compiling an encyclopedia. In everything except a fundamental similarity in language we are as unlike each other ethnologically and ideologically as the Eskimos are from the Chinese or the Danes from the Watusi! This observation is in no sense meant to be pejorative, and if any criticism is implied it belongs equally to both sides. To clinch it I say, unhesitatingly, that the British and Americans have irrefrangible ties of friendship and respect; they have inviolable bonds of mutual concern and if ever any of these were severed it would be a calamitous day for humanity.

To engineer my first post-war trip in America proved to be a daunting task from the start. There were of course no transatlantic air services and all shipping was under the control of the Government. It was necessary to make a convincing case with the Ministry of Shipping in requesting a passage to New York and then the approval of the Treasury had to be sought. One became enmeshed in spools of red-tape and the hangover of war-time bureaucracy was still rampant in Whitehall. After interminable frustrations which then seemed insurmountable but now appear to have been ludicrously unnecessary, I found myself in possession of a first class return ticket from Southampton to New York via the illustrious *Queen Mary*—a superb ship which I already knew from stem to stern.

The boat-train from Waterloo indicated that the passenger list must be virtually all-male and so it apparently turned out to be when I and a dozen of my fellow-travellers assembled for the first day's lunch. I will never forget the meal because of an incident that happened as soon as we were seated. With unbelieving eyes we watched the steward unloading on our tables baskets of newly-baked white rolls and mounds of mouthwatering, dairy-fresh butter. It was a sight for the gods. For years we had subsisted on unpalatable ersatz bread smeared with a slick of 'marge' and now we gazed upon crisp white rolls and ample helpings of creamy butter all awaiting our gastronomic pleasure. And it didn't take long! Not a word was spoken. And as if by some magic, the delectable food suddenly disappeared from the table. There was an air of guilt around us but it gave way to roars of laughter as we all simultaneously realised that we had polished in minutes enough rolls and butter to have fed a war-time family for a month!

And if that meal had started with a startling surprise it was but a momentary day-dream compared with what was to follow, as we began the customary exploration of the mighty liner's elegant acreage.

Far from being an all-male company, we were astonished to discover that the ship was virtually over-run with young girls, each one of whom seemed to be carrying a baby! It was a nightmarish revelation and it seemed that infant-carrying mothers were swarming all over the ship-along the unending corridors, throughout the vast public rooms, along the wide promenade decks and even into the closed cocktail lounges and bars! It simply couldn't be real. Hundreds of girls and young women, accompanied by hundreds of screaming children! Had our first civilised meal given us hallucinations? No way. It was all too true and too real. We soon discovered that we were aboard one of the famous 'Brides' Ships' which the two crack ocean-liners had recently been converted into. The unusual passengers were apparently young British girls who had married American servicemen stationed in the British Isles. When the Yanks went off to fight the war in Europe they left behind them in Britain a bevy of young brides who had, in due course, produced a battalion of little Yanks of varying colours and sex. When the war was over the American troops had been shipped back directly to their own country and the two Governments later decided that the 'brides' and their babies in Britain should be re-united with their husbands on the more hospitable shores of the United States. And to ferry these mothers and children across the Atlantic the two *Queens* had been commandeered for that specific purpose.

Thus did we find ourselves—a handful of assorted males—surrounded by hordes of excited mothers and howling babies on a 'Brides' Ship' heading for New York via Halifax, Nova Scotia. It was a rather shattering experience for us and as first-class paying passengers many of us resented the intrusion of these newly-weds and newly-born who were guests of the Government but who were behaving as though they owned the ship.

'Out-of-bounds' notices in certain parts of the ship were ignored or torn down and the brides and their brats—who seemed to evoke no sympathetic interest from anybody on board except the over-worked nurses and harassed doctors—were in full and noisy possession of the liner.

It has to be confessed that the brides for the most part did not exactly represent the cream of British womanhood, but it has to be conceded that the miscegenation in war-torn Britain had produced some very beautiful and sturdy infants.

All day and night the tannoy would blare forth messages like 'will Mrs X return to her cabin immediately where her baby is ill', which indicated that some of the young mothers had left their offspring unattended while they roamed the ship. The infants were of course all war babies reared on rationed foodstuffs with insufficient nu-triment and consequently, with the plentitude of food available on board, the inexperienced mothers had over-stuffed their babies—as well as themselves. Many were taken ill and several of the children did not survive the journey, especially after the call at Halifax where a well-meaning populace had showered chocolates, fruit, ice-cream and goodies on mothers who had probably never seen such things since they themselves were children.

There was one spot on the ship which we managed to keep more or less exclusive to ourselves—the rather beautiful library and its adjoining writing room—and here some of us sought sanctuary from the maternal lemmings who seemed to be everywhere.

One afternoon I dozed off in a luxurious armchair—most of the ship's furniture and costly decoration was still in wraps after its trooping activities—and I remember being rudely awakened by two tiny tots clambering over me. They had wandered into the deserted library and they had pounced on a sleeping 'daddy' to play with.

Like all normal fathers I am very fond of children—preferably single or in pairs—but definitely not in battalions. I discovered that these two smelly intruders were not without babyish charm and we quickly made friends. Then through the doors of the library came mother to claim her missing offspring for whose intrusion into the 'out-of-bounds' area she murmured an apology. We chatted for a while and she introduced herself as Margaret and the babies as Walter and Susan. I reflected at the time how comfortably and creditably Marge, Walt and Sue might have fitted into family life in Rochdale, Barnsley or even Neasden, and I wondered how they would fare and function in the alien environment of the over-powering United States, to which they were now committed. The mother, clearly a bright, petite level-headed young person was obviously fearful of the ordeal that awaited her in America where she was to fly down from New York to Georgia to meet her 'husband' and for the first time his parents. I got the impression that the in-laws were well-to-do cotton growers, anxious to see their son's children but a bit dubious about his choice of a 'bride'. I sensed her predicament especially when she confided that they were not married. I wished her the best of luck as she took her two bonny kids back to her cabin. What would become of this nice provincial girl who had probably never been outside England in her life?

Her 'ordeal of reunion' was something all the other mothers were about to face and it seemed to me that the procedure which had been planned by the authorities was crude, unimaginative and bound to result in confusion and possible heartache. The 'fathers' had been instructed to queue up on the quayside of the pier where the *Queen Mary* would berth. Most would be able to recognise their 'brides', all of whom had been allocated vantage points along the rails of the Promenade decks—a rather risky perch, I thought, for excited young girls with babes in arms!

I suppose I was not alone in speculating about the shock of recognition which must erupt when the pier-head confrontations actually took place. The last glimpse which most of these young mothers had caught of their departing spouses was a nostalgic vision of virile American manhood smartly attired in those slick expensive uniforms of GI's, airmen and sailors, a profile that lots of unattached maidens in embattled Britain often found irresistible—just how irresistible was attested by the hundreds of war-brides and war-babies presently on board the good ship *Queen Mary*!

At any moment now the girls were about to behold their war-time romeos standing pat on their home ground and kitted out this time in their typical everyday 'civvies'—variegated, vulgar, unglamorous—so far removed from the spit and polish elegance of the well-paid, well-dressed American servicemen who had captivated blushing brides in Britain. The better to observe what was likely to be a unique spectacle, I positioned myself on the rails of the boat-deck a few feet above the line of brides, so I was able not only to observe the tense anxious faces but also to catch some of the random remarks of the girls above the excited hubbub which always pervades the arrival, or departure, of an ocean liner.

Historic, unique, adventurous, dramatic though the event might be, I felt it had an air of anti-climax; it seemed a drab, unromantic, ill-organised affair, bereft of any sense of welcome or warmth that an English-speaking country might have been expected to extend to an accretion of young English immigrants—American now by marriage—who with their numerous offspring were about to be absorbed into the community life of the New World. The American flair for display and dramatic effect had produced no monster wedding cake! No white ribbons, confetti or chimes cleaved the yielding air to lend a nuptial touch to the scene, the statue of Liberty hadn't whispered 'Bring me your brides' as the ship queened by; there was no epithalamium to voice the nation's greetings to its newly acquired and newly-wed female citizens and there were no cheer leaders to send a thrill of pride along the spines of all those English girls who had opted for the stars and stripes. The only note of welcome came from an out of tune brass band which tried futilely to enliven the proceedings with 'Anchors aweigh', but its discordant strains were overwhelmed by roars and shouts from the waiting husbands and the echoing shrieks and screams from the emotional wives whose rendezvous with destiny drew nearer by the minute as the ship gracefully inched its way to the over-crowded quayside. By now mutual identification was easy and the frantic signalling from the shore was answered by flailing arms from young ladies lined up on the promenade deck. I spotted one man, conspicuous in the rear of the queue, who was desperately trying to attract the attention of a tall fair-haired girl standing almost beneath me. He was a heavily built fat young man and he was dressed in the all too familiar garb of a truck-driver—peaked cap, bulging anorak, denim pants and thick leather gloves. Suddenly the blonde girl seemed to recognise the frenzied signaller—her line of vision to the quay coincided with mine. But she appeared unmoved and unresponsive at what she saw. Then her face became distorted as she raised her hands to her half-open mouth. 'Jesus Christ,' I heard her gasp, 'is that 'im?' 'If it is I'm not getting off this blasted ship.' She then squeezed her way from the ship's rail and I watched the signaller on the shore relax his oscillating arms. No doubt he thought his impatient bride was going below to the landing deck, the quicker to reach his fond embrace. But she was, as I learned later, one of the several disillusioned girls who adamantly refused to disembark or to have any contact with the waiting bridegrooms. They resisted the entreaties of welfare officials who came aboard and the purser told me afterwards that two had locked themselves in their cabins and refused to come out until the ship had turned round for its journey back home.

Before I went ashore I had seen more than enough of the pathos, the drama, the comedy, the joy, the humiliation and the disenchantment that had marked this altogether astonishing reunion on the waterfront of New York. It was an unforgettable experience.

My first post-war scouting trip to America was a memorable trip in every way. Perhaps the whole sojourn was pleasantly coloured by the abundance of food and drink and the sense of freedom which was so intensely felt after the restrictions, tensions and terrors in blacked-out, devastated London which we had endured for four long years. It was easy to become a bomb bore in those days because so many Americans desperately wanted to know at first hand 'what it had been like'. I found most of them were woefully ill-informed about the conditions in war-time Britain and some of them tended to exaggerate their own domestic ordeals of deprivation, inconveniences and shortages during the war years. I'll never forget the look of martyrdom on the face of a New York hostess as she confided to me that for months they had never seen roast chicken and that at least twice a week they had to dine off hamburgers! In spite of that they never ceased to send us their 'Parcels for Britain' and they could never know how heart-warming and acceptable these gifts were to the recipients. American hospitality and spontaneous generosity are unsurpassed in the world.

On the literary scene I found that I had virtually the field to myself. It was an embarrassment of riches. I was inundated with offers of recently published books, manuscripts and future projects and I was able to pick and choose. And since my time was limited to the life-expectation of my dollar advance I couldn't give proper consideration to all the procurements (trade name for literary properties) that were available. Consequently I turned down many a then unknown author who was later to become famous. I remember one agent tipping me off about a forthcoming book which he predicted could be a winner. He couldn't let me see the manuscript but I could pre-empt it if I bought the author's previous book and thereby obtained the option on the new work. I quickly read the already published novel and while I found it readable and well written I thought it completely unsuitable for the British market. I therefore turned it down and so automatically lost *The Robe*, ultimately to become one of the biggest bestsellers of all time. I did pick up a resounding winner called *Miracle of Bells* by Russell Janney, an author with whom I became very friendly. The book did exceedingly well until the release of the film which was so bad that it killed stone dead any further sales of the book. That has happened many times in publishing.

On one of my subsequent trips I bought what I figured was an unusual book with a tremendous sales potential. It was a short manual on the rules and play of a new game that seemed to be, as they say, sweeping America. It was an Argentine rummy game called, appropriately enough, Canasta. I speedily learned to play it and before I reached London I was already hooked on the game. I got in touch with my friend Frank Owen, editor of the *Evening Standard*, and offered him the serial rights of this book free, in the hope that the resultant publicity could set the game alight in England and so rocket the sales of my book—the only available one on the subject.

Frank sought the opinion of his bridge editor and the latter apparently took a dim view of the book—and indeed of the game—his verdict being that it was in no sense a rival to bridge or even to gin rummy for that matter and he considered it quite unlikely to catch on in conservative Britain. So it wasn't serialised and the book managed to tick over until the country subsequently went Canasta mad. In the wake of this there was the usual flood of instruction books (like there was years later with the revival of Backgammon) but I reprinted my book several times as the 'original' book on Canasta and it stayed in print for many years.

On a trip shortly after this one I got wind of another game which was fascinating the American public but was as yet unknown in England. I made contact with the owner of the copyright (he was an engineer who had actually invented the game himself) and he granted me an option to produce and sell 'Scrabble' in the British Isles. I considered this something of a scoop so I cut short my USA trip to return to England in order to launch as quickly as possible the new pastime, the literary flavour of which lent itself so appropriately to promotion by a publishing house.

Making the scrabble boards was no problem (it was a printing and binding job) but finding a manufacturer for the numbered letters was something else entirely.

I literally tried everywhere and everything—cardboard pieces, lino, plastic, cork, wood, ceramic—all to no avail. Because of existing post-war import restrictions I couldn't bring in the sets complete from America and nothing which could be produced in England made economic sense. We needed some one hundred and ten pieces for each game and on an initial order of ten thousand sets the total number of letters would be over a million so the very size of the order frightened off most potential manufacturers. To add to my mounting frustration the American inventor wrote to tell me that he had it on the highest authority that the game had been introduced to Buckingham Palace and that the Royal family were already avid devotees! Discreetly 'leaked', this news would have given the advent of the game in Britain a tremendous boost. But I soon realised that I was well and truly stymied on the production of the letters. Then one day a scout who I had commissioned to find me a producer of the pieces telephoned to say he had solved the problem. He had found a firm who could make the letters in extruded plastic and specimens were actually in the post to me.

I and my colleagues were thrilled to bits, especially since latest news from America told us that 'Scrabble' was now selling like the proverbial hot cakes. And when I received the specimens we were overjoyed to find that they were not only perfect but the price was right too. We could put a retail tag on the game of fifteen shillings—about half the USA price—and still make a profit after royalties.

We were obviously on the brink of a bonanza. But I sensed danger when I saw that the follow-up letter from my scout was postmarked Dusseldorf. Could it be that the supplier he had so miraculously found was a German firm? Alas, it was and this would rule it out irrevocably so far as I was concerned. It was my policy (as the reader may now be aware) not to do any business with Germany. It was a principle I had never abrogated—I still haven't—and it was therefore unfortunately necessary to inform the American owner of the game that my interest as the potential British producer must be aborted forthwith. I simply said that the production of the plastic letters presented an insoluble problem for me and regretfully I had decided to proceed no further with the project. I thanked him for his kindness and his patience and I closed the file on what must have proved a financial gusher, had commercial common sense prevailed over conscience and principle.

Today, over twenty years later, I often recall this episode when I play Scrabble, at which, perhaps by a sort of primogeniture, I happen to be singularly adept.

I concluded my first post-war trip to America with a useful bag of literary 'goodies', several pairs of nylon stockings for my wife and an inner satisfaction at having made numerous contacts with agents, publishers and authors which should—and subsequently did—stand me in good stead in the years to come when I had established a commanding lead in scouting expeditions to America.

One thing I looked forward to with happy anticipation was the return journey on the *Queen Mary*—five days of luxurious inertia with nothing more arduous to do than eat, sleep and read manuscripts. As expected, there were very few passengers aboard and mercifully no brides and no babies! But never underestimate the inevitability of coincidence! One afternoon, I had finished reading the galley-proofs of a rather pedestrian non-fiction book when, in the soporific calm of the almost empty main lounge, I fell asleep. I must have been dreaming about Brides' ships, because I awoke suddenly with an uncanny feeling that war-babies were crawling all over me. And indeed they were; it was no dream fantasy but rather, as it turned out, an almost incredible coincidence. The mother of the infants rushed over to prevent them from doing a hatchet job on my galley-proofs (I completed this later!) and to our mutual amazement we recognised one another—the trio was none other than Margaret, Walter and Susan to whom (four weeks earlier) I had bid farewell on the eve of their homeward journey to the deep South. What in heaven's name were they doing aboard the *Queen Mary* eastward bound for Southampton?

I quickly organised a little tea-party for us in the lounge and while we were doing post-war justice to the sandwiches and pastries, Margaret told me a poignant story. As she had feared, the prospective parents-in-law gave her a cool reception and within a few days this had turned to outright hostility. Her 'husband' was utterly dominated by his mother and father and he offered her no protection or comfort. But the children were apparently welcome and soon happily installed in the huge Georgian mansion that gave upon the endless acres of the cotton plantation. However the situation deteriorated and it came to a dramatic climax when the mother-in-law, obviously the 'boss' of the ménage, came up with a proposition. They would be prepared to 'adopt' the children legally; Margaret would go back to England, they would pay all her expenses and give her a generous 'redundancy' payment as well. In other words, they offered to buy her babies if she would renounce them. She had listened carefully but non-committally and then a couple of days later she sought out the British Consul, and induced him to provide her air fare to New York. The babies travelled free. Silently and secretly she and the children had crept away from the parental home leaving most of their belongings and they were well on the way to New York before their absence was discovered. She had no trouble getting a return passage on the *Queen Mary* since she was already registered as a war-bride and thus was free, apparently, to go back home if for any reason she changed her mind about settling in America.

'I gave up a good job in a beauty parlour to make this journey,' Margaret told me, 'and I will go back to it now. I can look after the kids and nobody can claim them. So it's goodbye Georgia', she concluded cheerfully.

I admired her courage, her strength of purpose and her sensible North Country practicality in coping with a tragic situation. Uncle Sam, I felt, had lost a worthy daughter as well as a very promising nephew and niece! I hope Marge, Walt and Sue found happiness in their native land. They deserved it.

13

Interlude
Mit Huns

For years I waged a one-man war against Hitler and his Nazis.

It began in the early 1930s when I took over the editorship of the *Sunday Referee* and built it into one of the most influential journals in the country. I had gathered together a team of writers the like of which had never been seen before under one masthead, and I don't think it has been excelled right up to this very day. Aldous Huxley wrote an article every week for me under the banner, 'In My View'; Bertrand Russell contributed a column in which he had freedom to say what he liked; Compton Mackenzie conducted the 'Mustard and Cress' feature made famous by George R. Simms (the founder of the paper). Constant Lambert wrote each week on music; Mr William (later Lord) Mabane, MP, wrote on politics; Osbert Sitwell had a weekly feature; Richard Aldington was chief book reviewer, and other regular contributors included Henry Williamson, John Bickley, Stephen Embleton, Victor Neuberg, Dr Harold Dearden, Bob McGrory (Stoke City's famous manager) who wrote on football. Edward March (later Duke of Richmond) wrote on motoring, Leslie Baily was tv editor, W. Hayter-Preston (Vanoc) was literary editor and for good measure I signed on Walt Disney whose 'Silly Symphony' I serialised weekly.

With this galaxy of writing talent, I raised the circulation of the paper from 40,000 to 160,000 copies, in those days a very substantial sale for a newspaper that didn't buy its readers with free insurance offers, sets of Dickens, electrical gadgets and other meretricious aids to circulation.

And it was with this weapon—a widely read and powerful independent organ of public opinion—that I conducted a ceaseless battle against a movement which since it started in 1923 had posed, in my view, a menace to Europe and to the world. As I have said earlier in this memoir, no national newspaper has ever launched a campaign that eventually succeeded, and all that I can say about my anti-Nazi crusade was that it sounded the very earliest warning about the true horrors of Nazism and it exposed what was in store as Hitler and his gunmen proceeded to seize power in Germany.

But Britain had just emerged from the roaring twenties when life was gay and carefree; it was the day of jazz and the flapper and as the thirties emerged the spill-over of let's have fun was in full spate. The nation was in no mood for introspection and the prevailing attitude was that if things were bad in Germany it served the Hun damn well right! The horrors of the First World War were well within living memory and since that had been the war to end all wars what was there to worry about? With only twelve years of peace on the slate, it was far too early to be thinking seriously about the antics of two bogey-men with funny names like Schickelgruber and Mussolini in far-away Europe!

What people didn't believe—nor wanted to believe—was that World War I never really finished in 1918. But a few of us knew that every day which passed was bringing us ever nearer to the resumption of hostilities.

When in Easter of 1933 I ran a leader page feature (with pictures) exposing the secret lives of the Nazi hierarchy, it lifted the veil for the first time on the thugs who were ruling sixty million Germans. It was a sensational article and I followed it up week after week with more startling revelations and denunciations, all of which could have justified Hitler in throwing a bomb at me. (He did—twice—a few years later!)

I was accused by some of being a scaremonger, which I could easily afford to ignore, but I was deeply offended when certain Jewish organisations to whom I conveyed tangible evidence of the Nazis' incipient war on the Jews, roundly declared that my exposures would simply create anti-semitism in this country! It was years before British—and American—Jewry realised that their brethren in Europe were being slowly exterminated.

I had in Berlin in those days a resident reporter who seemed to have access to unique material for sensational dispatches—all of which I published week by week. Apparently I had the field to myself in exposing the Nazis and even if the British public were not sitting up and taking notice, I had reason to know that some of the gangsters themselves in the Wilhelmstrasse most certainly were.

In one exclusive story we revealed that the Germans were secretly building up an air force in direct breach of the Treaty of Versailles. Subsequent events in Germany showed that this information had been absolutely accurate, but at the time few were willing to believe it. One exception was Sir Robert Vansittart, who always had the measure of the Nazis.

Even more of an eye-opener was the story I ran about a German chemical firm being engaged in the secret manufacture of poison gas and on this I invited trouble. Within a few weeks of publication I got a writ for libel from the chemical firm concerned and although, at first, I welcomed this threat of litigation as a heaven-sent opportunity to get some world-wide publicity for my campaign against the Nazis, I could see danger signals. I trusted my Berlin correspondent implicitly; I knew his information was reliable but the onus of proof would be on us and we soon realised that it might be difficult—if not impossible—to get corroborative evidence to justify our allegations. Our private informers would 'clam up'. They could hardly be expected to risk coming out into the open against barbarians who were already meting out brutal punishment to all opponents, particularly to defenceless Jews.

So the libel preliminaries went normally into gear and although I capitalised on it as far as I could, I knew that this could be a costly action if it went to court, but I couldn't imagine a British jury awarding the now Nazified Germans anything but contemptuous damages. Nevertheless, the pre-trial expenses would become steep and I wasn't mitigating the situation at all by keeping up my relentless attacks week by week.

Then some weeks later I got a request from the German Embassy asking if I would see one of their officials who would be pleased to call on me. And in due course there appeared in my Tudor Street offices a very spruce and impeccably attired individual named Bismarck—every inch the traditional monocled German diplomat—and as was to be expected he exuded the essence of charm and sweet reasonableness. The Embassy—and via them, the Nazi Government—had noted with deep regret (he said) my continuous attacks on the new regime in Germany and since our two countries enjoyed such good relations, was it not a pity that a 'leading British newspaper' should adopt so hostile an attitude? He was sure it must be based on a misunderstanding of the true situation. The Nazi party was not anti-semitic; all they were trying to do was stem the flow of Jews (the Ostjuden) into Germany from the Eastern frontiers. This invasion was a key factor in the German economic situation, he explained, and it was not only a serious problem in itself but it was obviously having serious repercussions on the vast Jewish population within Germany. (He could say that again!)

I gave Herr Bismarck the impression that I was listening intently to this diplomatic brain washing because I knew there was a punchline somewhere in the offing; and it wasn't long in coming.

My polite and knowledgeable visitor then confided that he 'had been informed' by his commercial attaché that legal proceedings had recently been instituted against my paper on behalf of the firm of Schering Kalbaum alleging libel and defamation, and he wanted to assure me that the good offices of the Embassy would always be entirely at my disposal in order to effect an amicable settlement of this unfortunate matter—again of course purely in the interest of maintaining the bonds of friendship between Britain and Germany!

It's fantastic how, in diplomacy, one hand—as the Germans themselves say—washes the other.

With traditional editorial politeness and charm, I told the man from the Embassy that I had fully understood his explanations and his 'kind offer of intercession' but regrettably I would not be able to take advantage of his services since I had no intention of dropping my campaign against Nazi Germany. Quite the contrary, it would be intensified. And indeed it was. When a little later on the Nazis burned down the Reichstag, this is what I editorialised:

It looks like Gotterdammerung in Germany. The stage is dark, and the only forms that can be distinguished seem monstrous to civilised eyes—Easter Island shapes, devoid alike of understanding and feeling.

It is clear that the flames of the Reichstag have consumed not only the symbol of democracy, but the last vestige of political morality in a country which, for the past century, has been in the vanguard of civilisation.

111

Men of the Hitler type are the flowers of a system which functions primarily for the individual and condones, with cynical indifference, the economic and political manipulation of the mass with every instrument from religion to the machine-gun.

We are now witnessing in Germany the end to which this system must ultimately lead.

Wars and gun-rule will be the order of the coming day and it is certain that the Hitlers of the world will spend all the evil wealth of the past with lavish hands.

Then mankind will wake up, or perish.

And quickly following this, I splashed across four columns a dramatic interview which Einstein gave to my Berlin correspondent, Nesta Lyall, when they met in Brussels where the exiled scientist was living in May 1933. This is what he said:

'Hitlerism, if unchecked, will lead to a world war. Hitler is heading for war.

'The stage is set for war. The craving for power which characterises the governing class in every nation is hostile to any limitation of the national sovereignty.

'This rebirth of violent national feeling, which has been initiated in Germany by Hitler, is not only a disaster for Germany herself, but also for the whole world,' he said.

'Hitler understands how to raise this instinct to the power of a collective psychosis. He knows that the hate-lust is more easily inflamed in the presence of a visible and tangible enemy. That is why he has incited the Nazi fury against the Jews. They are a convenient target ready to hand for the shafts intended in the near future for other races, at present outside the Nazi bowshot.

'The world must be warned.'

Remember this was six years before the war broke out and no other British newspaper was publishing stuff like this.

By the summer of 1933 the world seemed at last to be generally alerted to the real menace of Nazi Germany. Adolf Hitler himself was now the dominant political force in the whole country (the following year Hindenburg made him Chancellor) and *Mein Kampf* was the bible of his followers.

There continued to pour forth from Germany stories of Nazi atrocities, particularly in the concentration camps where the opponents of the regime, together with countless Jews, Catholics and socialists, were being incarcerated like so much cattle. Always the powerful German propaganda machine denied these dreadful allegations but the stream of refugees reaching England from Hitler's Reich brought ample confirmation to those who wished to hear.

I decided to challenge Hitler himself on this vital matter. I gave instructions by telephone to my Berlin reporter that I proposed to telephone direct to the Chancellor to ask if he would agree to an 'independent enquiry' into the atrocity stories. This conversation, we learned later, was monitored by the Germans and consequently our attempts to make direct contact with the Fuhrer were frustrated.

But Nesta Lyall, who was on leave in London and had powerful friends in the German Foreign Office, advised that I should send a cable to Baron Von Neurath (the German Foreign Minister) which he would be bound to accept.

Here is the wording of the cable which I sent off:

Are Herr Hitler and the German Cabinet prepared to admit and assist an independent non-political committee appointed by the *Sunday Referee* to investigate the alleged brutalities perpetuated on Jews, Socialists and Roman Catholics; the committee to be formed exclusively of non-Jewish elements under the Chairmanship of a personality with world-wide reputation for impartiality?

Miss Lyall, familiar with the procedures in the Wilhelmstrasse, followed up the cable by contacting Neurath's secretary direct. He switched Nesta over to an official at the Foreign Office who admitted that my cable had been received but he said the Foreign Minister had asked him to reply saying that the proposal was 'quite impractical'. The paper would receive a reply from the German Embassy in London. It was duly delivered.

All the while this inter-European drama was being played out by phone and cable, my editorial people were hanging on breathlessly in the office waiting for the next move. It was an original and daring ploy and we had managed at least to get through to the Nazi Foreign Secretary. It was a good Sunday paper lead-story whatever the outcome. (The page is reproduced in the illustrations to this book.)

Among the well-known people whom I had approached to join the proposed Commission of Enquiry were Mrs Sylvia Parkhurst and a famous judge recently retired. Both agreed to take part.

But, of course, the last thing the Nazis wanted at that time was an investigative body which would inevitably have discovered the truth about the concentration camps if nothing else. Their blank refusal was evidence enough that they had something to hide!

Well, it was a good try but it didn't come off, and so the march of events proceeded—with a succession of dramatic coups and strokes culminating at last in the invasion of Poland—and then the Declaration of War.

Until I left the paper some time later, I didn't let up on my anti-Nazi attitudes and I never have! A newly-founded magazine, *Picture Post*, started by a refugee from Germany—one Stefan Lorant, a Hungarian journalist—took up the cudgels against Nazi Germany in a most vigorous way. It was echoing what I had written six years earlier.

Among the members of my *Sunday Referee* staff in those historic days were William Mabane, MP for Huddersfield, who (when I was in Leeds) wrote a weekly parliamentary sketch for my *Yorkshire Evening News*.

We were very close friends—we almost grew up together—and when I moved to London he became my parliamentary commentator. He was an able as well as an ambitious politician, extremely handsome—as was another boon companion of mine at that time, 'Bobby' Cunningham-Reid, DFC (member for Marylebone)—and I so well recall Willie confiding to me when we were once enjoying that very pleasant pre-war social amenity—tea and strawberries on the terrace of the House—that he would finish up one day as a Cabinet Minister. He did, as Lord Mabane. But at what a price!

After the war, we lost touch for many years but one night in 1955, or thereabouts, I spotted him in a box at Covent Garden with his newly-acquired rich South American wife. His hair was snow-white, his face lean and deeply furrowed and his tall gaunt figure had developed a stoop. He was the archetype of the political elder statesman. Although Willie was exactly my age, he could easily have passed for my grandfather!

Also on my *Sunday Referee* staff at the time was one Hans Peter Guttmann, a lean and cadaverous-looking German who had been a journalist and a publisher in Germany before he fled from persecution as a Jew (strictly non-practising) in Hitler's Reich. I had put him in charge of the paper's publishing advertisers and he did well.

From time to time, Guttmann would ask me to sign official forms in which I undertook to be responsible for the conduct and the maintenance of certain persons desiring to leave Germany—usually en route to America via England. The Home Office had, of course, to vet these applications before issuing the necessary entry permits and it seemed that the tolerant bureaucrats of Whitehall readily accepted the editor of a national Sunday newspaper (known for his anti-Nazi stance) as guarantor for the assortment of refugees in transit through England.

Guttmann occasionally brought some of these *émigrés* in person to see me and to express thanks for my assistance. One character I well remember was the brilliant cartoonist Berger—but I must have signed papers and accepted responsibility for scores whom I never even set eyes on!

As the situation in Germany grew more desperate, so did the exodus of Jews from the Third Reich increase proportionately, and I soon found myself facing a 'conveyor belt' of these applications for 'entry permits' not only from Guttmann but from others including a barrister friend of mine, Mr Leslie Solley (MP for Thurrock), who had heard of my 'escape route' activities. The news had indeed got around and I must confess the situation became a little embarrassing. I feared Whitehall might very reasonably decree that my signature was becoming a little too familiar and frequent so I discreetly suggested to my parliamentary correspondent—life-long Liberal and stalwart defender of human rights—William Mabane, MP, that he might care to sign a few of these application forms! And to his credit he did so without demur. I dreaded to think how many exiles from Germany could have descended on Willie and I at any moment demanding that we implement our guarantees to give them succour so that they should not become a burden on the British taxpayer! I am happy to say not one of them ever did.

I heard nothing more about my libel action with the German chemists nor did my successor as editor, James Minney, when eventually I left the paper to join the Argus Press. Guttmann, who had developed an almost canine devotion towards me, insisted on coming too and I found him a job in the advertisement department of my new organisation.

I will now skip a year or two here to tell how one night Guttmann's wife telephoned me in great distress to say the police had picked up Peter and were sending him to an internment camp.

The war, of course, had just started and the police were doing one of their routine round-ups of foreigners resident in England. I asked where Peter had actually been apprehended and his wife said, in Chelsea. This was good, I told her. I promised to do what I could and said I would call her later that night.

I happened to have a good friend stationed at the Chelsea Police Headquarters—one Inspector Nat Thorpe (formerly of the West End Station and later with the Fraud Squad). By a stroke of sheer luck I not only managed to get him on the phone, but it turned out that he was actually one of the officers who had taken Guttmann into custody. 'You've got to let him out,' I pleaded with Thorpe. 'He's absolutely loyal to this country; I have known him for years and I will vouch for him unconditionally. I am prepared to let him carry on his job if you will release him.'

'All right, he's yours,' replied Nat, who never liked those panicky drives against people whose only crime was that they were foreigners. 'But remember,' warned the tolerant cop, 'I put him in your care. You'll be responsible for him—whatever he does.'

'Responsibility accepted and thanks a lot, Nat; I hope I can do the same for you one day!' I joked.

To the joy but utter disbelief of his wife, whom I telephoned immediately, Peter was back with her in less than an hour.

He reported for duty next day and his huge, expressive dark eyes—so typical of the consumptive—said all he was not able to put into words. I thought to myself that if one day I should ever ask this man to jump into the Thames for me, he wouldn't hesitate to do it! Giving him back his job got me into hot water with the directors of my company. 'Is it right,' they questioned 'that we should be employing a German when we were actually fighting Germany?'

I replied that we were fighting Germany to preserve (among other things) that freedom which permitted me to employ an 'enemy alien' in time of war!

They took my point and Guttmann stayed on.

It was very soon after this particular incident that I decided to go into business for myself. For years I had made money—lots of money—for other people; I had turned failing companies into profit-earning concerns and I had reached one of the highest positions the newspaper world could offer. I hadn't the resources to buy a paper of my own—although I had bought many a one successfully for my employers—but in starting my own business I would at least make money for myself—if indeed I managed to turn a profit at all.

One of the few people to whom I confided my dreams was an old friend and colleague, Harry Ainsworth, then editor of the *People*. We lived near each other in Leatherhead and when he heard the news, he turned to me with a fierce look and in his broad Lancashire accent he said, 'Eh, lad, you must be out of your fucking mind. There's a war on; you've got a big job in journalism and you suddenly decide to go into something unknown. I'd forget the whole bloody thing if I were you!'

I disregarded his vehemently expressed but well-meant counsel.

Another who knew of my decision was the faithful Guttmann—who seemed to know everything about everybody! He came to see me and in his usual vociferous, dramatic, staccato manner (it would have been pure Prussian in any other German) he said, 'I come with you. Whatever you do; wherever you go, I come too. The money is not important. You will be a great publisher and I want to join you.'

He was irresistible and almost implacable. I told him I was taking a plunge in the dark and he would be well advised to stay in his own job where he was secure.

He came with me. I gave him some shares in my new company and a modest salary, and he was deliriously happy. We all worked day and night and very soon it was apparent that the old established publishing house of W. H. Allen & Co. (founded in the eighteenth century) was now safely reborn and well on its way to high endeavour.

117

It would be nice to record that my faith in my so-devoted, inseparable associate was justified and perhaps even rewarded, and that he prospered and had grown old in my service and when the parting of the ways came, it had been a mutually happy severance marred by no ill-starred memories.

Well, of course, life isn't like that—at least not in my version of the text.

By the merest off-chance—a misdirected phone call—I learned one day that Guttmann was secretly negotiating to buy for himself a small publishing company (Hammond & Hammond Ltd) which was on the company register, but currently dormant.

It was too incredible to be true but nevertheless I did a bit of sleuthing only to find out that it was indeed regrettably a fact. But worse was to come. I found that day after day he had been copying all my business records and duplicating the list of the company's customers and authors. He was artful as well as devious, for when I confronted him with my accusations he didn't deny or protest—what he had done (he tried to explain) was entirely in my best interests! London was at the mercy of German bombs. Any moment we might be hit and lose all our precious records. It would take months to re-establish ourselves. But lo and behold if such a calamity should happen, we would have a complete duplicate set of records immediately available. What forethought! What typical Teutonic thoroughness!

I dismissed him on the spot and I watched Guttmann walk dejectedly down Essex Street towards the Embankment. His forlorn mien and his leaden steps reminded me so sadly of that film scene where Charlie Chaplin makes his exit, broken and despised, at the end of the 'party' to which nobody had turned up.

I never saw Guttmann again and so far as I was concerned the book was closed—except for a postscript!

After the war ended I noticed one day a legal announcement in *The Times* saying that one Peter Hans Guttmann was applying for British naturalisation and anyone who wished to oppose his petition should write, etc. etc.

He duly became a British subject, because nobody entered any objection!

14

Interlude Mit Huns (Cont.)

Many people—far too many in fact—have accused me of bigotry, vindictiveness and even racialism, in my attitude towards Germany. I deny it absolutely.

I hate no one, not even those who have acted evilly against me personally, and I have never asked anybody to emulate my anti-Nazi attitude or even to subscribe to my views about Germany. It is entirely a personal matter, concerned only with my inalienable right to choose my own friends and to decide precisely with whom I wish to do business.

What the Germans did is within my own memory and indeed the memory of millions of other people still alive, and it is something I will neither forgive nor forget. I put the whole issue very clearly in an article which I wrote in 1943 when I made this positive declaration . . . 'I have vowed that, after the war is over, I will have no personal contact with any German who was in Germany during the war years. I will not set foot on German soil; above all, no business dealings!'

This article is reproduced in full in the appendix if anyone should want to read it. I don't retract a comma. Nor have I ever departed one iota from my original vow. It is no vendetta. I haven't consumed myself with hatred or nursed some unattainable desire for revenge, and it must be said that I personally suffered no physical hurt from the Nazis; none of my relatives went into the ovens.

I know, however, a very great deal of what the Germans did and if ever I need to refresh my memory I take a look at two photographs that came to me from German official sources. One is referred to fully in the article mentioned above.

The other illustration depicts a vast queue of women (mostly elderly) and children winding its weary way to the 'Bath houses' which can be seen silhouetted on the horizon. Some of the children are holding on to the hands of what must be their grandmothers and other little ones can be seen cowering in the arms of their terrified mothers. On either side of the pathetic queue are the inevitable SS guards in their enormous great-coats with rifles at the ready, urging along these dangerous, desperate enemies of the Third Reich! It is the last journey of these doomed beings. Like six million other human souls, they would never come back.

Reflect on this: over nine hundred thousand children (i.e. nine Wembley stadiums full)—all under the age of thirteen were murdered by—no, not by Hitler, Goebbels, Goering, Hess, Von Papen or the other top Nazis—but by those nice blond young Fritzes and Hans and Heinrichs and Wilhelms whom we used to see in their millions (on the TV screens) 'sieg heiling' the Fuhrer at their pre-war rallies. It was they who carried out the orders; it was they who burned seven hundred Czechs alive in Lidice; they who stoked the incinerators of Treblinka, Lublin, etc., and it was they who manned the 'death camps' throughout Eastern Europe with such highly-praised efficiency.

It wasn't Himmler—but one of his underlings—who wrote to his assistant: 'It is with particular joy (mit besonderer freude) I note that a train has been carrying every day five thousand members of the Chosen People to Treblinka. In the name of the Reichsfuhrer, I thank you sincerely (herzlich)!!'

There's gratitude for you!

I once published a huge book that gave chapter and verse for hundreds of incidents like the foregoing—all officially documented and authenticated. There is now a vast library of such writing but I have never ceased to stick my own oar in whenever necessary, and I have written scores of articles and letters as well as making numerous speeches on various aspects of the dire subject.

About twenty years ago, on one of my annual visits to America, I wrote two pieces in the *New York Times* about the USA attitude towards German war guilt and also about a sudden recrudescence of anti-semitism in Germany. I mention these two articles (they appear in the appendix) because the public reaction was really quite astonishing. I got literally hundreds of letters endorsing my views, quite a few violently opposing me and remarkably enough, many from inside Germany together with extracts from German newspapers.

In one article I suggested that the practical and dignified action for the remnant of Jewry still in Germany was to quit as quickly as possible—where there are no Jews there could be no anti-semitism!

It is no exaggeration to say that these two pieces in New York's leading daily newspaper caused a furore. The United Press put out a summary on its home and foreign services and the stream of letters which reached me indicated that I had raised a sore matter of conscience—had we been too hasty in forgiving the Germans and welcoming them back to the comity of Nations? Clearly a great many Jews thought so—now that I had drawn their attention to it! One person who had obviously been deeply affected telephoned me to ask if I would undertake the famous nationwide American lecture tour to propagate the views set forth in my articles. He promised to underwrite the whole of the costs and if it took a year to accomplish he would pay me handsomely for the sabbatical that would be necessary for me to take from my publishing activities. 'I am a rich man,' he urged, 'and my cheque-book is entirely at your disposal. Meet me at the Harmony Club tomorrow and we will draw up the plans,' he implored.

It was, of course, utterly impractical and I never met this fervent admirer.

I used to get into all manner of scrapes and embarrassments because of my outspoken utterances in America. The German element there is still enormously strong and numerous, and it is my firm belief that it was those former Germans (many of them Jews) who spearheaded the all too premature movement to forgive the Germans and resume business relations with them.

Particularly—and lamentably—has this been so in my own profession which, in America, is very much in Jewish hands. Like the *émigré* publishers in Britain—who include many highly successful houses—the American publishers were in the van of the concerted effort not only to 'make it up' with Germany but also to 'muscle in' on the astonishing post-war prosperity which the vanquished nation enjoyed—largely as the result of Marshall Aid, the absence of any military or naval burdens or expenditure on armaments, and the abrogation of all war debts and reparations. No wonder their economy flourished!

MMW–5 **

The German publishing industry around that time was, of course, almost non-existent. The Nazis had burned the books, slaughtered many Jewish authors and publishers and driven into exile the rest of its literary heritage. It was, therefore, of prime importance that the German government should lose no time in restoring Kultur to the land of its birth! And the first priority was the organisation of the great Frankfurt Book Fair. Heavily subsidised by the Government, the enterprise was lavishly promoted. The hospitality was fabulous and the event itself was generally acknowledged to be something of a triumph for Germany's restoration. There were those, however, who suspected something gruesomely ironic in the fact that the Germans timed the fair to coincide with the Jewish high holidays, especially Yom Kippur.

But this fortuitous clash of dates didn't deter the world-wide Jewish delegations and indeed on one occasion the very fact itself gave rise to a joke that became international. The two Kings of the Frankfurt jamboree were two Jewish publishers who had escaped persecution in central Europe.

The ever increasing success of this Frankfurt Buchmesse irritated me beyond measure, and my patience broke when I read that the 1960 event was acclaimed as the greatest. Frankfurt, where they used to burn books, was now the literary Mecca of the civilised world.

So I sat down and wrote an article for the organ of the British Book Trade, *The Bookseller*, on 'Why I never go to Frankfurt'.

As soon as the editor (the late Edmund Segrave) received the manuscript, he telephoned me to say he dare not publish it. He admired the article but it was too political and not really a publishing matter. On the contrary, I told him, it was very much a publishing matter, and since it wasn't libellous, blasphemous or obscene, it was his editorial duty to publish the article as sent. He had never before refused any contribution of mine and I had written many, and been paid for them. But he seemed adamant.

Well, he must have had second thoughts for later on he decided he would indeed publish the article but in the form of a letter over my signature—a procedure to which I had no objection. All I wanted was to give my views auditory recognition.

The editor then wrote me a remarkable personal disclaimer in which he confessed that he agreed with every word I had written and that his attitude to the Frankfurt Fair was exactly the same as mine. But he still lacked the courage to feature the piece as an editorial article although he did print it verbatim as a letter. (You will find it fully in the appendix No. 2.)

The whole Frankfurt bit came up again soon after the massacre of the Jewish Olympic athletes in Munich, when some of the American Jewish publishers took the opportunity to express their disapproval of my 'boycott' of Frankfurt. I answered them in a published article.

'I'll tell you the principal reason why I never go to Frankfurt,' I wrote. 'It is simply out of respect for the sacred memory of those thousands of Strauses, Goodmans, Weidenfelds, Bernsteins, Meyers, Deutsches, etc., etc., etc., who only a few short years ago were being hunted down in Germany, not as terrorists or guerillas or freedom fighters, but as so much Jewish vermin to be shovelled by the million into gas chambers and incinerators—built specifically for that very purpose.'

I have never been able to visualise the annual Jewish pilgrimage to the Frankfurt Book Fair without mentally equating it with those endless, pitiful queues of men, women and children treading their last journey to the insatiable charnel-houses that the Germans so carefully built, and some of which were so very near to Frankfurt am Main itself!

Nor do I ever cease to be appalled by the monstrous reversal of all ethical values that has resulted in Frankfurt of all places becoming today the 'cultural and literary Mecca of the world'. For it was here, within a stone's throw of the Buchmesse, that the greatest literary *auto-da-fé* in all history took place. And this is the shrine to which publishers, authors, agents and booksellers from all parts of the world now come each autumn to pay homage to the *BOOK*.

I was accused by publisher Roger Straus (of Farrar Straus and Giroux) of being 'uptight' (whatever that means) on the subject of Frankfurt. If I am he certainly ought to be. Does he forget that not so long ago a famous hotel (he stayed there recently) once displayed over its portals a notice that said—

NO DOGS OR JEWS ALLOWED

The notice has gone now. Why? Are the dogs and the Jews so improved that they are now freely allowed in the *gasthaus*?

My abstention from the German literary market place cost me, over the years, a great deal of money. At one time I could have sold to German publishers the rights of many books I published as well as large quantities of children's books which were so scarce in Germany.

I called once on a small publisher of art books in New York named Abrams who offered me a History of Art containing some superb illustrations. I immediately did a deal to take ten thousand copies for sale in England with an option on further similar books. I possessed an import quota which would cover the transaction. As I was leaving the little office from which Abrams and his partner operated, I took a last look at the lovely art book I had contracted to buy and to my horror I discovered it was actually printed in Germany! I promptly cancelled the order and thereby sacrificed a handsome profit since a book like this was an obvious winner.

I learned that Abrams went on subsequently to publish more of these German-printed art books and he succeeded hugely. A few years ago he sold his entire art publishing house for millions of dollars to the *Times-Mirror* group of Los Angeles.

I hate to have to say this, but the American Jewish publishers literally put Germany's dormant post-war publishing industry on its feet and it was the Jewish publishers who were so eager to publish books by or about notorious Nazi blackguards which many gentile publishers—including the late Sir William Collins—refused even to look at.

The depth of human degradation and abasement knows no limits when the good old cash nexus is at stake. It is a defensible assumption that among German post-war publishers, there must have been, shall we say, a sprinkling of ex-Nazis or simple Jew-baiters or perhaps even some dyed-in-the-wool Jew killers. They can't all have disappeared virtually overnight with the other twelve million members of the Nazi party!

They probably found it easy to swallow their pride in sitting down to do business with visiting Jewish publishers. But where, one might ask, was the Jewish pride? Buried, no doubt, beneath a mountain of Deutschmarks.

These are matters that have always deeply troubled me because they go to the very roots of all the things on which I once set so much store—human dignity, principle, integrity, moral courage, even-handed justice and that sense of rightness which is applicable in given situations. I truly believed that these were the fundamental moral imperatives.

It should be clearly stated and plainly seen that the question of Germany's guilt is essentially a matter entirely between Jews and the Germans. Other people, other ethnic groups, are concerned only secondarily. Hitler did not make war on professing Christians or Catholics, per se, nor was their destruction in any way a tenet of his philosophy. He chose right from the start to vilify only the Jews and to categorise them as a sub-human species. He degraded them publicly. Do you recall those photographs of bearded rabbis cleaning the streets of Berlin amid the jeers and cheers of the amused German onlookers? Do you remember how Hitler's favourite crony, Julius Streicher, delighted his boss—and at the same time the whole German nation—with foul caricatures of the Jew which he published every week in his obscene paper *Die Stuermer*? Do you recall the Nuremberg laws by which the Jews—only the Jews—were deprived of all their rights, banned from all professions and forbidden to buy even the necessities of life from shops displaying the sign, 'Jews not admitted'?

And how German motorists laughed at the road sign which warned, 'Drive carefully, sharp curve! Jews seventy-five miles an hour!'—typical heavy Kraut humour which so well reflected the prevalent contempt for everything Jewish. And all this was *before* the war—when Jewish traders in America, Britain and France were still doing business with the good Germans who so despised them openly.

I have picked these few facts from the voluminous records simply to emphasise that it was the Jews and only the Jews whom the Germans wanted to destroy. Had they defeated Britain, America, France, Italy and Russia, they would quickly have made peace treaties and in due course life would have gone on normally in all those countries; except for the Jews. The victorious Germans would have seen to it that there were few Jews left anywhere in the world. The lists of leading Jews marked down for liquidation

125

in the various defeated nations had already been drawn up.

The British list is no longer any secret. I saw it years ago and noted with some satisfaction that my name was on it. I have in my possession a copy of Hitler's official newspaper, the *Voelkischer Beobachter*, containing an exposé of me as a British editor of deep anti-German persuasion.

Had we lost the war—as we damn nearly did at one period—I wonder how many Jewish publishers would now be planning to go to the Frankfurt Book Fair next year?

A hoary legend that needs exploding is the myth that, but for Germany's generous reparations payments, the State of Israel would have collapsed economically. It is sedulously propagated by guilt-ridden Germans and even some Israelis believe it. So much so that shortly after the cash settlement was finalised, the redoubtable Ben Gurion publicly embraced the German Chancellor, Konrad Adenauer, at a celebration in New York. I could never have believed such a piece of blatant hypocrisy could be possible had I not been present at the gathering and seen it. What everybody conveniently forgets about the generous German reparations is that in order to make such payments possible, America cancelled a debt of two billion dollars which Germany owed her. In any case, the total wasn't much less than the value of the hair, gold teeth, bone-ash, skin and glycerine which the Germans extracted so meticulously from six million Jewish corpses.

At the height of the controversy aroused by my articles in the *New York Times* concerning German guilt, I was asked to give an address on the subject to the Overseas Press Club in New York—a famous forum for debates of international interest. When I got to the Club I found to my surprise that a German visitor (Prince von Hollenstein, I think it was) had been invited to present the case for the 'new German generation'. He was accompanied by the Ambassador and apparently he had made a request to speak first, to which I didn't object, even though I hadn't been notified that he was to speak at all. He had newly arrived from Bonn and apparently he was starting out on a lecture tour of the States, so he had his brief all well rehearsed whereas I didn't even have a note prepared. Mine was to have been an impromptu talk to fellow journalists.

The Prince—every inch a Prussian aristocrat—plunged straight away into a propagandist spiel in which he painted a glowing picture of the new Germany, described by him in ringing tones as Europe's stronghold of democracy! Toleration was now the watchword of the people whose war-time errors (as he termed them) were long forgotten. It was now a nation dedicated to the preservation of human rights, law and order and with peaceful intentions towards all mankind. Anti-semitism had ceased to exist, he finally declared, as he sat down to thunderous applause. It was a cunning but convincing performance and I was a little dumbfounded.

Can a juggler follow the top of the bill?

I thought fast. This calls for some direct action, I figured.

'Ladies and gentlemen,' I began. 'You have just listened to a perfect piece of German propaganda, carefully prepared and deftly delivered. I personally don't believe a word of it but we can soon find out whether the speaker is honest, truthful and sincere. He says there is an entirely new Germany today and he asks you to believe what he says is true. He comes to us with a message of hope; Germany has expiated her sins. She is reborn. I am a witness of this truth, he says. The Jews can live in peace and without fear in my Germany today. I personally vouch for it, he assures us.

'You have heard him say that he represents this new Germany and like his regenerated brethren, he is not afraid to speak the truth. Well, let's test that claim here and now. I hereby challenge this emissary from the new Reich to stand up before us all and declare publicly that, "I, Prince Von Hollenstein, am truly ashamed of what my people once did to the Jews and I now state in the name of the new Germany that it shall never happen again".

'Let him make this simple avowal before this great gathering of international newsmen,' I said, 'and his noble words will wing their way to the corners of the earth.

'To my knowledge no German has ever publicly acknowledged his nation's guilt or pledged his word for the future. Therefore let this representative of the new Germany now do so and if he does you are entitled to believe all he has told you tonight. I challenge him to make this declaration.'

It was now my turn to sit down to a roar of applause. But did the speaker accept the challenge? He did not. I overheard the Ambassador telling him not to reply—and he didn't.

So after a few minutes of deadly silence, I jumped up and shouted into the microphone: 'There's your answer. Now you don't need to believe a single word of that specious propagandist diatribe you have just heard. It's a tissue of lies.'

Something near pandemonium ensued but I will never forget the number of people who came to thank me when I finished the speech which I had originally been invited to make.

In a more amusing vein was an episode one evening after dinner at the New York home of my author Ilka Chase, renowned hostess and collector of celebrities.

I was enjoying a post-prandial coffee and cigarette with some of the male guests when a strikingly handsome German came and sat beside me on the settee. He was an Eric Von Stroheim to the life and all he needed to complete the picture of the immaculate Wehrmacht officer was an Iron Cross dangling from his black tie.

'You were British officer in war, I presume!' he rapped out and without waiting for a reply went on, 'then I ask you a question which still worries me. In 1943 it was my duty as U-Boat officer to obey instructions of Grand Admiral Doenitz and to fire on survivors from sinking cargo vessel struggling in Atlantic Ocean. Our order was "No more prisoners". Tell me, in my position as Commander of U-Boat, what would you, an English officer, have done?'

I thought for a moment about this brutal confession of heartless murder, and then a wave of fury swept me. Here in the elegant atmosphere of a sophisticated Manhattan dinner party, a stiff-necked Kraut had the temerity to ask me if I would have murdered drowning sailors in mid-Atlantic. He had certainly come to the wrong man.

'I'll give you an answer that you won't like,' I blurted out, but he countered this quickly with, 'Please, please, I must hear vot you say.' I could sense the discomfort and embarrassment of the other guests around us, but no one uttered a word.

Looking straight into his blue eyes, I said with calm deliberation, 'The reason you fired on helpless seamen is purely and simply because you are a coward. You belong to a nation of yellow cowards and bullies. When you Germans are whipping defenceless victims or strutting about in your jack-boots shooting hostages and gassing children, you feel big and brave. But at heart you are all brutes and

128

cowards. And now I will prove to you why you, personally, are a typical Nazi coward—if any man spoke to me like I am now speaking to you, I would brain him on the spot.'

'I do somezin better zan ziss,' he hissed between his clenched teeth.

Now here it comes, I thought, I've overdone it at last. I had a quick vision of a Wagnerian melodrama in which insulted Hun whips out tiny Mauser, shoots me and then commits *hara-kiri*.

But nothing like that happened. He rose to his full six feet two, clicked his heels together with a resounding crack, bowed from the waist and then literally goose-stepped straight out of the room.

'Whatever's happened to Heinrich,' cried our startled hostess as she observed the sudden and dramatic exit.

'I believe he forgot his jack-boots,' I volunteered cryptically.

15

Memento Mori Interlude

Whenever my diminishing faith in the perfectibility of mankind reaches a very low ebb—as it does with fearful frequency the older I get—I sometimes seek a little solace and comfort from my steadfast friend, informant and silent (but so eloquent) companion of the past fifty-five years—*The Times*.

There, I turn to an unobtrusive section of the journal headed 'In Memoriam' and you might, at first glance, think that reading an ostensibly lugubrious column like this could only serve to intensify any sense of despondency or despair. But you would be so wrong, for here indeed is a fount of inspiration and spiritual uplift. I read these elegiac messages with reverence and awe and wonderment, because, if you have eyes to see, you will find here something which puts to shame all the selfish, mean materialism of human affairs. It doesn't really matter if only a few people read these announcements. Intrinsically, they are private and personal. They weren't written to convince, to persuade, to impress, or to propagate something. They are merely acts of remembrance, motivated only by a pure, abiding and ineffable love. They bespeak a disinterested love that I think must be akin to holiness.

If, for instance, you would like to rekindle your belief in that old-fashioned thing called parental love, read the following:

Captain Robert Glanfield, only son of Lt. Colonel and Mrs Herbert Glanfield—remembered always with love, our dear son Bobbie, who died August 13, 1945.

That was over thirty years ago. How deeply this mother and father must have loved their 'Bobbie': a love undiminished and untarnished by the passage of time.

Nor can time have withered the affections of the writer of this simple declaration:

In loving memory of Private William Wentworth Axtell, killed in action near Arras, May 4, 1916.

Maybe sixty years is only as yesterday in the calendar of true love.

To me, a fully paid-up and long-time member of the Cynics Club, the divine beauty inherent in these simple expressions of selfless love has an air of shattering unreality in the present days of violence, venality, hatred, duplicity and cupidity. It is almost incredible—but heartening—to realise that there are still people who will take the trouble and effort to remember (with love) someone or something that once was precious; to proclaim publicly and unashamedly an unquenchable devotion, a love that does not die.

When a man is impelled to put into cold printed words a tribute to the 'loving memory of my darling wife who passed away twenty years ago' he is responding to an inner voice that has no kinship with ambition, commerce, money-making, or the sordid minutiae of ordinary life.

In proud and tender memory of my dearly beloved husband, July 1945.

In proud and happy memory of my brother killed at Gommecourt 1916.

Dora, dearly loved wife, mother and grandmother, 1968.

Reflect on the time lapses in each of those anniversaries. In the years between, wars have broken out—thrones have fallen, revolutions have exploded, cataclysms have racked the earth—a million things have conspired to obliterate old personal griefs and individual losses; the balm of forgetfulness has anodyned uncountable human miseries; yet nothing of all this has shaken the fidelity or assuaged the ancient sorrow of those who—out of enduring love and infrangible devotion—have chosen everlastingly to—Remember. How uniquely moving is the bitter-sweet language of so many of these

131

verbal memories: 'My dearly-loved only son'; 'my adored and sadly missed husband'; 'my wonderful mother'; 'my never-to-be-forgotten wife'. If these sentiments don't tug at your very heartstrings as you read them, consider yourself to be a much more annealed cynic than I am.

Contemptuous as I have tended to become about people *en masse*, I nevertheless salute all those who write 'In Memoriam' notices, for by such acts of super-erogation they involuntarily proclaim themselves to be nice people, principled people, lovable people (To Love, You Must Be Lovable), the sort that I have so seldom met in the flesh in my lifetime.

There are certain religions which contain in their liturgy special prayers to be recited annually in remembrance of a departed parent, relative, or friend and there is one faith in particular which attaches so solemn and mandatory an importance to the recital of these memorial prayers that men sojourning in foreign lands will often go to great lengths to find an appropriate place of worship wherein they can honour the anniversary of a dead parent.

This is an ingrained discipline which seems to melt the hardest of hearts. I have known formidable tycoons, avowed unbelievers, petty gangsters and big-time crooks who never fail to carry out this duty of remembrance even though to the sceptical observer, it seems to reek of superstition and hypocrisy. To produce a son (rather than a daughter) who will one day say 'Kaddish' for him, has rejoiced the hearts of Jewish fathers since the time of the Second Temple.

All of which goes to confirm my belief that the 'lest we forget' motivation is one of mankind's impelling powers. If you doubt that, let me remind you of the annual ceremony at the Cenotaph in Whitehall—which some soulless people now wish to see discarded. Here you will find the highest expression and consecration of Remembrance that the human mind can conceive. I have always considered this event to be the most moving, solemn and soul-stirring observance in the whole calendar of mundane affairs. On such a day as this, I believe that the very heavens open and the countless souls who gave up their lives in the great wars come back to see—and to hear—what we have learned or gained by their sacrifices.

Perhaps the quiddity of the event itself is enough—hundreds of

132

thousands of people indulging in a simple rite of remembrance, whispering in their secret hearts:

> I shall remember while the light lives yet
> And in the night time I shall not forget.

The Queen never misses this ritual of homage and recall, and the spectacle of her slight, neat figure bowed in reverence before the marmoreal, austere Cenotaph during the two minutes silence is a picture imprinted indelibly on the minds of millions around the world who have participated, actually or vicariously, in this ceremony of remembrance.

Like the devoted authors of the 'In Memoriam' notices to whom I have here paid a small tribute, the Queen and her husband are proud to proclaim in public each November that the quality of pure unselfish love transcends all, and that the attribute of remembering is, itself, a divinity within us. So, from where I sit, these must be two nice people—even for that reason alone.

I think I could die happy in the knowledge and certitude that thirty or forty years hence somebody would remember me—with love.

16

Interlude
Show Biz

The novel may be dying—it has been expiring regularly for the past seventy-five years—but one star in the publishing galaxy is alive and well and continues to shine brighter than ever—the previously mentioned showbusiness book.

In the book trade today on both sides of the Atlantic—and indeed on the Continent of Europe—the show biz book is very 'big biz'. There is always at least one show biz book on every bestseller list and a major new work in the category can command an advance of anything up to 500,000 dollars! The eventual earnings may well treble that figure.

It would be a reasonable guesstimate that actor David Niven, who followed up his initial success in the genre (*The Moon's A Balloon*) with two further hits at the jackpot, has already netted a return of not less than half a million. Doris Day, who lost practically every penny of her enormous earnings as a top film star, recouped some part of her losses with her autobiography which became a world bestseller. Jacqueline Susann, who was Doris' best friend, insisted that I publish the film star's book, which like so many similar autobiographies was written for her.

The record-breaking advance payment which we had made to Margot Fonteyn for her memoirs was perhaps less than half of her total take when all sales are grossed up. The biggest non-fiction advance ever at that time—half a million dollars—was paid to my author Gerold Frank for his official biography of Judy Garland, fifty per cent of which was bank-rolled by Helen Meyer of Dell for the paperback rights alone.

The record advance in 1976 for fiction was the million and point 3 dollars handed over to the author of *Ragtime*, a very much overpraised novel by my friend Ed Doctorow, who left a desk job in

American publishing to seek the big time as a novelist, and in the following two years this record was broken twice. Writers of popular fiction like Irving Wallace, Irwin Shaw, Harold Robbins *et al*. can pull down six-figure advances on a new work that still exists only in the author's brain, and a literate author like Saul Bellow can win a Nobel Prize that is worth just short of £100,000.

So clearly there's big money in publishing and some books which only rated a modest initial payment in advance have gone on—via hardcover, paperback and film rights—to earn their creators wealth such as no author prior to the twentieth century ever dreamed of. Quite a few writing doctors have made fortunes from their literary efforts—Dr Spock, Dr Fishbein, Dr Alex Comfort, Dr David Reuben—to name just a quartette. Reuben's book *All You Want To Know About Sex—And Were Afraid To Ask* set a new style of Socratic question and answer dialectic instead of straight, third-person narrative.

There is ample documentary proof that my pioneering efforts with the theatre book paved the way for the astonishing evolution of the present day show biz book.

Once upon a time a book about the theatre was a publishing 'dog', permanently at the bottom of the literary third league along with books on racing and boxing.

The vogue really began about thirty years ago when I published Gertrude Lawrence's autobiography *A Star Danced*. It caught on at once and I followed through with similar books about Alicia Markova and the Barrymores, both of which did extremely well. Then I published the biography of a theatre itself—Dalys, a long-forgotten West End house that was once the home of musical comedy.

It was the unexpected success of this particular book that led me to commission the historian of the British stage—W. MacQueen Pope—to write the histories of London's most famous theatres. We started off with Drury Lane, the full story of which could provide material for six separate books. *The Lane* was a winner from the word go, and it sold a record-breaking (at that time) twenty-five thousand copies. We were all delighted in Essex Street when we learned that the Queen had accepted a leather-bound copy as a wedding gift—presented to her by the administrators of Drury Lane.

135

estionably, this success set the seal on the show business
Ve had set the pace and rival publishers began to climb on to
d-wagon—but timorously at first.

Although I went to America twice a year in those days I never
managed to sell the rights on a single one of my top-flight theatre
books. One would have thought that Drury Lane would be a
pushover—it is the ambition of every actor, British and American,
to play 'The Lane'—but it was turned down by almost every New
York publisher and nearly always with the same excuse: 'The
Americans love the theatre but they don't buy books about it.'

How different is the story today! An usherette in a movie house
could be a potential author, with her *Follow My Torch* topping the
bestseller list!

It might be thought that a long experience of publishing this kind
of book—I challenge anyone to disprove the claim that I have
published more than any other publisher in the world—could have
produced a formula for instant success, but nothing of the kind has
ever emerged. This is a market which is utterly unpredictable and
many publications that seemed destined for bestsellerdom turned
out to be dismal flops; too often, the cake was bigger than the oven!

On the other hand many a publication that lacked high promise at
the start became a runaway hit—sometimes overnight.

Much depends on the 'subject' as well as on the author, but if the
subject appeals to the reader's special interests, he is likely to buy the
book—no matter what it costs. If, primarily, the reader is allergic to
the subject—or the author—you couldn't give the book to him for
free. Many a stage or screen celebrity, having over-estimated his
popularity or misjudged the strength of his following, has suffered
shell-shock when he discovered the public just wasn't buying his
newly published life-story. Straight away, of course, he blames the
publisher. Couldn't see a copy of the book anywhere; certainly it
hadn't received enough advertising or promotion! Every possible
excuse except the shattering truth that he just wasn't popular enough
to induce the public to fork out a few precious pounds to read all
about him.

The public will never know what goes on behind the scenes to get
a book off the ground. The press interviews, the TV and radio
appearances, the book-signing sessions, the launching parties, the

TOP: Country's youngest editor (author) makes presentation to Yorkshire's oldest journalist (Arthur Tidman). BELOW LEFT: author (aged 16), dispatch rider in First World War. BELOW RIGHT: Mr and Mrs Goulden with publisher Michael Joseph on *Queen Mary*.

CAVALCADE

2D — Registered at G.P.O. as a Newspaper

The British News-Magazine

... ROYAL VISIT TO U.S.A. ...

Cavalcade Suggestion is Heartily Endorsed on all Sides :

Cavalcade Suggestion is Heartily Endorsed on all Sides :

Ambassador's Blessing

HAPPIEST PICTURE OF BANK HOLIDAY WEEK
—a King, in shorts, joined his young subjects in camp. (see page 3)

LAST WEEK CAVALCADE put forward the suggestion that the King and Queen might graciously consent to visit America next year.

The proposal was prompted by the wonderful personal triumph which their Majesties had achieved in their State visit to Paris.

It is CAVALCADE'S view that George VI and Queen Elizabeth could weld the two great English-speaking nations into a lasting bond of friendship, just as, by their magnetic personalities, they have cemented afresh the Entente Cordiale.

There would be no political significance attaching to such a visit. It would be purely a gesture of friendship and goodwill as between the great democracies.

Never was the time—next year—more propitious for a Royal visit to America. The New York World Fair will be a focal point of the universe. Britain will be represented at this mighty exposition, and their Majesties might grace the opening of their British exhibit would be an event to fire the imagination of the two nations.

Since CAVALCADE made the suggestion it has been inundated with letters approving and supporting the proposal. A selection of letters appears elsewhere in this issue.

The project has the blessing and support of the American Ambassador in London, Mr. J. P. Kennedy. Having thus stimulated interest in the matter CAVALCADE and its readers will await the outcome.

Brisk, Accurate, Complete

CAVALCADE

2D — Registered at G.P.O. as a Newspaper

The British News-Magazine

... WE MAKE A SUGGESTION ...

A Visit by the King and Queen to U.S.A. Next Year Would Benefit the Whole World

PERSONAL SUCCESS—Never before in history, perhaps, has a State visit been acclaimed so emphatically a personal success for the two chief guests as that which George VI and Queen Elizabeth concluded in Paris last week.

THE spectacle of a very human man and his wife receiving with simple dignity and grace the homage of a great nation has captured the imagination of a world grown accustomed to the frenzied theatricals and martial pomp of the sawdust Caesars.

FRIENDSHIP—That the reigning house should be the means of advancing the nation's prestige overseas is no new thing in Britain's history. It has ever been one of the supreme duties of Kingship to foster and improve the spirit of "bon voisinage" as between this country and its neighbours, near and remote.

THE most recent Edwards and Georges of the Royal line have added glorious pages to the story of international relations. And now comes the personal triumph in Paris of George VI and Queen Elizabeth to shed new lustre on the record of Royal devotion to the cause of peace and good will beyond the shores of our own islands.

ANGLO-FRENCH TIE—To have cemented the Anglo-French accord at a time when Europe stands in need of a stabilising force is a noble achievement, the more remarkable because it has occurred within what ought to be merely the 'probationary' period of the new reign.

ABROAD, at the first time of asking Their Majesties have created the same splendid impression, the same genuine response, the same democratic appeal, which their frequent journeyings at home have aroused. The Nation—the World—stands to benefit if such missionary work abroad could be extended.

ought to be submitted now for the gracious approval of Their Majesties.

THE time is propitious. Next year America will celebrate one of the greatest international events of the century—the New York World Fair. It would be a soul-stirring gesture—an invitation to attend the Fair.

THE NEW LINER—They might make the maiden trip of new Mauretania the occasion for the crossing to America. More than that, it could be happily co-ordinated with a visit to the Dominion of Canada so eagerly sought by so many loyal Canadians.

A ROYAL visit to America would exert tremendous power for good in innumerable ways.

PROUD indeed would Britons be to know that their Royal House was the binding link for the three great democracies of Western World.

WORLD ENTHUSIASM—It needs but a few moments' thought to visualise the tremendous enthusiasm that would be aroused, the incalculable benefits that would accrue if it became known that the English-speaking Republic of America was to have the chance of acclaiming George VI and Queen Elizabeth, just as the Republic of France acclaimed them so unforgettably last week.

CAVALCADE will welcome views on the suggestion from readers, both sides of the Atlantic.

SMILES in which most of the World would join if Roosevelt were to be host to George VI and Queen Elizabeth

VISIT TO U.S.A.—CAVALCADE therefore makes the suggestion that in the interests of Anglo-American relations—in the interests of democracy—plans for a Royal visit to the United States of America next year

Brisk, Accurate, Complete

These reproductions encapsulate the story of my proposal for the royal visit to America in 1939 (see *Interlude with Royalty*).

CAVALCADE

The British News-Magazine

2ᴰ Registered at G.P.O. as a Newspaper

OUR SUGGESTION ACCEPTED BY THEIR MAJESTIES

ON this page five months ago "Cavalcade" made a bold and unprecedented suggestion.

It urged that in the interests of world appeasement and Anglo-American relations their Majesties might be persuaded to visit America next year.

The proposal — unprecedented because no British monarch has ever visited North America — captured the imagination of both English-speaking nations.

In spite of the fact that the British press reported that such a visit was unlikely,

"Cavalcade," in August—again on this page —stated that the visit would be officially announced in the King's Speech to Parliament—eleven weeks ahead!

His Majesty made the announcement this week. Story of this proud achievement on page 2.

ARMISTICE WEEK REFLECTION

Twenty years ago this week the Great War ended. Question the world is asking to-day is "Did the fallen die in vain?"

Illustrations herewith are thought compelling. In Armistice week, Above, a poppy seller at the Garden of Remembrance on Sunday ; at side, a cartoon from "Candide" bearing the caption, "I wonder if they know the fruits of their victory!"

Brisk, Accurate, Complete

CAVALCADE

The British News-Magazine

2ᴰ Registered at G.P.O. as a Newspaper

..OUR SUGGESTION MAY BE HISTORIC..

Royal Visit to New York, Mooted by "Cavalcade," is a Possibility, says Court Official

TRANSATLANTIC ENTENTE CORDIALE

A SUGGESTION made by CAVALCADE three weeks ago is destined to become historic.

Already it is a major topic in the two greatest English-speaking countries of the world ; at the moment there is the strongest possibility that the proposal will materialise.

RARELY has an editorial suggestion aroused such international interest. On July 30, following the triumphant visit of the King and Queen to Paris, CAVALCADE suggested that a visit to America by their Majesties next year would be an event of far-reaching importance— a mighty gesture of democratic solidarity.

LIKE so many of the world's good ideas, it was a simple enough proposal, yet it had not previously been articulated.

CAVALCADE, in urging that their Majesties might be graciously pleased to accept an invitation to visit New York next summer, advanced the belief that such a visit would cement for all time the friendship of America and Britain.

NEXT year the great New York World Fair will be opened. At this event of the century Britain will be the largest foreign-nation exhibitor.

Would it not be possible, asked CAVALCADE, for their Majesties to visit New York at this memorable time—perhaps to open the British exhibit?

NO sooner did the suggestion appear on this page than it was flashed to U.S.A. and Canada. It was immediately front-paged throughout the American continent.

Ambassador J. P. Kennedy, in London, signified his approval of the proposal personally to the Editor.

Grover A. Whalen, President of the World Fair, cabled to CAVALCADE his whole-hearted co-operation. Stalls letters and telegrams of congratulation on a splendid suggestion poured into these offices.

LAST week-end a broadcast throughout America announced CAVALCADE's suggestion. It has fired nation-wide enthusiasm. And now the British Press has heard of it! The great national newspapers are also making it front-page news.

It was headlined by London's EVENING STANDARD on Monday, with an exclusive statement by a Court official at Balmoral "that a Royal visit to New York next year was a possibility."

THE American papers, without exception, acknowledged CAVALCADE as the source and inspiration of the suggestion.

The British newspapers are silent about it. It is CAVALCADE's experience that most British newspapers never re praise anything achieved by a contemporary journal.

BUT CAVALCADE is not seeking kudos.

It desires only to see the proposal come to fruition, because it is convinced that the Transatlantic Entente Cordiale which it has proposed may be a turning-point in the world's history.

And there is reason to believe that it will take place.

AMERICA'S FIRST LADY: MRS. FRANKLIN ROOSEVELT —she may be hostess to George VI. and Queen Elizabeth next year

BRISK, ACCURATE, COMPLETE

TOP: Jacqueline Susann (left) with my wife and self – we were close friends of the famous author.
BELOW: A book promotion 'gimmick'. A diamond was the prize. Glamorous Elizabeth Harrison chose the winning number.

An extract from *The Bookseller* – in 1945 which dubbed me 'publisher-in-ordinary-to-the-newspaper-profession'.

DON'T FORGET YOUR INNINGS Get 'YOUNGER'

WILLIAM YOUNGER...

Sunday Referee

FINAL EDITION

FOUNDED IN 1877 BY PENDRAGON

THE NATIONAL NEWSPAPER FOR THINKING MEN AND WOMEN

No. 2907

REGISTERED AT THE G.P.O. AS A NEWSPAPER.

LONDON, MAY 21, 1933.

PRICE TWOPENCE

HITLER REFUSES A DIRECT CHALLENGE

Our Offer to Send Over an Independent Inquiry

"YOUR PROPOSITION IS QUITE IMPRACTICABLE"

GERMAN FOREIGN OFFICE AND THE Sunday Referee

HITLER IS AFRAID

CASES WE SHOULD LIKE TO INVESTIGATE ON THE SPOT

THE "Sunday Referee" has issued a challenge to Hitler, which, apparently, the latter refuses to accept.

On Friday last we sent the following cablegram (reply paid) to Baron von Neurath, the German Foreign Minister.

Are Herr Hitler and the German Cabinet prepared to permit and assist an independent non-political committee appointed by the "Sunday Referee" to investigate the alleged brutalities perpetrated on Jews, Socialists, and Roman Catholics, the committee to be formed exclusively of non-Jewish elements under the chairmanship of a personality with a world-wide reputation for impartiality?—Editor, "Sunday Referee," London.

BARON VON NEURATH.

KURSAAL FIRE THRILLS

INSURANCE BOON FOR MOTORISTS

PREMIUMS CAN BE CUT BY HALF

NEW SCHEME

UNDERWRITERS' "BIG BONUS" POLICY

By a Special Correspondent.

A NEW system of motor insurance which will result in considerable saving to careful motorists—in most cases the premium works out at half the present rates—has been launched by an influential body of Lloyd's underwriters.

It takes the form of a double sum policy under which premiums are practically based on a driver's experience and road record, not on the horse-power and value of his vehicle.

It is being offered to car owners, and the first step in a "war" between the established companies...

EUROPE'S LOVELIEST FOR BEAUTY CONTEST

Some of the fourteen European Beauty Queens, photographed in Paris, who have left for Madrid, where they will compete for the title of Miss Europe

NEW JEWISH BOYCOTT

Great Mass Meeting to be Held in London—Mayors Denounce Hitler

HERE is the latest news relating to the German situation.

Herr Hindenburg is not likely to remain many days longer in the German Cabinet...

MARLENE IS STILL FEMININE

WHY SHE ABANDONED HER MALE ATTIRE

MARLENE DIETRICH...

How I challenged Hitler in 1933 to permit an independent British enquiry into the German atrocities accusations.

THE MEN *who are* RULING GERMANY

A Searchlight on the Private Lives of the Nazi Leaders

UNSAVOURY CHARACTERS

ADOLF HITLER.

CAPT. GOERING.

THE chief fear of the men who are now ruling Germany is a public exposure of the moral deficiencies of the leaders of the Nazi Party.

The first act of the German Government after seizing power was to muzzle the Press. Not a word concerning the known crimes committed by the Nazi leaders was allowed to be published. Unfortunately, however, this ban could not be extended to the foreign Press, but every effort was made to block the channels of information abroad.

In some cases foreign newspapers were actually threatened with legal proceedings if they dared to com-...

This uneasiness was increased when two young girl friends of Hitler committed suicide; but nothing substantial could be drawn from this tragedy.

Hitler's personal secretary, Hess, gave the following answer to awkward questions: "I know that there is nothing wrong in this particular case." This cryptic statement increased rather than allayed suspicion; and rumours are now clustering thickly about the Chancellor's name.

The case of Captain GOERING is altogether different. Something more solid than rumour is at the ...

... devoted to political agitation. He became an official of the Nazi party as soon as he left the University. Frustrated ambition urges him forward.

Goebbels is a cripple who is striving to compensate his bodily defects by political success. He is a thoroughly unscrupulous careerist. First a friend and ally of the Strasser brothers against Hitler, he afterwards betrayed the Strassers shamelessly. He incited the leader of the Berlin Brownshirts, Captain Stennes, to revolt against Hitler, but when he saw that Hitler was the more powerful force he dropped ...

... circulation. It is a crime to make such a man the leader of young people, and it is well known that Roehm abused his military power in an unspeakable manner.

It is two years ago since the German newspapers shocked the country by printing Roehm's letters to a friend. These letters proved the moral depravity of the writer, and nearly every sentence was obscene.

Roehm's Confession.

Accused, Roehm declared he wrote the letters were forged. He went to Court, but as soon as the case began he withdrew the charge and thereby ...

RUSSIAN CARGO

... on Russian trade ... tly had the effect ... the backs of the ... engineers, Messrs. ... Macdonald, who ... on. Their petition ... s up to the time of ... l no response, and ... that the breaking-... ial relations is in ... responsible for de-... lease. ... el from the first

---

IN MY View

By ALDOUS HUXLEY

French Art

I HAVE spent much time recently in a study of French art.

It is most impressive—not, perhaps, so uniformly grand and lovely as the Italian, lacking, no doubt, those astounding peaks of dramatic intensity, into which the earlier Dutch and Spanish exhibitions occasionally soared—but still, in its own way, extraordinarily fine.

*   *   *

Moreover, French art has a special and peculiar interest which all its predecessors were without. For the French school is the only one of which it can honestly be said that its recent productions are fully the equal of its achievements in the past.

What, for example, is nineteenth-century Italian painting compared with mediæval and renaissance Italian painting? What is modern Dutch art by the side of Dutch art in the seventeenth century? The answer is: nothing.

Beside the old Dutch and Italian masters their descendants seem naïf, existent. We do not notice the ...

... 1877
... UNDAY REFEREE."
... ET, LONDON, E.C.4.
... N CITY 0844.
... FRL, FLEET, LONDON."

WEATHER:
the greater part of the mainly mild and rather wers or occasional rain, ditions in the North will

OOK: Continuing same-cooler, especially in the

LIGHTING-UP TIME
London Bridge, 4.45 a.m.

m.; SETS: 7.19 p.m.
a.m.; SETS: 1.17 a.m. to-

... $10 p.m.
according to Greenwich ... Summer Time Act day ... hour.

This was the first article ever published exposing the Nazi gangsters who had seized power in Germany (see *Interlude mit Huns*).

TOP: As a member of the Newspaper Society, I was invited in 1927 to tour and see Canada from coast to coast. We were the guests of the Government.

BELOW: The author with George Lansbury who helped to promote my campaign for pensions at 60.

Two of the many loyal staffs I gathered around me during 50 years. TOP: the *Hull Evening News*. BELOW: the *Sunday Referee*.

Members of the Goulden family. Five are in publishing; one is a children's author with 30 books to her credit.

SHOW BIZ IS OUR BIZ

Every publisher 'specialises' in something.

For a great many years *our* speciality has been the 'show-biz book' – a generic term that includes the whole world of entertainment.

Since we commissioned the late W. Macqueen-Pope to write his famous histories of the great London theatres, we have established a veritable corner in this particular market. We now publish more books of this kind than anyone else.

Today we are acknowledged to be the leading publisher of show-biz books, and few can rival us in the promotion and marketing, of these titles.

Consequently when an author or an agent has a major work in this particular category, his first choice is W. H. Allen. We've never had a flop!

A selection from our list of show-biz best-sellers

Julie Andrews	Cecil B DeMille	Festival of Opera
Jean Anouilh	Drury Lane	Edith Piaf
Fred Astaire & Ginger Rogers	George Formby	Cole Porter
	Clark Gable	Rex Reed
The Barrymores	Eva Gabor	Rodgers & Hammerstein
Leonard Bernstein	Greta Garbo	David O. Selznick
Humphrey Bogart	Judy Garland	Frank Sinatra
Burns & Allen	George Gershwin	Richard Tauber
Maurice Chevalier	Lillian Gish	Irving Thalberg
C B Cochran	Sheilah Graham	Ethel Waters
Gary Cooper	Helen Hayes	Darryl Zanuck
	Veronica Lake	
	Hedy Lamarr	
	Jessie Royce Landis	
	Lily Langtry	
	Gertrude Lawrence	
	Franz Lehár	
	Beatrice Lillie	
	Markova	
	Ethel Merman	
	Marilyn Monroe	
	Ivor Novello	

W. H. ALLEN

The first public acknowledgment of my success in establishing the 'Show-Biz' book as a viable publishing category (see *Show Business Interlude*).

AIR PAGEANT

and

Opening of the

HULL MUNICIPAL AERODROME
HEDON ROAD

By

𝕳.𝕽.𝕳. 𝕻𝖗𝖎𝖓𝖈𝖊 𝕲𝖊𝖔𝖗𝖌𝖊

Thursday, 10th October, 1929

☐ ☐ ☐

Air Pageant Committee :

THE RT. HON. THE LORD MAYOR OF HULL (Counc. B. Pearlman)
COL. THACKWELL (Chairman)
CAPN. H. SLINGSBY
REV. F. H. NEWCOMBE, M.C.
CAPN. N. BLACKBURN
CAPN. N STACK, A.F.C. (National Flying Services)
COL. PENNINGTON (National Flying Services)
CAPN. G. THOMPSON
MR. S. DARMODY
MAJOR B. UPTON
MR. J. N. L. POLLOCK (Hon. Treasurer)
MR. MARK GOULDEN (Hon. Secretary)

Proceeds in aid of Hull Rotary Club's Infirmary Appeal and other Charities

Frontispiece illustrates Bristol Fighters and has been kindly lent by the Bristol Aeroplane Coy., Bristol.

A memento of my pioneering efforts for civil aviation in Britain. Hull was the nation's first municipal airport (see *Interlude with Wings*).

provincial tours, the advertising lay-outs, the literary luncheons—all this has to be engineered and orchestrated and it means hard slogging, nerve-racking 'deadlines' and above all else, a thumping great publicity budget!

As a staunch believer in the value of advertising and a glutton for publicity and promotion I never lost an opportunity of indulging my predilection for these methods of selling books.

It was looked on askance in the early days and the more conservative publishers considered it brash and even vulgar.

But in the task of getting public recognition and acceptance of your particular product (ugly word) and to compete successfully against hundreds of rival claimants I go along with the philosophy of Mazeppa, the worldly-wise stripper in *Gipsy*—'you gotta have a gimmick!'

And here are a few gimmicks which I conjured up over the years. To promote a novel about the diamond trade, I once gave a launching party in a West End casino and every guest got a chance to win a real diamond. The 'draw' was made by glamorous Elizabeth Harrison, who wore a hundred thousand pounds worth of gems loaned by a progressive publicity-minded jeweller named Andrew Grima.

To celebrate the publication of the late Jackie Susann's novel, *The Love Machine*, I hired a 'one-armed bandit' lavishly decorated with hearts and flowers and rigged so that three hearts would win the jackpot. Since we had prizes for nearly all the three hundred guests, the machine was further rigged so as to produce a jackpot every other pull! It was a gimmick that kept the party going and proved immensely popular.

Launching a rather beautiful book on Japanese flower arrangements (Ikebana) we induced Japan Air Lines to loan us half a dozen sloe-eyed stewardesses to take the cocktails around at a party at Moyses Stevens where background music from *Madama Butterfly* completed the oriental atmosphere!

For the jacket illustration of one of her sexy novels, Jackie Collins wanted to show a row of shapely girls' legs. I therefore advertised for interested young ladies to come along and be auditioned at our offices in Essex Street. Mary Quant put up the prizes. Long before the appointed time, there was an ever-increasing queue of hundreds of leggy lovelies. A situation was building up that needed some quick thinking and swift action because our premises would never hold a fraction of the would-be competitors. I telephoned the adjacent Waldorf Hotel and explained the situation to the manager who, sensing a bit of useful publicity, promptly put the ballroom at our disposal. We ushered the girls across to the Aldwych and the leg-judging presented a nice scoop to the press and TV cameramen who had suddenly materialised. The subsequent pictures were used in practically every paper in the country. I can recall no similar stunt that got more press mileage than this leg-show.

Jackie's husband, Oscar Lerman (owner of Tramps and Rags), who is himself no mean promoter, thought the whole thing, improvised as it was, a stunning success.

I once booked the entire White Elephant on the River restaurant for the launching of a major book by Robert Carrier, the famous writer on cuisine. The gimmick here was that Robert and the chefs from his own restaurants took over the kitchens and cooked a superb dinner for over two hundred and fifty guests. It was a memorable gourmet occasion.

To get Liberace's autobiography happily on its way, we took over the huge restaurant at Biba's when that glamorous Kensington emporium was at the peak of its fame. We entertained over six hundred to dinner and when I told the guest of honour that he would have to make a speech, he—a performer who had faced audiences all over the world—was quite terrified. He got through it successfully by gripping on to my wife's hand during his witty speech!

Incidentally I expected this flamboyant artiste would be something of an ego-maniac with his outrageous costumes, his ostentatious candelabra and his aura of glorious technicolor, but he was nothing of the sort. He was modest, thoughtful, well-mannered, sincere and the possessor of a deep humility, for all of which I admired him and enjoyed his company. For the occasion Biba's cooks served an after-dinner dessert cake in the shape of Lee's famous piano which certainly struck a nice chord!

Once I hired the Savage Club's facilities within the Constitutional Club to put on a 'black tie' dinner party for Alec Waugh. It was a double event—the publication of his latest novel and the celebration of his seventy-fifth birthday. This was in every sense a very charming occasion with a distinguished guest list and it was generally accounted one of the best ever given by a publisher. Style and charm don't really ever go out of fashion!

When I published a book by David Frost on 'That Was The Week That Was', the focal point of the publishing party was a special programme put on by David and his colleagues from their very popular television show. It was impromptu but quite brilliant. This must have been David's first ever celebration party.

Gatecrashers are always a problem at these publishing functions and no one so far has devised a practical method of excluding uninvited guests. I remember one big after-theatre supper party at the Savoy (for Noël Coward) when we almost ran out of food and drink. We had invited three hundred people and four hundred and fifty turned up!

The presence of 'royalty' at some of these gatherings may be prestigious but it can also be something of an 'over-kill' wherein the real object of the celebration gets relegated to a back seat. In spite of themselves—but sometimes I think rather deliberately—there is a tendency for a royal guest to hog the show.

Once upon a time, it was rather beneath the dignity of an author to take too prominent a part in the promotion of his book. He was a cut above the sordid commercialism which, after all, is the root of these social shenanigans, and apart from liberally helping himself—and his friends—to the publisher's Moët and Chandon, he tended to keep slightly aloof and unapproachable.

There is no such reticence any more. Most authors now throw themselves whole-heartedly into the promotional 'back-up' and even though the chores may be arduous they all seem to enjoy it immensely. No better promoters have appeared on the literary scene in years than a couple of ex-Prime Ministers (Heath and Wilson) whose personal appearances grossed up the sales of their respective books and kept booksellers' cash registers tinkling throughout the country—and abroad!

I never came across an author with more personal popularity than Michaela Denis who, you may remember, penetrated the jungle alongside her husband Armand to capture—on celluloid—the ways of wildlife, and to entertain the public with their remarkable films—and books.

It was almost an embarrassment to walk down the street with Michaela. Autograph hunters stopped her almost every yard of the way—workmen scrambled down scaffolding, taxi drivers froze their cabs, she was hailed from passing buses and lorries and—astonishing to relate—she never refused anyone her signature. She was always smiling and she greeted everyone in her delightful French (Cockney) accent with the heart-warming words, 'You are all my very good friends—I love you.'

When we sent her up to Manchester to sign copies of her first book *Leopard In My Lap*, the vast crowds prevented her from getting to the bookstore venue. The fire-brigade had to be called out to clear a path for her in the end!

Her Belgian husband was a handsome man of considerable culture and extremely knowledgeable about the jungle and its dangers. He was also inexplicably mean and at one time Michaela didn't possess a suitable dress in which to attend a big BBC reception. My wife came to the rescue by lending her a mink coat!

She had a remarkable power over animals and would sometimes carry about with her a mongoose or a snake which scared the pants off everybody. But they were always impeccably behaved.

I once possessed a very valuable and highly-bred Siamese cat. He was indeed so highly-bred and aristocratic that he spoke to no one. He never sat on anybody's lap, he never purred and he would take one cross-eyed glance at a visitor and then disdainfully walk away.

But not with Michaela. She came to dine with us one evening and while we were having cocktails, 'Tim' stalked into the room and, ignoring everybody else, he walked directly to Michaela and jumped straight on to her lap. She literally talked to him and he replied in the squeaky staccato with which most Siamese cats converse. Never had he spoken to anyone before and those who knew of Tim's supercilious, unfriendly, aloof nature, were amazed. Michaela had really reached him and we had to literally prise him away from her when at length she had to go in to dinner.

Michaela told me that she had got this strange power over animals—and over some humans—from a woman witch doctor she had become friendly with on one of the Denises' forays deep into the African jungle. She had imparted secrets to Michaela—which remained secrets—and I am quite sure that what she had learned from the jungle soothsayer exercised a profound effect on Michaela's life-style ever afterwards.

17

Transatlantic Interlude

It looked like being a 'dull crossing'.

I had accepted the invitation to sit at the Captain's table chiefly because on this occasion I happened to be alone and there was always a chance that the table company might be interesting if not stimulating. But from the sprinkling of 'invitees' who appeared at the first meal (which the Captain never attends) it seemed to have the earmarks, as I have said, of being a rather dreary trip. Unless you are the completely extrovert, uninhibited type— which I am not—your table companions can make or mar an ocean voyage.

Like many another seasoned traveller, I always had an affectionate regard for the old *Mauretania,* which in common with most of her sisters on the North Atlantic run, was elegant, swift, stable and 'friendly'—the latter being a subtle something that belonged only to certain ocean liners. It is almost indefinable but, as any Atlantic 'commuter' will tell you, it did exist and one could sense it almost as soon as the last mooring rope had been cast off.

It was by now a little late to cajole a single-seater-table from the purser since the ship was booked solid and in any case the Captain's invitation card is virtually a 'command' and you would need to have a plausible excuse for turning it down.

So there was nothing else to do except wait to see what the evening would bring forth when the Master would preside over his circular table set for a dozen assorted passengers, among whom one might (with a modicum of luck) find a congenial neighbour. It is no small ordeal to have to endure about a dozen meals in succession with a company of people who may not be altogether simpatico, especially when the normal exchange of polite conversation has dried up, as it tends to do after a couple of days at sea. Besides, everything and everybody looks so much better at night-time in the first class dining saloon of a great passenger ship when the company assembles for

141

dinner, and in those pre-war days—you could be reasonably assured of seeing a well-dressed, sophisticated crowd converging on its designated places, amid soft lights and sweet music.

As was to be expected, the Captain's dinner party arrived punctually but as the Master was making the usual introductions between his guests, I noticed he adroitly skipped a gap in the seating plan to my left which was, of course, to his right.

Apprehensively, I figured that if this spot were to remain vacant for the rest of the trip, I would have to sneak up one place or keep conversation going with the Captain across a disconcerting void.

Well, on the first night the dining saloon filled up rapidly. The room was abuzz with animated voices, customary clinking of tableware and the popping of corks when suddenly there appeared in the entrance to the restaurant what can only be described as a vision of loveliness—a tall beautiful girl exquisitely gowned and white-gloved, her corn-gold hair coiffeured with orderly disarray and piled high on her head.

The Chief Steward immediately took her in tow and it was with a frisson of excitement that I realised the path he so skilfully carved for her amid the ocean of tables was heading straight for us!

As I watched her approach, I mentally echoed the line that Byron whispered to his soul when first he saw his divine cousin, Mrs Wilmot: 'She walks in beauty like the night . . .'

The Captain—an old hand at the social game—was distinctly flustered as he took over command of the 'Goddess' from the head-steward and he fluffed his lines as he made the formal introductions to the pop-eyed guests. Smilingly she took her seat, perfectly controlled and perfectly at ease and—cliché or no cliché—I have to record that her radiant smile seemed to light up the whole table!

It was as though she had known us all for years; she had no mannerisms and she got the conversation off to a free and easy start by telling us her late arrival was due to the fact that she thought there was a mouse in her cabin! But the room-steward, whom she had hastily called, assured her after careful investigation, that the ominous squeaks came from a wardrobe door and he cured it in a matter of moments! It was a nice feminine touch and the Captain's comment that it would indeed have been 'a jolly lucky mouse' got the predictable round of laughing acquiescence and thereafter the relaxed and happy guests tucked into the superb fare which the great passenger ships proudly provided in those opulent times.

And so, I reflected with smug satisfaction, this lovely creature is to be my table companion for the next five days; whereupon I offered up a silent prayer of thanks to White Star/Cunard for this unexpected and highly appreciated bonus! The first evening was a resounding success and it looked as if it wasn't going to be a dull trip after all!

During the night as we crossed the Humbolt Straits (a notoriously bad patch) the weather turned a little nasty and it worsened towards morning, which was not unexpected since the voyage coincided with the vernal equinox, a period that is unfavourably known for its sudden squalls and gales.

There is nothing like a rough sea to suspend social life aboard an Atlantic liner and as I went into lunch the next day, I was (thoughtfully) armed with a copy of a current bestseller which would act as my companion should I find myself to be a solitary luncher!

I was not surprised, therefore, to see the many forlorn-looking empty tables in the restaurant but I was certainly surprised—and delighted—to see that my lovely table companion was safely enthroned in her seat, surrounded by vacant chairs, including the Captain's, whose absence indicated that the turbulence was not yet over. The prospect of having her all to myself during the meal would have been appetiser enough but a few 'white ladies'—a popular aperitif of the moment—quickly thawed out any fear of coolness that the stormy weather might have blown in. Later on a divine white burgundy did its share in making this a mid-Atlantic lunch to be remembered.

At our table the night before, you could have literally heard the whirring and clicking of the mental computers of the guests as they tried to fathom who or what was this super-girl who had descended so unexpectedly upon us. There was, no doubt, a lot of wild guesswork since her name, when she was introduced, afforded little clue to her identity nor was the printed passenger list any more helpful next day.

But being the good newspaperman I was in that time, I had little difficulty in 'getting her story', aided, I might add, by the lovely lady herself who I soon learned had no discernible inhibitions. She was the principal buyer of one of the most famous New York fashion houses and she was making her biannual trip to Paris for the *haute couture* collections, a chic chore she had undertaken for many years, which helped to explain why she was such a 'good sailor' and why she spoke fluent French.

She was a native New Yorker and she had just a slight suggestion of the loquacity to which most American women incline. But she was lucidly articulate; everything she said was beautifully modulated and interspersed with musical laughter. She stood garrulity on its head. She was a fascinating talker and I readily confess to being a bewitched listener.

Sitting beside her, you marvelled how bounteous nature had been in bestowing so much beauty on one individual! She looked beautiful, her voice was beautiful, she smelled beautiful and she ate like a beautiful woman should eat—which unhappily is something you don't always behold in beautiful American women!

It may be fancied that the lapse of time and nostalgic memories have woven a web of romance and fantasy around the events here recorded; maybe present imagination has o'erleapt past reality. But this is not so. I am not given to hyperbole and by inclination and training I am a faithful and accurate chronicler of events. Apart from any professional and business expertise I may have, I say with some confidence that in four diverse matters I am ready to pit my judgement against all-comers:—perfect pitch in music, the fine points of football, appraisal of a literary work and the appreciation of female beauty. In all of which I have had a long apprenticeship and a considerably longer post-graduate experience!

So in recalling this transatlantic interlude, I have not exaggerated nor have I attempted to fictionalise a mundane incident. In my time-scale it all really happened yesterday.

I remember that at this delectable lunch we sat everybody out—including most of the impatient table-stewards—and there were no other guests in the dining room when finally we got up to go. As I retrieved my book, the Goddess spotted it, saw the title and exclaimed, 'Oh, please may I borrow this? I meant to get a copy when it hit the bestseller lists. I am a quick reader and I promise to return it to you before we dock. Is it good? I adore all his writing.'

Delivered with the infectious enthusiasm she seemed to display towards any object of her desire, she was of course irresistible. Eloquence is dumb when beauty pleads.

So she took the novel and with a light-hearted *à bientôt*, she wended her way towards the bank of elevators in the foyer.

It was customary in those days for all guests at the large 'official' tables to reassemble as a group after dinner in the ship's main lounge and to form a circle, often enlarged by seasoned passengers coming up to greet the Captain or to say hello to other old shipboard acquaintances. It was all very friendly and informal even though a certain barrier of exclusiveness did surround the 'Captain's group'. And on the particular journey of which I write, there appeared to be quite a procession towards our 'circle' and without commenting on it, we all knew perfectly well what the central attraction was!

Protocol allowed the Captain to have the first dance and since I was number two table-companion, I would be next in line for the pleasure of dancing with the loveliest girl on the ship.

And if we had discovered an affinity for amiable table talk at luncheon, we were quickly aware of an even stronger kinship on the dance floor. I had always been a little allergic to tall girls as dance-partners but on this occasion, since I felt seven feet tall myself, there was little disparity in inches between us. And since I knew she would be 'devoured' as soon as we left the floor I made the most of it—as indeed we both did!

It might easily have been my last dance with her, for we had hardly resumed our seats when two of the senior ships officers—the Chief Engineer and the Senior Surgeon—bore down in a concerted outflanking movement towards our crowded table. They were both handsome 'sea-dogs'—and they both knew it—and I figured that henceforth it would be difficult to compete against the gold-braid and the Van Dyke beards, and I spotted even further competition from two predatory Atlantic 'romeos' who had insinuated themselves into a couple of ring-side seats in our circle. Odds of four to one were a little daunting!

Fortunately, on board we had a ballet troupe returning from their American tour and although these nimble young ladies are notoriously indifferent ballroom dancers, I found one who moved like a

145

feather and followed like a shadow so I 'hogged' her for the rest of the night, occasionally flashing a signal to the Goddess as she span round the ballroom locked in the embrace of a nautical Adonis or a civilian heart-throb!

In the days and nights that followed, I saw the lovely one always at meal times and I don't think it was altogether a one-way magnetism that caused our paths to converge at other times during the voyage—which, from almost every possible aspect, was one of the happiest any lonesome traveller could wish for.

Came, then, the 'last night'. You can literally cut the air of anticipatory excitement that pervades the atmosphere aboard a big ship as it begins its land-fall. All the chips are down, gone are social formalities and class distinctions; everybody seems to be on a 'first name' basis with everybody else and any reminiscence is excuse enough for another round of drinks! Thus do the final hours slip by: fond farewells are said and fatuous promises of 'future re-unions' are made as the liner itself begins to say goodbye to another human cargo, soon to be replaced by the next one on the turn-round.

I have never liked farewells or partings of any kind; not even 'being seen off at the station'. So on this penultimate stage of the *Mauretania*'s voyage I did some perfunctory hand-shaking and while the mountain of baggage began, imperceptibly, to raise itself on the landing-deck, ready to be off-loaded in the morning, I slipped quietly away to my cabin. One always used to eat and drink far too much on these glamorous transatlantic trips and invariably my 'last night' routine was not to sit up till dawn guzzling with jolly, transient 'friends', but to enjoy a good night's rest before plunging back into the hurly burly of everyday life on the morrow.

As was the prerogative of a faithful client of the shipping line, I had been allocated a much sought-after cabin. I had with me a small portable radio (scarce in those days) and by skilfully attaching it to the couplings of the port-hole I was able to bring in a lively continental programme.

So with *'eine kleine nacht musik'* and the balm of the day's 'last cigarette', I felt nicely relaxed, content and unencumbered (I always sleep 'in the raw') on this calm spring night as the swift ship sailed towards the coast of Northern France.

I drowsily ruminated on a voyage that had promised to be a

'winter of discontent' but which had been made 'glorious summer' by the presence of an unforgettably beautiful girl whose companionship had given wings to five days that might so easily have dragged their feet.

Such are the vagaries of fortune and such were my somnolent reflections when suddenly I heard a distinct tap on my cabin door. Instantly wide awake, I called, 'Who's there', and I half expected to see some 'drunk', lost in the corridors of maritime power or a night-prowler out for an eve-of disembarkation 'stick-up and quick getaway', enter the cabin.

My bed-side light afforded only a penumbral view across the room but I could discern the door gently opening to admit—not a marauder—but an apparition in a vermilion and gold Japanese kimono. It was the Goddess herself and her loose flowing gown rustled silkily as she turned to close the door and so shut out the noisy merriment of a party going on down the corridor.

She spoke in a conspiratorial whisper after seating herself at the foot of the bed.

'I nearly forgot your book,' she murmured. 'I shall be getting off at Cherbourg in a few hours so I won't have a chance to see you again.' There seemed to be a note of sadness in her voice.

'It's a lovely book,' she added, 'but the ending made me cry.'

Astonished, bewildered, excited, I couldn't collect my wits to utter even a half intelligent remark. It was all too unreal.

Here in my cabin was the exquisitely beautiful creature who had bewitched us all at the Captain's table. Invariably happy and affable, she had nevertheless always seemed a little distant and unattainable, but now, unbelievably, I was alone with her in my own cabin.

It simply couldn't be happening.

Then she stood up to reach the bed-side table and put down the book and as she rose the wide kimono slipped to the floor and with a deft twist of her fingers she plucked pins from her hair, letting it cascade down her bare shoulders—a golden Aurora enfolding a living naked Madonna.

Intermittent flashes from the beams of the Bishop Rock Lighthouse coruscated eerily through the now dark room and faint sounds of music from the radio mingled with the susurration of the waves as they caressed the hull of the speeding ship.

'Son et lumière' by courtesy of the sea and the sky! What else could you wish to complete the magic of a spring night?

Across the years, when recalling happy memories of that glamorous night, I sometimes get to speculating as to what a High Court Judge, a Cabinet Minister or even a Bishop might have done in exactly similar circumstances to those that befell me in that strange and unexpected interlude.

It is an intriguing—perhaps cynical—thought but I am reasonably certain that taking everything into account, your guess is precisely the same as mine.

18

Interludes With Fate

Some of those 'firsts' mentioned in an earlier interlude with which I have been credited are worth recalling, if only to prove that journalism and publishing are both innovative professions and that there will always be new ideas waiting to be 'Eureka-ised'.

I was the first publisher to make a scouting trip to America after the war.

I was one of the first newspaper editors in the country to put news on the front page. I laid out the *Observer*'s conversion to this style.

I was the pioneer of sponsored radio programmes in the British press.

I was the second publisher in Britain to produce mass-sale paperbacks.

I pioneered the show business book—one of publishing's most successful evolutions.

I installed the first Intertype headline-setting machine in the provinces.

I appointed the first-ever radio-editor on the permanent staff of a newspaper.

I co-invented a matrix-drying machine that revolutionised the casting of newspaper stereo-plates.

I was the first publisher to raise the price of the novel to £1.

I was the first British publisher to put the famous Tarzan books into paperback and also to sell over one million copies of any soft cover.

I was the first publisher to print the poems of Dylan Thomas, whom indeed I discovered.

All of this 'I witness' stuff may not be very much to boast about but then I am not boasting. I am simply setting down some of the scoring points of various rounds fought over the years by a moderately successful journalist/publisher.

Publishing in England is very much a dynastic affair and many of the nation's top publishers were lucky enough to inherit an already well-established business. I started my career from scratch at the age of thirteen and, like my Manchester friend, the gifted music critic and panegyrist of cricket, Neville Cardus, I 'read' English literature in the academic confines of the Carnegie Free Library!

Although my job on the local evening paper—affectionately known as the 'ha'penny arsewipe'—was the lowest form of human activity in newspaperdom, I knew that nothing could stop me becoming, one day, an editor—which indeed I achieved in surprisingly short time.

All I inherited from my father, a music teacher with a profound knowledge of the liturgy of Judaism—and a weakness for consistently backing also-rans—was a strict Jewish orthodoxy much of which I have never abnegated.

I could easily have finessed my entry in Who's Who with an ambigious 'Clifton and Cambridge', because I was born in the former and started my journalistic career in the latter.

But Carnegie and Pearlson would be more accurate and truthful—the Pearlson factor being a certain rabbi's son, Gustave, who was my unpaid mentor, tutor, confidant and counsellor and also my faithful friend. He was a very strange person, the kind one rarely comes across any more. I have met in my lifetime only three persons whom I regarded as geniuses. One was Dylan Thomas, another was a relatively unknown author called Janet Frame, and the other was this said Gustave Pearlson. Not more than five feet tall, with a head exactly like the portraits of Shakespeare, he could not have been less impressive outwardly. But his erudition was utterly incredible; he could talk learnedly and write exquisitely on a multitude of subjects and he spoke five languages fluently. His memory was prodigious and he had an interminable flow of anecdotes about practically any famous personage you could happen to mention. His short legs dangled from the piano-stool as he played Chopin divinely. He was a Hebrew scholar and Talmudist of formidable attainments and he was the author of a deeply researched and finely written History of Jewish Persecution. And above all, 'Gussie' was a great womaniser, even though his physical attributes were by no means Gablesque. But his mind was irresistible to women and he was the living proof of two favourite theories of mine: there are no virtuous women, only incompetent men, and that nearly all women prefer intellect in a man rather than pulchritude.

And it was due wholly to my unimposing but intellectually magnificent Gus that I first looked through the windows of art, literature, music and philosophy. To be in his company was sheer delight and no college don could have imparted to an ardent pupil a fraction of the wisdom, knowledge and learning that this wonderful little man lavished so willingly and affectionately on me. I never had the chance to thank him properly. He finally went to live in his beloved Paris, which he knew intimately, and there he must have died unsung, unremarked and probably penniless since he had the usual intellectual's contempt for money.

Maybe we'll meet up in the next world where no doubt he might be teaching the Angelus to the angels—hopefully (as they say) to the lady angels!

From my mother—a former school teacher—I got my first love of fiction, for on my trips to the Carnegie Library I would always bring home her favourite authors—the good ones like Gissing, Somerset Maugham, May Sinclair, D. H. Lawrence, Henry James, etc., etc., and always the escapist novelists like Mary Braddon, Mrs Humphry Ward, Ouida and so many others now long forgotten.

In my apprentice days, the reporters would vie with each other in doing what were called descriptive pieces, anything beyond the routine reporting of current happenings, and it was usually the star descriptive man who got the best assignments. Many of us sent pieces to other journals because the journalist then was grossly underpaid and had to supplement this income by becoming a 'penny-a-liner'; that is a leg-man who sent news to other papers and agencies for which he received payment at the rate of one penny for every line of news that was printed. The 'lineage' connections of some senior reporters were as secretive and remunerative as the perks of top-rank hall porters!

Nothing made me happier than trying my hand at a descriptive piece and I developed something of a flair for writing these extra-mural contributions. Before long I managed to get one into the *Manchester Guardian* miscellany—an accolade which increased my height to ten feet tall! It was the first of many others.

I have mentioned earlier that I am something of a believer in pre-destination. I think that fate can intervene at a certain point and in a quick stroke alter the entire course and direction of one's career.

Here's a pretty good example. One day I received (I didn't seek it) an invitation to fill the post of assistant editor of the *Times of India*—as a preliminary step to assuming in due course the editor-ship of the paper. It was a stupendous offer—handsome salary—regular leave to the company's retreat in the hills, mem-bership of the leading Bombay club and automatically a knighthood at the end of the mission. It was utterly irresistible and I promptly handed in my resignation as managing editor of the Hull group of papers. I promptly ordered my colonial gear at Thresher and Glenny in the Strand; I booked my outward passage on the P & O, and a paragraph with pictures in the *Worlds Press News* (I still have the cutting) informed the newspaper trade of my impending depar-ture which, up to then, had been kept under wraps.

Then, a few days after completing my exodus plans, I was intro-duced quite fortuitously to the Indian manager of Reckitts, the worldwide organisation, whose headquarters were then in Hull. This man had spent twenty-five years in all the major cities of India and none knew the country more thoroughly than he did—par-ticularly Bombay.

'Let's lunch one day and I'll tell you all about it,' he said, and so eager and excited was I to get this vital first-hand information that we fixed the very next day for our meeting.

And we lunched for well over three hours, at the end of which I rushed back to my office, and sent a long telegram to the *Times* people in London explaining why it had suddenly become utterly impossible for me to go out to India!

I withdrew my resignation (which delighted my co-directors), I cancelled my steam-ship ticket and also my tropical kit. What a narrow escape! My friend from India had opened my eyes. I would never now see those pale hands beside the Shalimar!

'First thing you'll have to learn,' warned my frank friend, 'is to drink whisky—casks of it. Very soon you'll pick up malaria—I'm full of it, and it never leaves you. In your job you will mix with the élite and if you don't drink—or can't—you'll be ostracised. In any case you will cut yourself off so completely from everything that happens in England and Europe that if you ever go back you'll be a stranger. Every two weeks you'll go down to the harbour simply to look at the liners arriving from Britain, just to give you a nostalgic whiff of home. Having cut myself off from my own country all these years I could never get a job in England. And neither would you. You won't save a penny and your ultimate knighthood will be a burden unless you have private means to keep it up.'

That was more than enough! My dreams of Empire were shattered but I was profoundly grateful for this man's objective and invaluable advice.

But it didn't quite end there. The two men with whom I was negotiating (Read and Pearson) wouldn't accept my withdrawal. I had signed a contract and they could hold me to it! However, they 'deduced' that salary might be the stumbling block and the probable cause of my change of pace, so they would be happy therefore to increase my pay by three hundred rupees a month!

But in the light of what my Indian friend had told me, I was adamant, I wouldn't have gone even if they had offered me rubies as well! And it was only after a lengthy and at times acrimonious correspondence that the impasse was surmounted.

Fate would seem to be a bit of a time-waster. If fate ordained that I be offered the editorship of the *Times of India*, why did it also ordain that the Reckitts Blue messenger should cross my path and influence me to reject the offer? I don't know, do you?

Not dissimilar was the offer I got of a job in London, which also came fortuitously. I had written an article in one of the trade papers in which I said that the pace in British newspaper trends was being set by the progressive Northcliffe group of papers. It inspired a telegram from Northcliffe himself asking if I would like to join this 'progressive group', to which I promptly answered 'Yes'.

So I went up to London to see the editor-in-chief—whose name now eludes me—and I came away with the offer of a job at the sub's table, as a starter to get my hand in. Later the same night, I met some of the staff at the Press Club and they seemed to be a very tough, hard-drinking bunch who had little to say that was complimentary about the 'salt-mines' in Carmelite Street where they worked—at such times as they weren't boozing! One particular scribe with the imposing title of Captain Nichols—I think he wrote the gossip column in the *Evening News*—took me on one side and earnestly advised me to stay in the provinces. 'They will squeeze you dry here,' he warned, 'and then they will discard you like an old rag.'

I didn't relish the role of a wrung-out dishcloth in the street of adventure, so I went back to Hull, a little subdued perhaps and maybe a little wiser.

But my ambition ultimately to get to London was undiminished, and only a few years were to elapse before I followed in the footsteps of Garvin, Spender, Donald and the others from the Hull newspaper nursery on the way to Fleet Street.

19

Interlude With Mailer

Unique among all the professions is the grapevine which flourishes in the purlieus of publishing. The delicate tendrils of this ubiquitous plant vibrate with the news, the gossip, the comings and goings in the literary scenes of all countries and there is a continuous stream of messages—to which are acutely tuned the ears of commissioning editors, sponsoring editors, indeed all who are concerned with what goes on in contemporary publishing.

'The word is out' that a big new literary property is in the offing and instantly the scouts go into action.

Who's handling it? Is it under option? Who can steer it our way? Will it serialise and paperback? Is it filmic and therefore a big money project? These are some of the initial flashes that agitate the minds of publishers when a special tip-off wings its way along the grapevine. No other business that I know of depends so heavily on inside information of this kind to generate its source material. Of course, the vine has its fair share of empty rumours and false news, but by and large it is dependable, accurate but rather amorphous in its origins. It's like trying to trace the birthplace of the latest funny story!

One day in 1975, I got a whisper via the literary tom-toms that a very big show business project was in its embryonic stages and, because of my personal dominance in this particular genre, it was easy enough for me to stake a claim on this new venture.

The proposition was a volume of really exquisite photographs portraying in a variety of seductive poses the most photogenic woman in the history of the cinema—Marilyn Monroe. I had already published two full-length biographies of this queen of glamour, one of which included (as a centrefold) the famous nude photo of Marilyn which library-subscribers to the book promptly pulled out from their borrowed copies!

The picture-book idea had emanated from America and it was in the hands of two friends of mine, Bob Markel the chief editor of Grosset & Dunlap and his assistant Stanley Corwin. There was already world-wide interest in the subject when the initiating editor conceived the stunning idea of getting Norman Mailer to contribute a text to accompany the pictures. This text would be in effect a brief biography of La Monroe but written in the typical Mailer manner of highly convoluted sentences, abstruse philosophy and the searing analysis in depth that characterises the prose of this internationally famous author.

But there was apparently a daunting obstacle to the smooth working out of this saleable package deal of glowing narrative and superb photography. Mailer didn't know Monroe and there wasn't time for him to do the necessary biographical research into her career.

But Mailer is a man of subtle resource and lively imagination and very quickly he resolved the dilemma of getting the Monroe story without tears! He would draw on the two full-length biographies which were already in existence—*Marilyn Monroe* by Maurice Zolotow and *Norma Jean* by Fred Lawrence Guiles. I had published both these books in Britain and both authors were very close friends of mine.

Mailer proposed to make no bones about the genesis of his source material—he would flatly and boldly acknowledge in his biographical text that he had relied on Messrs Zolotow and Guiles—each of whom had spent years researching their respective books—for the basic facts about the deceased star!

His agent indeed went to the length of actually telling Guiles that Norman intended to draw on his *Norma Jean* book.

Fred conveyed this good news to me in a personal letter in which he said he had given 'permission' for Mailer to make 'extracts' from the book. Obviously he was tickled pink to get this accolade from such a literary lion.

'The resultant publicity ought to help sell my own book,' cooed Fred. 'Don't you think you should rush out an immediate reprint so as to cash in on this boost,' etc.

My reply must have shaken Fred to the soles of his feet.

'You can do what you like about the American rights on your

book,' I admonished him, 'but you have no *locus standi* whatsoever concerning extracts from the British edition. I am the sole person with power to grant any such permissions. You must therefore immediately notify Mailer's agent that any "permission" which you may have already given applies only to the American edition of your book.'

That meant, in effect, that Mailer could not sell his work anywhere in the British territory unless he first obtained my consent to the extracts which he proposed to 'lift' from Guiles' book. And that, of course, went for my other author, Zolotow, who also had already given 'permission' regarding extracts from his particular book.

I then officially warned Mailer's agent—one Scott Meredith, another old friend of mine—and also his American publishers (Grosset & Dunlap) that no extract from either *Norma Jean* or *Marilyn* could be made in Mailer's proposed work without my consent, so far as British rights were concerned.

It must be made clear that up to that moment I hadn't even seen the Mailer text, nor had I any idea how heavy were the extracts he proposed to make from Guiles and Zolotow.

All I knew at that time was what the naïve Guiles had told me and also what Zolotow had confirmed. (As the leading publisher of show biz books, I was of course anxious to see the completed work—text and pictures—of the Grosset & Dunlap book since it was right down my street.) Then I learned that Stanley Corwin (the emissary of the American publishers) was on his way to England with proof copies of the book. Because of the prior interest I had expressed in the project, Corwin naturally called me on his arrival in London, but he said that his principals in New York had requested him to show the book first to another British publishing house—Hodder and Stoughton. Indeed they were at that moment actively considering it.

I was startled by this piece of information, particularly since I was already holding an option offer of £20,000 from the *Sunday Times* for the serial rights on the Monroe book. The grapevine had telegraphed that I, in the normal course, would be publishing this major show business book in Britain.

My reply to Corwin was that he should at least do me the courtesy of showing me the material. I might, in any case, make a bigger offer than the rival interest.

He therefore promised to retrieve the proof-copy from Hodders so that I could read it over the weekend. He promised to deliver it personally at my office that very afternoon.

But to the surprise and chagrin of my editorial colleagues and myself Corwin failed to turn up. It was all very mysterious and on the following Monday it became still more mysterious when Corwin telephoned me to apologise for not delivering the manuscript and pictures as promised but he had just received 'instructions' from New York to close the deal with Hodders and thus it wasn't possible to show me the material! He himself was returning to New York immediately. He sounded very distressed and ditheringly embarrassed but I never saw the stuff.

What was the reason for this secretiveness and the sudden exit of the American negotiator? Never before had I 'lost' a big show biz book without even a chance of seeing the material, especially when we had established priority. We were quite dumbfounded but the mystery was solved three days later. Out of the blue I got a call from a former publicity executive of mine who imparted some startling news. 'I have just read the Mailer stuff,' she said, 'and it looks to me as though he has helped himself to the best part of your two Monroe books. You'd better get hold of it quickly and see for yourself. You'll be staggered.'

I thanked her (she was rewarded later for her perspicuity) and I promptly got a copy of the book (don't ask me how), into the hands of my lawyers (Oswald Hickson, Collier & Co.).

Members of their staff spent two whole days preparing the 'deadly parallel'—that is assessing and showing side by side how much of the texts of the Guiles and Zolotow books had been 'lifted' into Mailer's commentary. The result—as my informant had predicted—was staggering—almost a quarter of one book had been appropriated either 'verbatim' or cleverly disguised and transmogrified into Mailerese.

Working closely with my legal friend and copyright expert, Roy Furness, I first contacted Guiles and Zolotow. After listening to me they both immediately withdrew any 'permissions' they had previously granted to Mailer. They gave me full powers of attorney to negotiate on their behalf but of course I could deal only with the 'rights' covered by the British contracts, and this largely concerned Hodder and Stoughton who had bought Mailer's work obviously for publication in the British market.

I slapped in a demand for substantial payment for the un-authorised use of my copyright material and soon the transatlantic grapevine was buzzing with the sensational news that a foremost American author was being accused of 'plagiarism'.

The American press from coast to coast made hay of this story. Apparently Mailer himself was infuriated. In an interview he threatened dire revenge. 'No one is going to call me a plagiarist and get away with it,' he thundered. 'I do not need other writers' words or thoughts to make myself a book,' he exclaimed. Mailer's lawyer (the well known Charles Rember) joined the battle. 'What it means,' quoth this top-flight attorney, 'is that unless Goulden makes a full apology Norman Mailer will sue him for libel. The suit will go on in England and he will ask substantial damages.'

Norman himself went one better! 'I will go over to England and beat him up' (meaning me), he is alleged to have told reporters and I replied to this by saying I would be happy to take Mailer on at any sport—boxing, wrestling, running, anything except 'prose-lifting'.

I got a touching letter from Mailer's agent asking me to be 'merciful'. 'You would be surprised how little Norman is getting out of this job', pleaded Mr Meredith.

My own arithmetic suggested at least a quarter of a million dollars! The ultimate take was much more.

Then one evening the head of the USA publishing house—a gentleman named Roth—telephoned me at home and his opening gambit was the well known easy familiarity ploy.

'Look here, Mark,' he chortled amiably, as though we had been bosom pals for years (I had never clapped eyes on him). 'We're both publishers and professionals; surely we can settle this little matter amicably,' he urged ingratiatingly. 'Norman has made full ac-knowledgement and maybe we slipped up in not seeking your own permission.'

'Of course we can settle it amicably,' I replied. 'It's simply a question of arithmetic. How much will your author pay for using large slabs of copyright material without proper authority to do so.

159

You know the drill. You are a professional.' I quoted back at him his own kind words.

Expansively and genially he retorted, 'Shall we say a thousand dollars will cover it?'

'You can *say* it', I answered, 'but it's contemptuous and if that is how you evaluate a matter as grave as this I don't think there is any purpose in continuing this dialogue. I will therefore wish you a very good night.'

And so the battle of words went on. The *New York Times* ran a story in which they said Mailer was incensed about being called a plagiarist and they quoted Mark Goulden as saying: 'Mailer doesn't want anyone to call him a plagiarist: I will.'

'Better brush up on your karate,' cabled an old publisher friend from New York, 'because Norman is coming over to beat you up.'

But this particular Norman Conquest never materialised.

Meanwhile the book had been published in America and it was an instant and tremendous success. But it couldn't be sold in the British territory and Hodder and Stoughton, who had paid something like £30,000 for the rights, were stuck with an enormous first edition which the American publishers had printed for them. The text couldn't be altered.

So the two principals came to see me with a view to reaching a settlement. The last thing I wanted to do was harm a fellow-British publisher, especially since he was not really at fault.

They were both nice people and they were in no way culpable for Mailer's unauthorised use of the material. I was happy to meet them.

Had I really wanted to be bloody-minded and mercenary, all I needed to do was to keep quiet (when I knew the extent of the 'extracts') and simply wait for the book to be published with all the unauthorised passages permanently in print. The damages could have been punitive and the high-priced book would have had to be pulped.

One thing was clear at last. There was no mystery as to why Grosset & Dunlap didn't wish me to publish the Monroe book or even to get a glimpse of the raw material. Had I been allowed to see it and so spotted how liberally my copyright material had been used, I could have demanded to publish the book literally on my own terms.

Some years ago I was involved in an action wherein an author of mine had 'lifted' seven words from another author's work without acknowledgement. It cost me £700—exactly £100 per word. Figure what the publishers of the pirated Mailer material would have had to pay out on that basis!

But I agreed to a compromise with the Hodder people. A substantial sum would be paid over for 'usage' and this would be split three ways with my two authors. All costs would also be paid and a statement of the settlement terms would be published.

Both Guiles and Zolotow sent me thanks and congratulations—indeed my own firm of lawyers did likewise. The case had been conducted according to my strategy, and it succeeded.

Had the two authors given me authority to deal with 'world rights' on their works, I would have been able to show a really handsome result.

Setting down this interlude in a couple of thousand words makes it look like a bit of fun! It wasn't. It involved time, effort, strain, anxiety and a lot of frustration. The files on the case were over nine inches deep. The initiative was entirely mine; I fought hard for the rights of two authors and I think the whole thing was a resounding victory for the writing profession generally. It could never happen again.

20

Pot-pourri Interlude

Two letters which I wrote to *The Spectator* in 1965 are included in the appendix section of this book simply because they produced bigger responses than any of the other epistolary contributions that I have made to the press over many years.

The one about 'Shining The Ball' for some reason raised the ire of the cricketing fraternity to such an extent that you would have thought I had proposed turning Lord's cricket ground into public allotments! From all the centres where cricket seems to be played they hurled 'body-line' deliveries at me for daring to suggest there was anything wrong in a bowler rubbing the ball into his crotch to impart a shine to the leather! They all seemed to take it deadly seriously even though the letter itself was obviously written facetiously. One blimpish character said it was my dirty mind that was at fault by daring to even hint that the rubbing action might look like a masturbatory gesture!

Another outraged reader, signing himself a 'Member of the MCC', flatly accused me of trying to sabotage and ridicule a natural pastime that gives pleasure to millions—which I found a little imprecise since the writer didn't specify whether the pastime he referred to was the cricket or the massage!

Two cricket reporters chose to comment on the letter with ill-disguised scorn but a lady cricket fan from Germany wrote cryptically on a postcard, '*Bei Mir Bist du Shine*', which I considered to be a no-ball! A postscript to this correspondence was the fact that one of the Australian players in the 1975 Test series had to change his pants twice during one game, so incarnadined were they from his waist to his knees by the red dye from the leather ball. He looked for all the world as though he had just sacrificed a chicken in his lap! (See Appendix No. 8.)

The exchange of letters on the subject of British arrogance stemmed from an article in *The Spectator* from its German correspondent, Sarah Gainham, in which she said the cause of two world wars was 'the profound misunderstandings between England and Germany'. She went on to excoriate British salesmen in Bonn for using four-letter words about Germany and the Germans and she bemoaned the fact that she had experienced a similar attitude on the English roads when she was 'driving her Mercedes with German number plates' through the country recently.

The divine Sarah also slammed the 'Colonial' British for their patronising manner towards Europeans, reminding us that these continentals were 'our equals, in some cases our superiors'. Finally, she exhorted us to 'change our self-righteousness and our arrogance'!

As will be seen from the letter which *The Spectator* published, I gave this pro-German screed the clobbering it richly deserved but the editor of the paper (I think it was the late Iain Macleod) decided to add a sneering personal footnote and it was this unworthy and prejudiced addendum that so many people who replied to me—and the paper—resented very strongly.

Re-reading my letter, there is no doubt that it was a vigorous, vehement outburst but absolutely justified. So too thought hundreds of readers who got in touch with me at my home address. You could almost visualise the retired colonels from Bath and Cheltenham who had risen up in their wrath to stand by me in smiting 'Fraulein' Gainham. I found it very heartening. Personally, I have always loathed all knockers of this country especially those slimy creatures which creep out from under the woodwork—calling themselves Marxists, Trotskyites, Maoists, International Socialists or any other label that will effectively serve to disguise their Britishness!

Doubly repulsive are those stalwart Jewish defenders of Russian Communism, the leaders of which, so far as Jewry is concerned, have virtually taken over where Hitler left off. I hold Jews who play 'footsie' with Russian Jew-baiters and anti-semites as contemptible human beings. (See Appendix No. 6).

How many professional writers could bear to read something that they wrote half a century ago—assuming they still survive!

I faced up to this gruelling test in the course of researching material for these memoirs. Faded and fragile was a cutting I came across in a folder of memorabilia gathered from my earliest days in journalism and attached to it was a note recording that this was the very first descriptive piece (as distinct from straight reportage) that I ever got on to the leader page of a newspaper.

I was then a court reporter with very little scope to do anything except record the seamy side of life as disclosed on the charge sheets each day—'Carnal Knowledge', 'Keeping A Disorderly House', 'Causing Grievous Bodily Harm', 'Assault and Battery', 'Breaking and Entering', and other misdemeanours customarily dealt with in a court of summary jurisdiction. Sometimes there would be a promising item such as 'Attempted Murder', 'Manslaughter', or even 'Murder' itself, but in such cases the senior reporters would take over and 'do' the story, leaving us small fry to go and play snooker at the George and Dragon (sixpence a table!).

The little vignette which I wrote under the heading of 'Cheeky Face' was a real-life incident and I remember drafting it one morning when there was nothing more exciting on the 'Rexes' ('Rex v. the Defendant' was the title on the prosecution sheet) other than 'D. & D.'s' (drunk and disorderly) and some petty thefts—all of which were usually ignored by the court reporters unless some exceptional incident or angle came to light, and that of course would only be picked up if the bored scribes happened to be listening at the right moment.

On this particular day I did happen to be listening and when the 'prisoner' in question was brought up I sensed a story because he was undoubtedly the smallest criminal I had ever seen. Normally, the recital of his misdeeds wouldn't have awakened the half-snoozing magistrate's clerk himself and it was perhaps my nose for news that spotted a 'human interest story' (so beloved by news editors) in the case of 'Rex versus Tiny Tim!'

For a cub-reporter still wet behind the ears, it wasn't a bad first effort at by-line journalism. I would dearly love to see what one of today's fat-cat gossip-writers (pulling down £15,000 a year) could have done with a small incident like that bereft as it was of sex, scandal or bitchiness! (See Appendix No. 5.)

Publishers—especially those who try to be with it—have done much to cultivate the vogue word and thereby have rendered a disservice to the art of linguistics.

As a seasoned blurb-writer I have done my venal share and I have helped to give currency to some of those atrocious neologisms which tend to distort the meanings and debase the values of written and spoken words.

The word 'geriatric', for instance, became fashionable when some innovative hack thought it might be profitable to write a book that would do for old age what a lot of successful volumes had done for love, sex, health, fitness, dieting and beauty.

His book became a hit and jumping on to a promising hay-ride, as publishers always do, others got into the act and so geriatrics was born, providing a new genre in publishing.

The premise in most of these guides to longevity is that our youth-oriented society insists that the human body deteriorates with age and they go on to prescribe the ways and means to beat biological disintegration. All this inflationary prose about the ageing processes is, in my view, harmful because it keeps alive the myth of inevitable decreptitude although it pretends to debunk it.

Time is not toxic and vigour does not vary inversely with the chronological age of an adult. Most doctors are guilty of perpetuating the error that time poisons the human tissues, that as the years go by we simply wear out. It just isn't true. We are not machines subject to metal fatigue. The body is a living organism that is perpetually being renewed, repaired and revitalised and the only poisons that harm us are those we introduce by wrong eating and drinking and smoking and, above all else, by wrong thinking. Accepting the false belief that we are doomed by time is the sure way to inevitable decline and the reading of silly books about 'gerentology' merely draws attention to subjects that people can afford to ignore. Just before Artur Rubinstein plays the opening bars of the Emperor concerto, I am sure he doesn't say to himself, 'Ought I to be doing this at eighty-nine?', and I vow that Picasso didn't question himself when he painted one of his three-breasted ladies on his ninetieth birthday.

Any elderly reader who contemplates buying a book about growing old or how to retire would be well advised to spend the money on a nice bottle of Burgundy. It would be cheaper, jollier and much more health-giving.

It's *how* you die, not *when* you die, that matters!

Apropos de rien: when I published the unexpurgated hardcover edition of Frank Harris's hitherto banned book: *My Lives and Loves*, I sold the paperback rights to Corgi books in England for an advance of over £20,000, a record-breaking fee at that time.

After paying half the advance, they suddenly got cold feet. 'What happens if you are prosecuted and your edition is confiscated?' they asked. 'You wouldn't expect us to pay the other half, would you?'

Reply: 'You have signed a contract for the paperback rights. I shall demand the second instalment to be paid in full. Whether you publish the book or not isn't my concern. However, your remedy is quite simple: insure against our book being prosecuted.'

Sequel: Lloyd's offered to cover it, although in the end we were *not* prosecuted. The second half of the advance was duly paid up and the paperback edition is still on sale today—ten years later!

I once made a lot of money by co-inventing a mechanical device used in the production of newspapers.

It had long been my belief that 'colour' in newspaper printing could be the thing of the future and I began investigating the possibilities along with a highly skilled works-manager named Harris who was then in my employ. We experimented with various methods whereby a newspaper could introduce a second colour into its text pages and its advertising columns. Here I must interject a technical note. Newspapers are printed from curved lead plates which are cast from papier mâché moulds or matrices. These matrices are impressions of the actual type that makes up a newspaper page. They are placed in a 'matrix-box' into which molten lead is then poured. When the box is opened a curved plate emerges ready, after trimming, to be locked-on to the cylinder of a rotary printing press. In order to print a second colour (say red) you would need two plates that were absolutely identical, so that when the red plate overprinted the normal black plate, it would be in accurate register.

Well, try as we would we simply couldn't get two given plates so perfectly 'twinned' that the resultant register on the printed sheet would be spot on. There had to be cause for this disparity, even though it was out only by a hair-line. Then, one day, I did a 'Eureka'—it hit me that any difference in the two plates must be due to shrinkage (caused by moisture evaporation) in the respective matrixes while they were being cast. I rushed to tell Harris of this brain-wave and he agreed that this might be the secret. The problem then was how to control the shrinkage, and after more experimenting we devised a matrix-box that would hold each mould absolutely firm and rigid so the plates could be cast dead accurately. It was a simple solution but it worked, and from the rough prototype he went into production with our precision 'matrix machine', which we named the Gouldris (a combination of our names). It found a ready market not only among newspaper proprietors who wanted to offer their advertisers a second colour but also from those who wished to improve the quality of their monochrome printing, for it was soon apparent that the perfect plates produced by our machine improved the standard of printing normally achieved on high-speed rotary presses. With a little judicious publicity, we were soon coping with a stream of orders, especially from abroad, and at £150 a time we were soon in a profit situation. With Income Tax at less than two shillings (10p) in the pound, we were able to retain a sizeable portion of our extra earnings.

Then the big boys of press machinery jumped on to our bandwagon and very soon they were offering a much more sophisticated product than ours, although the principle of their apparatus was exactly the same as our Gouldris. We had taken out provisional patents but we knew we had no chance against corporate power so we pocketed our winnings and called it a day.

However, we had pioneered two-colour-run-of-the-press printing and we proceeded to cash in on it with big national advertisers who were quick to recognise the potential of this new development. And so were the big national newspapers, led by the *Daily Express*, who made a promotional splash when they offered two-colour printing to their advertisers. The *Express* had always impressed me as being the liveliest and most innovative of London's newspapers. To my mind—and my judgement merits some respect—it was always a trend-setter and the front runner of the popular dailies—and I think that is the position which it still holds today.

167

My admiration for the enterprise and the expertise (a word not invented then) of the *Daily Express* was such that I avidly followed every nuance of its make-up and every facet of its lively editorial policy. So much so that one morning at breakfast I was surprised to notice that the paper now sported an entirely new type-dress—a rare newspaper event. All headlines in those days were hand-set and a good make-up man working with a good comp could achieve some striking typographical effects.

I cast an expert and envious eye over the new style *Express* and I remember liking the whole effect immensely. But I suddenly realised that in the refurbishing process they had scrapped one particular type face which I had always thought was perfect headline lettering. I have no record by me but I think it was called 'Century'. Anyway, it had been dropped and without hesitation I wrote to the editor (whom I didn't know) asking if he would sell me all those discarded founts, assuming of course that they had not already been melted down!

Very promptly I got a letter back from a Mr Ralph D. Blumenfeld, telling me he was intrigued by the strange request I had made, and inviting me to discuss the matter with him in London. I found him to be a charming American, kindly, helpful and tremendously flattered that a provincial editor should have shown such a personal interest in the make-up of his paper. We had a splendid lunch at Andertons Hotel (it now lies buried beneath a Fleet Street office complex) and I went home with my type founts, which I soon melded into my own typographical facilities with great success. This off-beat introduction to 'RDB' was the beginning of a friendship that lasted until his retirement.

As a journalist and later as a publisher, I seem to have enjoyed good relations with the *Express* people and many of my former employees joined the roll-call at the 'Glasshouse'.

I knew Beaverbrook rather well, and during the early days of the war when I lived in a cottage adjoining the grounds of his home, Cherkeley, I had access to the best of the produce from Beaverbrook's nurseries and kitchen gardens. I have kept in my memorabilia an interesting letter of thanks which he sent me when he was Minister of State, and I enjoyed some good talk with him on two of my two hundred Atlantic crossings. I hold the view that

Beaverbrook's tremendous war services in 'getting the planes' were never properly appreciated or recognised.

It is a perpetual mystery to me why there aren't more cynics and disillusioned folk in the world today. For an unfathomable reason, the word cynic has become a term of opprobrium, sometimes used with a good-humoured slightly patronising indulgence—'Of course old George is a bit of a cynic you know!'

I am not being cynical when I say that the cynics are realists of the world. But there has grown up a false picture which depicts him as humourless, disgruntled, frustrated, withdrawn; a misanthrope with a chip on his shoulder, eager only to defame and denigrate. This is utterly false and it derives mainly from one of Wilde's famous rehearsed quips about the cynic being one who knows the price of everything but the value of nothing. The joke, of course, is that 'Old Oscar himself was a bit of a cynic'.

No, the true cynic in today's unlovely jungle is the man who has seen much and is not too pleased with what he has seen through. That is not to say he has become the enemy of society. He is the enemy only of sham, trickery and duplicity. He believes with Socrates, Diogenes and Antisthenes that virtue is not merely the only good but the highest good. And because virtue is so seldom rewarded, and the virtuous person so seldom seen, the cynic may be forgiven for refusing to accept what is specious, devious and venal. In time he acquires a spiritual carapace to protect him from the knavery, dishonesty and treachery—and the calumny—of his fellow-men but it doesn't mean that he is in a perpetual state of hostility towards the rest of mankind. Nobody is born a cynic, you become one by observing man's inhumanity to man, by encountering the hypocrisy, the outrageous lying and the sycophancy which are rampant in the social and commercial fabric of modern life.

And whatever else he might be, the cynic is no proselytiser. An iconoclast yes; a 'maverick' perhaps, but a converter no. He may have become disillusioned and disenchanted with the passing show but it isn't his aim to destroy it. That would be blaming the piano for the pianist's bad playing.

Perhaps there are few quicker ways to become a cynic than to go into publishing. Once upon a time it was supposed to be a 'profession for gentlemen'—whatever that means. At its lowest level today publishing is still something of a cottage industry, but in the higher brackets it is big business with everything that the ugly phrase connotes. It is corporate commerce in almost all its aspects—right from the manuscript of the author down to the order form from the bookseller.

Publishing is today a major industry and most of the big firms in Britain and America are largely in the hands of business entrepreneurs, cost accountants and (in the back room) tax lawyers. In the mad scramble to get new material for publication—without which you can't exist—it has become a cut-throat business like all others where the objective is profit—and without profit you will certainly cease to exist.

Here, as in all highly competitive enterprises, our indispensable friend the cheque book has absolute dominion. To get the best books, the best authors, the best marketing, the best promotion, the best production and to be housed in the best premises, you've got to have the best cheque book! Anybody who believes otherwise should retire to a Trappist monastery, or see a specialist. The publishers who will stay the distance and remain at the top of the heap will be only those who can pay the price. Financial dominance is the key to future success in publishing.

Like the other publishers of my generation I remember when you took an author to tea (the business lunch wasn't invented), talked pleasantly, amicably and knowledgeably about a projected new book, discussed terms (based fairly on what the book might earn), drew up a contract on a single sheet of paper, happy and content in the knowledge that it would be faithfully carried out.

Today it is customary to acquire a new literary property by bidding for it at a public auction as though it were a prize-bull put up at a fat-stock show. If your purse is long enough and you emerge as the winner, you then get a voluminous contract, every clause of which is predicated on the assumption that the 'other side' is a rogue and a cheat!

Having done the first leg of a 'big deal' you now have to discard the City gent's garb—the striped pants, the rolled umbrella, etc.—don the strip of a Barnum and Bailey barker and hang in there to promote your expensive package. Your reputation—maybe your service contract—is on the line and all the while the eagle eye of the accountant is watching you. Whether you have succeeded or failed will not be known until you read that eagerly awaited Book of the Year—the company's balance sheet! It's the bottom-line that matters.

Well, that's a synoptic view of how the publishing business operates at summit level these days. And it's just as much big business for the writers today as it is for the publishers. There are, of course, a few exceptions—but by and large any author can be seduced away from his regular publisher by a poaching publisher who offers better terms. Few fail to succumb.

I do recall one writer who refused to become a literary 'harlot'. She is my good friend and author Vera Caspary (with a string of bestsellers to her credit, including *Laura, Bedelia, Letter to Three Wives*, etc. etc.). One day in New York her agent said to me: 'I have a cable from a British publisher (one of the *émigrés*!) saying he will double whatever you offer for Vera's new novel. You will appreciate that it is my duty as an agent to notify Vera of this bid, much as I loathe it.'

'By all means,' I replied. 'Let's see what she says. A "blind doubling" of my advance is a tall order.'

As well as being a talented author and a highly-paid scriptwriter, Vera was also a nice Jewish girl from Chicago!

And this is how she replied to her agent: 'You can turn that lousy offer down!' And just to underscore her flat rejection she then dedicated the novel to me! That inscription stands today as a memento of one author's loyalty. It's an all-too-rare occurrence.

The only other instance I can recall from memory concerns another good friend and author of mine, Alec Waugh. It so happened that his American publisher (Roger Straus) had reservations about Alec's up-coming novel—*A Fatal Beauty*. He thought it was far 'too English' for the US reader and therefore he might have to reject it. I got into touch with Alec and told him not to worry because I would have no difficulty in placing the novel with an alternative American publisher if he so wished. But Alec wouldn't hear of it. 'All my books have been published by Farrar Straus in America and I do not wish to change my publishers', he told me.

I therefore went back to Roger and persuaded him to publish the book by taking a run-on of five thousand copies from my own

English edition. I am pleased to say it turned out well because Roger actually had to reprint the novel!

The loyalty of authors to their publishers is as much a myth as the legend that some of them write in a spirit of 'art for art's sake'—meaning, presumably, that monetary reward is of secondary importance!

In fifty years of consorting with writers of all shapes and sizes, dedicated or otherwise, I never met one who refused a royalty. Perhaps there is something onomatopoeic between Loyalty and Royalty.

I deplore the way in which many famous American publishing houses have fallen into the hands of oil corporations, film companies, motor manufacturers, transport contractors, and similar industrial conglomerates. Many of these proprietors couldn't care whether the end product is literature or fish and chips. What appears on the 'bottom line'—see how their foul jargon has penetrated the book world—is really all that matters. They beam with pride on the cavortings of their whiz kids and go-go boys, many of whom (like their bosses) are barely literate and if it weren't for the university presses and the few remaining independent houses, the publishing trade would inevitably degenerate into a vast merchandising operation like the paperback business (the mainstay of American publishing) has now become.

Wouldn't it have been lovely if the publishing profession in England had remained—or even pretended to be—at heart really 'a profession for gentlemen' where writers would be content to leave their interests entirely to skilled bookmen who would faithfully undertake to sell as many copies of each author's work as the traffic could bear? There would still have been bestsellers and riches for many; there would have been honest trading and fair competition, decent rivalry and above all some innate regard for the quality of learning, erudition and literature as well as a true interest in the future of letters.

Instead of getting £10 per word for a book which he hasn't yet written, a big-name author would have to be a craftsman willing to work for his living. Some publishers might even act as though good books were more than coronets! And there might even be a chance for emergent new writing talent!

But it'll never happen now. Mark my words!

172

21

Interlude Poetic

Music, except the atonal dissonances of Schonberg, Honegger *et al.*, lyric poetry and beautiful artefacts—particularly eighteenth-century French furniture—have been among my main artistic delights.

As a young man, I found that the poets seemed to say all the things I wanted to hear concerning the values that I so early cherished—but which alas, later on, slowly eroded as life became more materialistic and less romantic.

The 'Jewels five-words long' that I discovered in the works of my favourite poets fascinated me and I could retain the structure of a beautiful line ('and it rang like a golden jewel tumbling down a golden stair') just as one mentally records a lovely melody. Such things made music at midnight for me.

But it wasn't simply the metrical magic in the words of the poets to which I responded—I recognised the faithful adherence to truth in all things, which was what Coleridge believed to be the essence of the poetic creed.

I can still recite yards of poetry by heart—and I often do, especially when it is necessary to put a quotation from Shakespeare into proper context.

A sound and dedicated acquaintance with the glories of English poetry is, in my view, a useful apprenticeship for the subsequent appreciation and evaluation of prose, and that, after all, is (or should be) one of the essential tools in the publisher's trade. I don't really think this is the case any longer these days when the literary value of a work—or the publisher's ability to discern it—is of less importance than an ability to estimate its potential sale or to assess its filmic possibilities.

When I worked in the offices of Doubleday in New York, I attended the weekly editorial meetings of the Literary Guild, their famous and highly successful Book Club operation, and I was tremendously impressed by the quality of the readers' reports on books submitted to the committee for possible selection.

The Guild possessed a formidable rota of readers—any one of whom would present a succinct analysis of a given book that always commanded my admiration.

These assessors were knowledgeable people; they were unbiased and objective, and I recognised that their judgement—for or against—was thoroughly reliable as to the literary merit of the work under survey.

But unfortunately a book chosen for book club adoption (or for normal publication for that matter) is not always selected on the strength of its beauty of style or its elegance of expression.

Is it literature? is not necessarily the criterion. Is it saleable? more often is.

The opinion of a literary agent concerning a work is about as useful as a car salesman's advice about his impeccable second-hand car! But naturally no publisher takes much notice of the views of an agent whose sole function is to sell his client's wares for the highest possible price and also to protect his author's future interests against the rapacity and money-grubbing of those legendary monsters who convert gems of English literature into bestsellers or paperback gold-mines!

Nevertheless, agents may serve a useful purpose although I don't know precisely what it is. Many have their favourite publishers to whom they often give first refusal of much of what they have to offer—like the famous A. D. Peters who, when I once tackled him personally on the subject, unhesitatingly confirmed my allegation that he sent all his best material first to Collins and whatever they didn't want, he then submitted elsewhere. He was quite unabashed by the unfairness of this favouritism and since he held all the aces there was no point in arguing with him.

I once had an amusing showdown with a British literary agent who invariably had a stock answer to any inquiry that I made to him about a specific book. 'There are several other publishers ahead of you on this one but I will certainly let you see it in due course if it becomes available.' That's what he always said and consequently I rarely got a book from him: they never seemed to become available.

Those in front of me always got the priority—especially when it was a book of American origin.

One day I asked him to lunch with me at the Savoy and over a meal (far too expensive for a non-co-operator of his calibre) I broke the news gently to him. 'I've just come back from my half-yearly trip to America,' I said, 'and I want to tell you about a book that you haven't heard of yet. I met the author at a New York party who told me about his new novel. It isn't finished yet, but nevertheless the author has instructed his New York agent to let me see it FIRST for England. It will come through the XYZ agency in New York and as you are their representative in London, you'll be getting this particular manuscript shortly. I expect you to send it to me when it reaches you, as the author wishes.'

'What's the name of this book?' my startled guest enquired.

'It's one you couldn't forget,' I hastily answered. 'The title is *The Negro with the Crew-Cut Hair*.'

'But my dear Mark,' piped up this literary Ananias, 'I've had several requests for *Negro* (he was so familiar with it that he snappily abbreviated the title!): they go back months.' It was the good old predictable standard reply.

'Impossible,' I exclaimed with well-simulated fury, 'no other British publisher knows anything about it. The author actually lives in Florida and I happened to meet him on one of his rare visits to New York. It was a stroke of sheer luck.'

But my agent friend was sticking to his customary alibi—several other publishers were ahead of me on this one too!

'Look, Richard,' I said with pleading in my voice now, 'there must be some mistake. Are you prepared to let me see those requests which you say you have already received for this book? I can't imagine why the author should be lying to me. He said he'd told nobody but his New York agent.'

'By all means, dear chap,' he responded heartily. 'Let's go straight back to my office and I'll show you the letters.'

I accepted the offer with alacrity but as we were getting into our overcoats I turned to my trapped friend and said, 'I'll save you the trouble of getting those letters. It so happens that there never was such a book; there never was such a title, and you, my dear Dick, are therefore a bloody liar.'

175

He was stunned.

'So you tried to take the mickey out of me', he managed to blurt out as I left him standing in the cloakroom, immobilised by his guilt.

I had administered a well-deserved rebuke and I had nothing to lose, even if he retaliated by never giving me a book in the future He never had anyway!

Perhaps it was because of my long love affair with the muses that induced me to start a Poets' Corner in the *Sunday Referee* in 1933.

No other Sunday newspaper—nor any of the literary journals—published such a feature. This is how it came about.

It seemed that Arthur Calder Marshall—just down from Oxford—had told Hayter-Preston that their mutual friend, Victor Neuberg, appeared to be in pretty poor shape. This distressed Hayter-Preston—he was in Victor's debt and had a deep affection for the gifted but unrecognised writer.

Preston, who was my Literary Editor, wondered if I could give Neuberg a job on the *Sunday Referee* and I readily agreed to meet Neuberg. As a result of the interview Neuberg became Poetry Editor of the paper and it was decided to allocate him a weekly column within which he would conduct a poetry competition, publish some of the entries (with his own comments) and award prizes. I paid him a pathetic pittance for the work but he was nevertheless overjoyed at the prospect of 'working in Fleet Street'. He told Hugo Manning it was the first money he had ever earned and the spiritual harvest the position was to bring him was beyond measure!

The Poets' Corner made its first appearance in the *Sunday Referee* on 9 April 1933 and it was an instant success. Suddenly Victor, now a member of the same editorial staff as the Sitwells, Aldous Huxley, Bertrand Russell, Constant Lambert, Richard Aldington, etc., had become a power!

It is quite incredible how poetry has always been virtually the Cinderella of the Arts. Very few publishers want anything to do with writers of verse unless they are already well known practitioners in other genres or unless the publishers wish to appease the vanity of an established prose author in order not to offend— and possibly lose him.

176

The booksellers look upon poetry books with the same eager enthusiasm they would bestow on a publication about dog-racing in Wigan or deep-sea fishing in Outer Mongolia!

Every so often a reviewer will gather together a batch of recently issued versification and write a portmanteau notice that most readers of the paper will subsequently ignore and which will advance the art of poetry a few steps further towards its ultimate oblivion.

From time to time a journal or magazine devoted to the art has gamely struggled for survival but by and large the poets among us have to feed on their own enthusiasms. They are not catered for like the practitioners of needlework or pigeon-fancying or pop-art and if there exists an unacclaimed Milton he is likely to continue for a long time wasting his sweetness on the desert air!

Oddly enough it's very different today in America, a country which hasn't produced fifty notable poets since it first listened to the harmonies of its prairies and the lullabies of virgin forest and stream. The cult of poetry of all kinds—from the bawdy ballads of the Barbary coast to the sophisticated lyrics of New England—is a strong and powerful element in the cultural life and character of a relatively young nation.

There are American publishers who actually specialise in the publication of poetry and the catalogues of most houses usually carry one or two new poetic offerings. Informed and erudite critics help to maintain the place of poetry in the country's literary output. A poet really has a chance to shine in the American literary scene. In France, Spain and even in heavy-handed Germany, the flower of poesy is cultivated with delicate care. Only in Britain—birthplace of the world's greatest poets—an immortal galaxy spanning the years from Chaucer to T. S. Eliot—do we neglect our imaginative creators of beauty, elegance and wit. Nevertheless we are still a nation of poets and the gift of versification is a heritage of which we should be proud. The quality of so much poetry—unpublished and unsung—in this country is a revelation to those who take the trouble to seek it.

And this was indeed something we discovered almost from the moment we initiated the Poets' Corner. The response was astonishing and I shared Victor's amazement at the general excellence of the work submitted. We could have filled many weekly columns and our one regret was that we couldn't give more space to the feature.

Victor never doubted his judgement of a poem, which was his strength. He had now become a power to be reckoned with. He favoured no school or cult and he heeded only an inner *frisson* which whispered 'This is poetry'. Apparently he had this when he read a poem called *Chelsea Reach*, by an entrant named Pamela Hansford Johnson. He awarded it a prize and printed it in the issue of 23 April 1933. He gave a similar accolade to a contribution from one Laurie Lee (later to earn fame as the author of *Cider with Rosie*).

One day Neuberg and Hayter-Preston came to see me with a suggestion that, as a further inducement to poets, we should publish every six months a volume of poetry by the author whose submissions were considered to be the best during the period. I promptly agreed to the scheme and I said that additionally I would put up a cash prize. By this time we were getting a prodigious weekly batch of poems and by the time the new offer was announced over three thousand entries had been examined. The task of adjudication was formidable and Neuberg was assisted in his labours by two erudite volunteers, Leslie Minton and Beth Tregaskis. Much of the work sent in was often in handwriting difficult to decipher. One such was a poem beginning 'That sanity be kept . . .', which came from an unknown in South Wales, signed Dylan Thomas. It got the weekly prize. Another from the same source beginning 'The force that through the green fuse drives the flower' impressed Neuberg even more and his comment was, 'This is a large poem, greatly expressed . . . it is cosmic in outlook.'

Pamela Hansford Johnson wrote to Neuberg saying how much she admired the poems he had published from the Welsh entrant Dylan Thomas and she asked Victor for Thomas's address so that she could write to tell him of her admiration.

Victor was convinced that the next choice for the half-yearly prize (publication in volume form and a cash award) should go to the Welshman whose contributions had made such an impact on him. And since the final decision was mine I agreed to read some of the poems sent in by this regular entrant, and one night I took a batch with me to read at leisure.

I can now recall—forty years later—the excitement I experienced on a first sampling of this extraordinary poetry. It was so distinguished that I began to suspect its authenticity. Was this some clever, eclectic hoax? Do our poets steal from Homer? How could major poetic utterance like this—some of it sublimely lyrical, some of it abstract and difficult to comprehend—how could truly great poetry of this coruscating brilliance emanate from an obscure writer living in a small Welsh town?

The very next day I told Neuberg—as well as Hayter-Preston and a couple of other people whose literary views I highly regarded—about my reaction and particularly about my misgivings as to the validity of the work. Little Neuberg almost jumped for joy. 'Genuine? Of course this poetry is genuine: maybe we have found a genius.' Neuberg exulted.

Curbing his emotive enthusiasm a bit, I said, 'We can soon find out. Let's bring the writer up to London and put him through the wringer. We'll meet our genius face to face.'

I called my secretary—Miss Gwen Thomas (no relation)—and told her to write to one Mr Dylan Thomas of Swansea and invite him to visit us in London—at our expense. I instructed her to send him the rail fares and to book him for two nights at the Strand Palace Hotel which was a few minutes' walk from our offices off Fleet Street.

'I would like you all to try to be present when our discovery arrives,' I told my colleagues and within a few days—alone and unannounced—the mysterious sweet singer from Wales presented himself for our scrutiny and cross-examination.

You could hardly imagine anybody less like a poet than the bucolic curly-haired corduroy-trousered young man who nervously stood before us in my book-lined editorial room. He had been a fee-paying pupil at Swansea Grammar School where his father was Senior English Master.

And did we 'grill' him! We fired questions at him; we probed his background and his Welsh heritage; we traced his progress from school to little-magazine poet and he took it all good humouredly—he evinced a boyish charm that was rather endearing.

My lasting impression of the interview was his response to my blunt question as to how he actually wrote his poems. 'Oh well, you know,' he replied, 'I sit down and begin to write and it just flows and flows.' It was a simple, ingenuous statement but it was delivered in a slow, measured mellifluous voice which I shall never forget. The words 'flows and flows' became somehow onomatopoeic and it was hard to relate these honeyed sounds to the stolid, almost doltish face from which they emanated. I was fascinated by his speaking voice no less than by his gifted poetry.

I remember passing a note to Ted Preston saying, 'Victor is right—we are in the presence of a genius.'

Well, of course, the rest is literary history—albeit distorted by some literary historians. We awarded Mr Dylan Thomas the prize and his *Eighteen Poems* was duly published, the physical production being undertaken by the Panton Press. I paid the whole of the costs. Those are the bare facts. They are accurately confirmed by Jean Overton Fuller in her biography of Victor Neuberg published in 1964 by W. H. Allen. Cyril Connolly said likewise.

The genesis of Dylan's 'discovery' was also accurately related by Dame Edith Sitwell who wrote: 'Mr Mark Goulden and Mr Victor Neuberg invited the boy Dylan Thomas to London and to these gentlemen we must be ever grateful. They were indeed good friends to him.'

I saw Dylan only a couple of times in the years following my publication of his *Eighteen Poems* and by then he had degenerated into a drunken layabout haunting the pubs and the sleazy doss-houses of Bloomsbury. The cherubic face which had endeared him to us when he came to the *Sunday Referee* office was now replaced by an unkempt and dissipated visage which had all the stigmata of the incipient alcoholic. He had become the poet of the pub.

But when in 1954, after Dylan had fled London (as Rimbaud once had fled Paris): after he had sounded all the depths and shoals of fame, adulation, razzle-dazzle and dipsomania in Manhattan, the spent meteor finished up in the New York gutter, discarded and despised. And very soon after he did 'go gentle into that good night', there suddenly surfaced in Britain congeries of literati anxious to claim the 'honour' of having discovered the most original poet since Eliot, Auden, Herbert Read and Hopkins. All these claims were, of course, rubbish.

It seemed that a great many ardent poetic souls had early recognised the talents of the Welsh bard—which again is rubbish. Just before publication day of *Eighteen Poems*, I personally sent a note (together with a copy of the volume) to every literary editor in London and the provinces—a letter in which I urged the recipient to take a careful look at the book because I, as an editor, considered it to be the work of that ill-used word: a genius. This should, at least, have whetted the literary appetite of some of the professional press scribblers, but it didn't. So much then for the talent spotters!

The subject became, for a while, after Thomas's tragic end, a topic in the 'literary weeklies' and two letters which are reproduced in the appendix, speak for themselves. (See Appendix No. 7.)

Up to date there have been no fewer than twenty-three major books about the writer whose poetry was 'the most absolute poetry of the time', but few of them have got the facts right about the discovery of Dylan Thomas. So you can take the above simple narrative—told for the first time—as being the absolute truth. I was there.

22

Punch-line Interlude

As a bitter observer of the human comedy, I have never objected to a little mordant criticism when I happened to be on the receiving end. As the French say, '*A bon chat, bon rat.*'

But I intensely dislike those monstrous caricatures which some newspaper artists perpetrate when they attempt to portray well known people, notably in the Sunday papers. You get a blurred vision of a bloated animal festooned with strings, spaghetti and squiggles and somewhere in the midst of this mish-mash you can vaguely discern Healey's bushy eyebrows, Callaghan's protuberant nose, Heath's prognathous jaw, or President Carter's bunny teeth. If I were a victim of one of those cruel parodies, I would sue for defamation of features or at least slander of goods!

A few years ago *Punch* decided to run a feature about well-known publishers under the heading of 'These Looks Speak Volumes'. I learned that I was to be included in the series and they sent round their staff artist, Sherriffs, to do a 'live' sketch of me in my office.

I duly appeared in this *Punch* 'panorama of publishers' as number three and the text (as follows) seemed eminently fair but utterly uninspired, no doubt because of the undistinguished curriculum vitae of the subject!

THESE LOOKS SPEAK VOLUMES
After thirty-five years of catering for the literary tastes of the public—both as newspaper editor and publisher—Mark Goulden, chairman of W. H. Allen, confesses that he still doesn't know what they really want. Since the day he discovered an unknown young poet in Wales, brought him to London and published his first volume of verse—it was Dylan Thomas—he has quested and found a lot of new writing talent and this he

considers to be the real joy of publishing. His 'proudest' titles: all the books of Edmund Wilson because he is the greatest literary critic alive today: Robert Nathan's *So Love Returns* because it succeeded without 'sex, violence and horror': the novels of Rose Franken because they have sold over two million copies: Alan Sillitoe's *Saturday Night and Sunday Morning* because it was acclaimed the best 'first novel' of the fifties: MacKinlay Kantor's Pulitzer Prize winner *Andersonville* because it successfully raised the price of the novel to twenty shillings in England.

On the whole that was a nice write-up but the accompanying sketch—which you see below—I considered to be little short of a pictorial libel.

3. MARK GOULDEN

Reproduced by permission of Punch

I thought at first of buying up all copies of that issue of *Punch* and having them pulped. The prospect of that awful picture being gazed upon by thousands of patients in dentists' and doctors' waiting rooms for the next six months gave me sleepless nights, but I figured that the only way to mitigate the mischief was for *Punch* to publish some sort of disclaimer from me.

I therefore sent to the editor the following letter:

A PANORAMA OF PUBLISHERS

Sir,

I am grateful for the honour you have done me in hanging me on the line of your portrait gallery of eminent publishers, but by some grievous mischance you seem to have hung the wrong man!

The sketch which accompanies the biographical note is not one of me but of Manny (Sourpuss) Speigel, the notorious 'beer-baron' who rubbed out 22½ of Al Capone's legmen during the prohibition era in Chicago.

This Manny won dying fame because of his quaint quirk of carving or drilling his three initials (MSS) on the hides of his victims and this, plus the fact that he could neither read nor write, must have caused his picture to go into your files under the heading of 'publishers'!

His end was unspectacular. One day a huge volume of poems (The Canterbury Tales) fell from a thirtieth storey window on Madison Avenue and struck him between the eyes—a sort of 'poetic justice'. A wit at the inquest said poor Manny had been killed by a 'flying Chaucer'!

But that was his only connection with the book trade.

So Punch erred in substituting his picture for mine.

Yours faithfully,
Mark Goulden

I suggested that the editor might care to reproduce a facsimile of the offending sketch alongside a photograph of myself (which I enclosed) so that the readers of the esteemed journal could note the unfortunate transposition which had inadvertently occurred!

But as was to be expected, the assistant editor of a humorous paper lacked any sense of humour—or maybe he hadn't been 'assisting' long enough—because he sent a deadly serious reply to my allegedly comic complaint. This is what he wrote:

Dear Mr Goulden,

I'm extremely sorry that you dislike Sherriffs' portrayal of

184

yourself but I cannot accept your explanation. It seems to me far more likely that you felt a certain contempt for Sherriffs' abilities even before he started to draw you, and it was this that contorted your features into that unwonted sneer.

The rest of the portrait is considered very handsome.

Yours sincerely,
Peter Dickinson
Assistant Editor

Well, as they say in Madame Tussauds, 'Handsome is as handsome does!'

23

Interlude
With Authors

Few things delight the heart of a publisher more than his 'discovery' of a new writing talent. It doesn't happen very often; some publishers have never even made a notable 'discovery'.

But when a publisher gets a manuscript that is clearly the work of a person with literary ability, he sets the wheels in motion. And this is what he usually does; he gets one of his editors to read it in order to confirm his opinion that this may be something out of the ordinary. He might then seek the opinion of an outside reader, one of that venerable body of literati who report to publishers on manuscripts sent to them for assessment. They are usually good at evaluating the 'literary' merits of a work but they never commit themselves on the vital issue of sales potential.

If, with enough supporting opinion, he thinks the manuscript deserves publication the editor brings it up at the next editorial conference where the firm's whiz kids will toss it around. If the sales manager thinks he can sell enough copies for the resultant book to wipe its own bottom, a modest offer will be made to the author. The chances are that as a first effort it will lose the company money but the chances are also that the company has invested in an author of some promise. Of course, if the work in question is so manifestly outstanding that no second opinions are even necessary, then the procedure is different in so far as the publisher tries to grab the property for the best price he is willing to pay.

Much of the foregoing applies only to new writers—those with no track record. An established author submitting a new work—either direct or through an agent—gets a different treatment. If he has any sort of success record at all, it then becomes an arithmetical calculation. Will this new book get him over the top or is it just a pot-boiler where the author is trading on his name and past performance?

Far away and beyond all this is the known writer with a string of bestsellers to his credit. Such an author is usually tied up on a contractual commitment to his publisher but he is fair game for the unscrupulous pirates who have no compunction in trying to get this kind of author to make a switch. If his only contractual obligation to his current publisher is an option on his next work, then he is as good as free. No option clause in a contract can prevent a disloyal author going over to some other publisher for better terms. These contracts are not worth the paper they are printed on and the validity of an option has never been tested in the courts for the simple reason any claim based on it would be thrown out of court before the case could be got on its feet. Unless the option clearly specifies exactly the terms for the next work, it is meaningless; without stated terms, it is a contract within a contract and as such is *ultra vires*.

So, by and large, publishers are very much at the mercy of their authors and the situation will never alter because there still exists a sordid and unhealthy rivalry between publishers.

Some of the top publishers in the business happen to be the biggest poachers. One such is known to possess a form-letter which he sends to any author who has suddenly attracted the limelight or hit the jackpot. 'In the event that your next book may be free', is the opening gambit in this standard approach and few authors—and no agents—are inclined to reject a feeler of this kind out of hand. Provided the writer has a promising new work in mind, he could probably write his own ticket if he wants to exploit the interest already expressed by a publishing seducer.

It has to be said that nowadays there is no lack of material submitted for publication. Unrequested manuscripts—coming in over the transom as the trade jargon has it—pour in all the time even though a few pompous publishers actually refuse to accept work that has not been invited or commissioned. If everybody adopted this prissy attitude, there would have been no *Gone With The Wind*—the classic example of a bestseller that literally came to its publisher through the post. Banning unsolicited manuscripts merely makes life easier for commissioning editors.

So when a publisher finds a potential winner out of the blue as it were, he is entitled to make a little whoopee over it. It is now a commonplace that some highly successful books—mainly novels—were turned down by dozens of publishers before one lucky operator decided to give it a whirl. But there is very little nail-biting among publishers when one of their rejects makes a hit under the imprint of a rival house. A book is a book is a book! It's all part of the publishing gamble, for ours is one of the most unpredictable businesses in the whole realm of commerce. Any attempt to forecast the probable impact—and subsequent sales—of a given literary property is largely guesswork on the part of the publisher and his advisers, except if it is a new project by one of the dozen or so already famous top authors—in which case it's merely a print-out job for a computer as to its worth.

The general public doesn't get to know much about the genesis of a bestseller, particularly if it originally got the run-around from a batch of publishers. A writer likes to let his readers believe that his success was spontaneous and expected!

One thing about publishing which is absolutely certain is that the literary quality of a book is in no sense a guarantee of its success. Indeed, more often than not high literary quality may well be a guarantee of failure.

Many years ago, I picked up the British rights on a novel published in New York (by my old friend George Braziller) and written by a New Zealand author named Janet Frame. It hadn't taken off in America and I was quite sure it wouldn't set the Thames on fire if I published it in London.

But it was a brilliantly written novel, and it richly deserved publication even though it wasn't destined to be a money spinner.

Its theme was insanity—a killer subject in spite of two outstanding successes in the genre, and rarely has the melancholy and distressing human malady been more sensitively handled than it was in *Faces in the Water*, by Janet Frame.

When I published it in England it got the expected cool reception from the booksellers—it was a 'first' by an unknown and therefore carried the kiss of death—but the critics gave it raves, particularly the critics on the literary papers. A few of them have a nose for good writing.

A second novel by the same author* fared no better with the booksellers but it got even better notices from the reviewers, all of which goes to prove two things: one, the book retailer has little interest in the intrinsic worth of the product he sells, and two, good reviews have hardly any bearing on the sales of a book. The publisher has to do all the promotion.

After publishing two novels I thought it was time that this particular writer, so highly acclaimed by the critics, should meet her British publisher. I therefore got in touch with her agents but, astonishing to relate, they, like me, had never seen her! Did she really exist? Here was the inkling of a very promotable mystery angle. Unfortunately, as we were gearing up for a teaser press release on the missing author ploy, she actually turned up. However, she made it known that she was allergic to publishers and she didn't want much truck with agents either, it seemed. It was conveyed to me that this strange author shunned publicity, and although she was in London, her whereabouts were secret. But her agent did promise to send on to her a letter from me. I therefore wrote a note to say that I respected her desire for privacy and although I wished to meet her, I would eschew the customary invitation to lunch. I suggested that she should come to the office to meet me and I would arrange a 'sandwich lunch' for both of us, thus avoiding any public appearance. Apparently this idea appealed to her. She replied and we set up a date.

She arrived on the dot and after the greeting formalities—very stilted, very cool and very detached—we faced each other across my desk. What I perceived was a plumpish, rosy-cheeked, demure young woman, indifferently dressed, and bearing unmistakably that scrubbed, carbolic look which is the hallmark of people who have lived in institutions. This institutional aura is as easy to detect as is the 'Brixton shuffle' which characterises the gait of a man who has been 'inside'.

Well, this confrontation in my office turned out to be as trying a half hour as I can ever recall. I opened the conversation gambit as brightly as possible but after ten minutes, I realised this was

* *Faces in the Water* by Janet Frame (W. H. Allen, 1961); *Scented Gardens of the Blind* by Janet Frame (W. H. Allen, 1963)

decidedly a one-way dialogue—my visitor hadn't uttered a word or batted an eyelid. Nor did she break her silence during the next ten minutes, by which time I had completely run out of conversational steam!

She had simply continued to listen and to stare unblinkingly at me, sitting bolt upright in her chair. Unable to endure this ordeal by silence any longer, I am afraid I blew my top. 'Look here, Miss Frame,' I almost shouted, 'I've been talking to you for nearly half an hour and you haven't said a damned word. If you're not interested in what I'm trying to say about you and your work, please don't waste any more of my time,' with which admonition I moved towards the door.

But suddenly she unfroze and smiled. 'I have heard every word you have said,' she announced in a firm voice that had distinct Colonial overtones. 'And,' she continued, 'I agree and accept all your excellent advice.'

With that the whole ambience changed. Here, it soon emerged, was a woman who was not only a gifted novelist but an articulate speaker with a perfect delivery. I rang for the coffee and sandwiches and from thereon we chatted amiably during which I got the drift of her own astonishing life story.

It seemed that she had spent some time in a New Zealand mental home and during her incarceration she had written a short story which she gave to the superintendent to read. So impressed was this official by the writing that he took a chance and sent it up to the local broadcasting station. They promptly bought it and put it on the air as a star item in their fiction programme. Then she wrote another story—this time almost a novel—and when the superintendent read this new effort he at once entered it for a literary competition being promoted by the New Zealand radio station. It won the first prize!

It seems that Janet then left the institution and found her way to America where she contributed some articles to (of all media) the highly sophisticated *New Yorker*. She also wrote her first full-length fiction work which Braziller—one of the more literary publishing houses—immediately put into his list. This was the book I picked up during my scouting expedition to New York, and with which she subsequently made her debut on the British literary scene.

190

I learned from my now alert and very communicative visitor that she was at work on a new novel but I gathered she was doing her writing while actually living in Camberwell (of all places) with a coloured family! The reason for her working-class location was that she could be near to the famous Maudesley Hospital at which she was an outpatient. From what she told me about her proletarian surroundings (screaming children and ceaseless blaring radio) it seemed a miracle that she was able to do any work at all.

Before our interview ended, I made her a proposition. I would lift her out of her sordid and insalubrious environment; I would install her in a furnished flat for which the company would pay all expenses, and there she could get on with her writing, unworried by financial or any other obligations. One condition I imposed: as she had already written novels dealing with mental disturbance, she must now concentrate on an entirely different theme. She accepted the idea with evident pleasure and within a few days we had found her a nicely furnished apartment off Brompton Road, where she was happily and comfortably installed.

I sent to her four newly-published successful novels suggesting that she should read them in order to feel the 'trends' in current fiction. They were by famous writers and within a couple of days she had sent the books back to me together with a concise report on each of the titles. I want to say that I have never read a better piece of literary criticism in my whole career. She could have had a top job as a reviewer on any paper. It was an astonishing *tour de force*. She not only assessed the novels accurately, but she criticised some of the writing with compelling force and insight.

Obviously she didn't think much of the books and perhaps it had been a little indelicate on my part to have sent her some 'specimens'. As a writer she was head and shoulders above all the other four authors put together!

Well, I left her to settle in and hopefully to produce, in good time, the brilliant contemporary novel which I was certain she could do. For three months I heard nothing from her. Then one day came a letter to say she had urgently to return home to New Zealand on family matters but she would finish the novel and send it on to me.

In due course it came. It seemed to be a superb and imaginative effort and started with every prospect of developing into a great

191

book. But suddenly it trailed off and from thereon we were back in the old depressing atmosphere of mad people and doom and despair—the entire mixture very much as before.

Well, that sort of thing happens in publishing. Some writers simply cannot function outside a certain familiar environment.

Another gifted author of mine who, I think, suffers from a slight parochial obsession, is Sillitoe. It's all very well to say that these authors are writing about a particular milieu in which they are immersed and which they can interpret with a unique kinship. But surely the reader ought to be considered. He can become bored with too much loony-bin authenticity, too much Lancashire 'hot pot' or too many Nottingham black puddings!

It is a bitter irony that these two first-class professional novelists cannot produce runaway bestsellers like those which far less competent writers churn out with enviable regularity. A lesson that any author should learn early in his career is to listen to the advice of his publisher. It's free, and it's invaluable and when it comes to saleability, the publisher knows best!

I remember saying to Sillitoe when I told him I would publish his first novel (*Saturday Night and Sunday Morning*), 'If you put yourself in my hands, I will make a lot of money for you as I have for many others.' And I did.

With the passing of time, Sillitoe's 'discovery' has become a bit 'mythologised', like Dylan Thomas's earlier on. Credit for it has been claimed by all sorts of people—a reader, a film producer, a talent scout, a literary agent, a friend, an editor—everybody except the one person who decided to put the book into print—and that is the only factor that counts in the literary stakes. No punter backs a non-runner!

When the manuscript was given to me it was in a tatty state, which clearly indicated it had been around—as indeed it had—to practically every publisher in London. The professional reader Otto Strawson had recommended it but then he had recommended dozens of others which we never published. In reading a manuscript, I pay no attention to outside opinions. I have my own standards of judgement and my basic premise is that if I am impelled to go on after the first fifty or so pages, then the manuscript has something. It is easier to decide what is worthless than it is to make an affirmative decision.

But I have never made the 'yes' verdict lightly and having done so, I stick to it. I would not have been in any way prejudiced against *Saturday Night and Sunday Morning* had I known before reading it that twenty publishers had turned it down.

I finished it over the weekend and on the Monday I told Jeffrey Simmons to ask the author to come in to see me, just as I had done, forty years earlier, with a writer called Dylan Thomas. I am a great believer in meeting the author.

Alan stammered his thanks—and his incredulity—when I told him I would publish his novel and it was many weeks later that I heard from his agent that the book had suffered multiple rejections. 'If you hadn't accepted it, I would have then abandoned the book,' Madame Rosica Colin informed me.

For a would-be author to get a start somebody has to push the button, and if by chance you push the wrong button, the opprobrium is all yours. Nobody wants to know. It was your choice, and you are stuck with it. But let it be a success, let it hit the jackpot and then the 'Saints Come Marching In' to bask in the glory of the achievement.

'We told you so,' etc. etc.

'As a publisher, you must meet an awful lot of interesting people.'

I have been coping with that fatuity for nearly forty years. With a slight transportation of adjectives it could easily read, '. . . a lot of awful people' which could be just as inane but perhaps slightly more accurate.

Scattered over the pages of this book are references to various authors and others I have met professionally and in a few cases I have added a personal comment or two.

What follows are some random thumbnail sketches of a few of the more interesting people publishers are supposed to meet and from the brief details any reader can judge for himself just how 'interesting' they were—or are.

First, I should explain my general attitude towards writing-people. Mostly they are bores and the majority of them really believe that what they have written is a major contribution to the 'library of the mind'!

Probably eighty per cent of their entire conversation is devoted exclusively to what they have just written or are about to write. With some writers the psychosis reaches the stage of an obsession and most publishers do their best to dodge such clients—many of whom are so stricken with the writing bug that they are virtually paranoiac. One famous writer with whom I did business was so obsessed with the characters he had created that he really considered them to be living entities! In his more lucid and reflective moments he would say things like: 'I'm not sure I shouldn't have let Christopher seduce Rosalind just before she married Richard at the end of Chapter Three. After all, Dick was a dear friend of Chris.' His egotistic delusion was such he believed that I was just as familiar with these puppets as he was. The pay-off is that I had never read a word of any of his books!

There is a type of author who is an expert at fielding the brush-off. Try as you will to end the literary conversation by switching the subject to Siamese cats or the devaluation of the zloty, this cunning manipulator will soon weave it back on course to the vital topic of 'my book' and you are sunk.

There is only one other human genus I know that is totally immersed in its own particular vocation to the exclusion of all else—film people of every grade. Get a bunch of them together and there is no hope of discussing anything except 'grosses', Frankie's new part, Ziltches' latest flop, Angela's triumph in *Moon Over Monaco*, the Cannes Festival, or other scintillating subjects which the celluloid cognoscenti can natter about enthusiastically for hours on end. To anyone outside the magic circle of movie making, it is an unutterable bore, and the quality of the debate is usually in keeping with the mentality of the participants—intellectually well below zero!

However, let's make a start on our poly-snapshots.

Duchess of Bedford

A tough baby this, who knows what she wants and doesn't mind stepping on a face or two to get it. The masculine female *par excellence*. Her book, *Nicole Nobody*, was, in my view, as dull as ditchwater although a great many readers thought otherwise. Its sales impetus was guaranteed by a pre-publication release in which the Duchess alleged she spent three nights of love with a would-be rapist in a Manchester hotel! The publicity 'mileage' which this episode clocked up in every newspaper was unbelievable—as unbelievable as some people thought the incident itself probably was! Nicole is something of a perfectionist and she drove the art-editor and a few others up the wall to get each illustration right or just the way she wanted it! The editorial staff sweated blood to get the book out ahead of time—5 April—so that the Bedfords could leave England before a new fiscal year had begun. Editors and printers achieved a minor miracle by meeting the deadline. Plans were then made for a big launching party at Woburn House at which Nicole and Ian would officially say farewell to all their 'county friends'. It was to be a lavish affair—dinner, dance, black tie; guests from London to be coached to London and back, etc., all set to be one of the most stylish—and most costly—publishers' parties ever mounted.

As I joined the office meeting called to discuss the details of this jamboree, I remarked *en passant* to the Duchess (who was examining a copy of her book), 'Well, Nicole, how do you like it?' I was astounded to hear her reply: 'I don't!' She refused to elaborate or say what she objected to and I reminded her how hard the editorial people had worked to get the book out on time. I couldn't determine what was the reason for her displeasure. 'We are here,' I said, 'to discuss plans to celebrate in a sumptuous manner the publication of your autobiography, but since you hate the book, it would be a shocking waste of time and effort and money to do homage to a literary corpse. The festive occasion would be a wake, not a party. In the circumstances, therefore, we must abort the whole idea. As chairman of the company I will not sanction the expenditure of one penny on it! Regretfully, ladies and gentlemen, there will be no Woburn House party.'

And there wasn't!

Nicole, whom some of my colleagues adored, is a first-rate promoter and very professional. She did everything asked of her to publicise her book—here, in America and in her native France. As I have said, it got off to a good start, no doubt because of the 'glamorous nights' publicity and the book's snappy title—which was her own suggestion.

The Duchess heard about the book's initial success while she was in France (a few days after quitting England). She cabled my promotion manager saying, 'Does Mr Goulden still dislike me now that my book is a great success?'

I sent her a one-word reply, 'Yes.'

Duchess of Leinster

A rather pathetic figure, she was the author of a life story telling how a girl from Brooklyn married into the English peerage and found only disillusionment and poverty. Rafaelle should have been the central character in a real life Cinderella story but her noble spouse turned out to be a drunken layabout and today she has little left except a coronet and bitter memories. When we met to go over her book (*So Brief A Dream*) she was living in a tastefully furnished 'garret' atop a luxury block in Grosvenor Square, bravely trying to behave like a Duchess and expecting her book to have 'film possibilities' that might change her penurious circumstances. It didn't.

Duchess of Argyll

Because she is perennially newsworthy and uniquely photogenic, Margaret Argyll must be the most paragraphed and photographed Duchess in Debrett. She is accustomed to getting her own way but the gossip-hounds who relentlessly pursue her don't always co-operate. The *Express* keyhole hacks seemed unduly hostile while she was writing her autobiography, which was odd since Max Aitken is her adoring friend.

As the 'Deb of the Year' she was truly a trend-setter in style and beauty when such things mattered. Today she still is stunningly attractive and the living proof that the impeccably-dressed and perfectly-groomed woman can outshine—and outlast—the casual inelegance of jeans and T-shirts now the uniform of so many of our liberated, lazy lovelies!

Duchess of St Albans

The only Duchess of the quartette I have known who has any pretensions to literary ability. Her autobiography, written in instalments, does her much credit. Imaginative, artistic and charming. A nice person with no 'side' or 'bounce'; as likeable as her husband.

Kirk Douglas

I spent many hours with this 'nice Jewish boy from Brooklyn' trying to get him to put his story on paper before it's too late! He is still not quite able to comprehend his fabulous success as a film star or what has happened to the 'street smart' urchin who trod the well-worn path from the Lower East Side to stardom. Although very keen to 'tell all' he is too busy to keep his dimpled chin on the typewriter. Neither is he allowed to move far from the watchful eye of his able managerial wife, Anne—her own romance with Kirk would make a good prelude to his hoped-for autobiography.

Edmund Wilson

The foremost literary critic of this century. A man of profound erudition with a gift for making difficult things easily understandable in lambent prose—'Bunny' was a delightful companion, crusty at times, unable to suffer fools gladly, and, like me, often in trouble for not being afraid to speak up and speak the truth. He got on the wrong side of the British press for his alleged anti-British attitude. Critics would like to have damned him with faint praise but he was far too big for them. A headache to his publishers but a distinguished addition to any list. Towards the end of his career, his work was still brilliant but his books just didn't sell.

Here's a good story of my publication of his banned (in New York) book: *Memoirs of Hecate County*. One episode in the fictional work was considered pornographic by the 'censors' in New York and it was withdrawn from sale. Against today's undisguised scatology *The Princess with the Golden Hair* would rank as a drawing room story!

Nevertheless, my publication of the notorious novel was the first attempt to break the book-ban in Britain. It got off to a good start and it was well reviewed, but within three weeks I was visited by two officers from Scotland Yard's Vice Squad, who presented me with a long questionnaire to fill in concerning the book, its author, my company's credentials and a lot of other equally irrelevant and tiresome questions. I played for time because I knew two top national papers were about to review the book favourably and their opinions would strengthen our case—if, indeed, it ever became a case.

197

I told the officers to come back the following week to collect the completed document but before they left, I asked them (off the record) if they themselves had read and understood the book. One got the title all ballsed up and the other said he thought it was 'a dirty book', so I promptly clobbered him with the cliché that there are 'no dirty books, only dirty minds!'

It was no secret that I was hoping police action would be taken against me for publishing the book. A prosecution would generate some terrific publicity—the most eminent literary critic in the world would be accused; one of the oldest publishing houses in Britain would be the defendant and above everything else, there existed a big batch of reviews all praising the work, and more to come. We were bound to win if prosecuted and future sales would rocket.

But we weren't prosecuted. Two weeks after their visit, the detectives phoned me. The senior officer said, 'I have some good news for you, sir. The DDP has decided to take no action against you.' I thanked him, and nearly wept—for disappointment, not for joy!

Jacqueline Susann

Any pen picture of Jackie must inevitably include her husband Irving, because all their long married life they were almost Siamese twins. She was a very brave woman; never once did she—or Irving—ever hint that in the midst of her days death had marked her down. She was a cancer victim but it interfered in no way with her professional work or with her social life. Like so many successful women writers, she too was at heart 'a nice Jewish girl from Philadelphia', wedded to 'a nice Jewish boy from Manhattan'. Irving ranks as one of the best promoters in existence. The two of them wove their lives around Jackie's literary output—they talked of little else. If they hadn't both been such nice persons, they would have been quintessential book bores.

The uxorious spouses of women authors are in a class by themselves but Irving Mansfield's regard for Jackie amounted to something near adoration and his attitude towards her work as a novelist was that of an evangelist towards Holy Writ. I once had a very substantial offer for extracts from one of her novels, but Irving turned it down flat—the condensation would distort the story and especially the 'denoomeant'. With similar finality he rejected an invitation for Jackie to be a guest at the luncheon Foyles gave for Morecambe and Wise when we published their book.

Ben Perrick, the genial major domo of these famous literary lunches, heard that Jackie was in London and he asked me if I could bring her along as a top-table guest. But Irving wouldn't hear of it. 'If my Jackie isn't number one, she attends no functions,' he declared. 'She plays second fiddle to no one.'

And she didn't go. It was, perhaps, the first time an author had declined a Foyles' invitation.

Greater love hath no man!

E. Hayter-Preston

A 'literary' journalist in the tradition of H. W. Massingham, J. L. Garvin, J. A. Spender, W. T. Stead, St John Ervine, W. N. Ewer, Spencer Leigh Hughes, etc., Hayter-Preston for years wrote the brilliant Vanoc articles—which alone would have made the *Sunday Referee* famous. 'Ted' could write engagingly and knowledgeably on almost any subject under the sun. He was equally expert and authoritative in writing about art as he was in commenting on the human comedy. He possessed a wonderful vocabulary and he made words sparkle.

From the twenties onwards, he knew practically everybody in British literary and artistic circles but commercially—or materialistically—he never made the grade. He was destined to be always the modestly paid scribe instead of one of the nation's top writers able to command top fees. But he loved his work and was content to earn 'just enough to live on'.

One day the chief of a major film company asked me if I could find him a 'literary genius'—one who could assess books, manuscripts and ideas submitted as filmic material and on whose judgement the company could implicitly rely. 'I've got the very man,' I told him, and I arranged for Ted Preston to meet him. Before the interview Ted asked me what sort of fee should he propose. 'What have you in mind?' I queried, out of sheer curiosity. 'Well, as it is a part-time job I think £500 a year would be reasonable.' 'You crazy idiot,' I shrieked. 'Talk like that and you're dead! These are big

people; they think big so you talk big. The minimum pay must be
£3,000 a year.'

He was overwhelmed. Never had he earned a retainer like that.
But he got the job and the salary without demur.

Isidore Ostrer

He looked like a poet; he spoke quietly like a poet and as a matter of
fact he actually wrote poetry. But no fame came to him as a poet.
This refined, soft-voiced retiring little man was, in real life, a great
commercial tycoon. In films, in banking, in industry, in newspapers, in property—he won great renown. In the ferocious world
of big business, he was accounted a financial genius and he was an
economist and monetarist of outstanding ability. Inevitably he
became a millionaire but with this differentia—he was a generous
millionaire! I am positive he would have been generous without his
millions for he possessed that rare quality of being an innate, instinc-
tive giver, even in small things. I enjoyed his friendship for many
years, right up to the time in fact when he died in Cannes.

Few people knew him as intimately as I did and only a select
number merited his confidence. He was a great naturopath and
devised his own dietary system which no doubt prolonged his own
life; he was nearly ninety when he died. His unique gift as a healer he
had acquired from a long association with the pioneer naturopath
Dr Josiah Oldfield. And it was with these skills that Ostrer was able
to save the life of his devoted wife.

This is the story he told me. One dreadful day the doctors
informed him that his wife had contracted cancer and had only a
short time to live. With faith in his own curative abilities, he vowed
he would cure his wife's grave malady. He thereupon decided to
liquidate most of his British assets quickly, and without reservations. 'I could have got enormous prices for some of the
Gaumont-British cinemas and sites,' he once confided to me, 'but I
wasn't the least concerned with money. All I wanted to do was to get
Rosalind to South Africa as quickly as possible and begin the cure.'

They already had a home in the land of perpetual spring, and that
is where they went to defy the doctors' dire prognosis. For many
months Ostrer and his wife virtually isolated themselves from all
social activities and contacts so that the strict therapeutic regimen

which he had devised for his wife could be meticulously carried out. Gradually, her health improved and it seemed as though the millionaire medicine-man's faith and skill were being rewarded. Came the day when Ostrer was satisfied that his wife's malady had regressed and he brought her back to England for examination by the greatest specialists. She underwent rigorous tests, she submitted to minute investigation and scrutiny and at the end of the ordeal she was pronounced completely free of a disease that formerly had been considered irreversible.

To Isidore, the rehabilitation of his wife was a far greater achievement than any of the mighty commercial enterprises which he created in his lifetime.

Louis Stanley

Formerly a Cambridge don, Louis is a versatile writer on a variety of subjects from golf to grand prix car racing. His very lively pen is supplemented by some fine camera work and everything he does reflects the tremendous physical energy which 'Big Louis' has at his command. He works anything up to fifteen hours a day and travels hundreds of thousands of miles every year on the grand prix circuits, where he is as well known and as permanent as the chequered flag itself.

During his early married life he carried out an investigation into his wife's financial stake in her family business of Rubery Owen, the vast engineering company, and he discovered that what had been considered her modest 'interest' in the firm really amounted to a major share of the entire equity. After immense labour and scrupulous enquiry, he established his wife's financial holding and *locus standi*, and eventually took an active part himself in the racing car activities of the company, involving huge expenditure. He and his wife, Jean, attend every grand prix throughout the world.

Appalled by the mortality rate among racing drivers, due mainly to lack of immediate medical aid on the track, Louis invented and launched the first full-scale mobile hospital capable of dealing on the spot with every kind of serious casualty. It was an immediate success; every circuit installed one and up to date it has saved many valuable lives. It is now in general manufacture for civilian purposes and orders from the Third World emergent nations are pouring in.

Louis's company (Stanley BRM) was recently awarded the International Gold Medallion for export, and Louis himself received an individual award for 'exceptional meritorious services to exports'. Great things are expected from his own Formula One racing car driven by Larry Perkins.

Louis's splendid contribution to motor racing (he has written many books on the subject) richly warrants him a place in the honours list. It is long overdue.

Elizabeth Harrison

A sweet, good-time glamour girl, who turned literary after a stage career, she jumped on to the show biz book band-wagon on the strength of her successive marriages to two film-stars—Richard Harris and (by extension), Rex Harrison. Hubby Rex had already been 'dealt with' in volume form by another wife—Lilli Palmer—but neither ex-spouse told anything not already known or worth knowing about Sexy-Rexy. Life with Richard was also protected by the libel laws. So the book—like many similar 'apocalyptic' promises—was a bit of a non-book and consequently almost a non-starter in the literary hit stakes.

Leo Rosten

Undoubtedly the Mark Twain or Stephen Leacock of Jewish humour, he knows by heart every Yiddish joke ever invented. At the drop of a yarmulka he will tell you five hundred, unless stopped by the collapse of his auditor.

Garrulous, loquacious, talkative—all the adjectives of speak-speak, apply to Leo, but he's always interesting if you have the stamina. Do humorists possess a sense of humour? Lunching with Leo in New York soon after I published his record breaking success, *The Joys of Yiddish*, he told me about the fantastic fan mail he received. And the remarkable thing about these letters, he revealed, was that the majority came from non-Jewish readers! Never able to resist a pun, I remarked, ' "The Goys of Yiddish", as you might say.'

But Leo, apparently, was not amused!

Dame Vera Lynn

A sweet singer with a sweet nature who, starting from Cockney sing-alongs, warbled her way to fame and fortune. With a plaintive, pitch-perfect voice that deftly exploits the old-time music-hall nasal slur, Vera sits on a throne once occupied by another nation's sweetheart—Gracie Fields. And like many another celebrity, she is ably managed by her astute lawyer-husband, Harry Lewis. No breath of scandal seems to have wafted into Vera's life, which probably explains why her autobiography appealed to only a small portion of the millions to whom she has endeared herself.

Peter de Polnay

A cosmopolitan, widely travelled writer who once hit a literary 'six' right out of the ground, but during an innings which has now lasted over thirty years he has never repeated that smashing stroke!

After his success with his non-fiction opus, *Death and Tomorrow*, he settled down to write novels and now regularly produces two a year—with every prospect of maintaining this scoring rate for years to come! A real 'professional', this urbane middle-European is cerebral, imaginative and highly original. His books get consistently favourable reviews and if good press notices could sell books, he would be in the money. He lives contentedly in Paris like a Bohemian.

He once supported me enthusiastically when I used his latest novel (many years ago) as a gimmick at the British Book Fair (an abortive attempt to steal Frankfurt's thunder). I put up a big money prize for the visitor to the Fair who could suggest the best title for de Polnay's new novel, an outline of which was printed on the free entry form. It attracted a lively response and de Polnay made the final choice from among thousands of entries.

A co-operative author is a publisher's delight.

Dame Anna Neagle

One of the nation's favourite and enduring stars of the stage, musical comedy and films. Like another of my authors (Sheilah Graham), Anna began her career as one of Charles Cochrane's 'young ladies'. But her biggest role in life was as Herbert Wilcox's 'young lady'. Never did a husband worship a wife like Herbert did Anna. He not only 'promoted' her but he wove a protective cocoon around her so that his beloved and lovely Anna should not be contaminated by the cruel world! He even refused to let her see any press review that was the least bit unfavourable to her.

Perhaps over-protection takes away some of the spice of life. And because her career was 'un-spicey', Anna's autobiography failed to hit the jackpot. Like the queenly character she so brilliantly portrayed, the public 'were not amused'.

Another brave lady who concealed from the world a dread malady that afflicted her once, and which she completely vanquished.

24

Interlude With Menachem Begin

He is a slightly built man: but so was Lloyd George; he lacks inches—like Napoleon did; in a crowd he would be passed over without comment as no doubt Hugh Gaitskell might have been—swarthy and heavily bespectacled he would, in a synagogue, be the look-alike of scores of other congregants.

His English is good but strongly accented and his speeches always read so much better than their oral delivery. He writes intelligently and there are biblical overtones in what he says.

That is a biographical 'quickie' of one of my authors—Menachem Begin—who is today Prime Minister of Israel.

He reached his political eminence the hard way. He literally fought for it as indeed he fought for the deliverance of his homeland.

When I first met him in Israel soon after I had published his book—*The Revolt*—in 1953, he was living modestly in a small Tel Aviv apartment with his amiable but somewhat retiring wife. He had no palpable political power but he was still one of the most famous men in all Israel and it seemed to me that despite his isolation and unobtrusiveness, he was nevertheless the hub of a highly-geared political machine which one day must make a tremendous impact on the destiny of the world's smallest yet most significant sovereign state.

I was not impressed by his mien nor by his expressed views on current affairs. Anything less like a 'statesman' or the leader of a powerful underground movement would be difficult to conjure. In his homely parlour surrounded by a group of indeterminate but obviously 'dedicated' people, he most certainly did not emit the aura of anything resembling 'Israel's Man of Destiny'. But in no way did this detract from my long-held admiration for what he had done as the leader of the Irgun Zvai Leumi and of the many brilliant declarations of his unexceptional political beliefs. I was deeply incensed to find that wherever I went and with whomever I spoke in Israel, there was little but ridicule, contumely and contempt for Begin, the erstwhile leader of those Jewish patriots who had wrested the Homeland from the mandatory power. Some people denounced him as a 'fascist' and made much play with his alleged motorcade of jack-booted young followers who were 'trying to emulate Hitler's tactics'.

This defamation was I think inspired by some official Zionists and the top-brass of the Haganah forces, but it was almost universal and the calumny had even reached England, where Begin's name was vilified by countless people who had probably never seen him nor knew the true story of the Irgun's valour and sacrifices.

I had the greatest difficulty in finding a printer who would take on the production of Begin's book. It was refused by two leading firms with whom I did a lot of business. They said Begin was an enemy of Britain (wholly false) and that publication of his autobiography, which was critical of the Establishment, would give offence to the British authorities. I was under considerable pressure to drop the book. For in those days of paper shortages, printing restrictions and production economy the Government had undeniable sanctions readily available if called upon to deal with a recalcitrant publisher, just as they have today in dealing with firms who defy the wages policy. All of this increased my determination to print the book. It appeared in the summer of 1951 after Ivan Greenberg (a former editor of the *Jewish Chronicle*) and I had spent many weary hours trying to make the manuscript 'fail-safe' and to sanitise many glaring libels. The translation was done from the original Hebrew by another of my authors – Samuel Katz – and in spite of our combined efforts and vigilance, a writ for libel was slapped on us within a few weeks of publication!

Begin and others in Israel implored me to fight the libel case (it concerned the untimely death of the guerrilla leader Abraham Stern). They told me they had a wealth of evidence to refute the complaint but the thought of getting witnesses over from Israel and of trying to defend so-called Jewish terrorists before a British jury was too terrifying a prospect.

206

I had to settle the case out of court. But that was the only serious repercussion to my publication of *The Revolt*. And to emphasise what some British Jews thought about Begin (twenty-four years before he became Premier), the organ of British Jewry (the *Jewish Chronicle*) not only refused to review the book but they refused to accept any advertisement concerning it. I told the editor (without mincing words) that he was exceeding his duty as a responsible journalist in censoring a book that was an important historical work. He was adamant. Last year (1977) I again wrote to the editor, this time reminding him of his ban on Begin (twenty-four years ago) and asking him to publish a long-overdue retraction. But he was still adamant. He promised to 'wait to see' what Begin would do as Premier!

The hostility of many British Jews to Begin still persists, and strangely enough it comes mainly from that type of Jew who bends over backwards to avoid offending the Establishment. When Begin and Katz planned to come to England in 1972, there was a howl of protest from certain quarters. It was led by—of all people—a Jew, one Gerald Kaufman (today a Labour junior minister) and at that time a journalist on the anti-Begin *Jewish Chronicle*. But happily the Government was not to be influenced by Gentile or Jewish objectors. My friends, Begin and Katz, were duly permitted to come to England and I took a dig at the protestors in a contribution to the *New Statesman* headed 'The Begin Beguine,' which said in part:

It is lamentable but true that within some sections of the Jewish people the ghetto spirit dies hard. Unfortunately, there are still those who cannot rid themselves of the fallacy that the role of the Jew is to be history's professional martyr. They continue to believe that persecution and oppression is the Jewish destiny, so that when some obscene tyrant decrees that his final solution is the total extermination of Jewry, they are ready to go gentle into the night of unspeakable degradation and ignoble death. Thus, within living memory there occurred the ghastliest massacre in all history wherein millions of human beings went meekly to the gas chambers and incinerators with rarely an attempt to sell a life for a life.

It has always been my view that the deeds of the Jewish underground in Palestine afforded the first positive proof in centuries that, at long last, the Jew was prepared to fight back and to stand on his own two feet. The merchant princes and generous bankers were ready to give money to build the national home, but now there had arisen dedicated young patriots ready to give their lives. And that, after all, is surely the only way by which any oppressed minority has ever achieved freedom or statehood. This is an inescapable historical truth, however much we might abhor the violence, horror and bloodshed that is inevitable. I am perfectly certain, in my own mind, that but for the heroism, and sacrifice of the young lions of Betar, the Irgun, Lohame Herut Yisrael, Ha-Shomer, the Haganah, Orde Wingate's legions, and all other pioneer militant revolutionaries it is unlikely that a sovereign State of Israel would exist today. Indeed, it is conceivable that some mandatory power might still be ruling the country.

What these freedom fighters did above all else was to give the world a new image of the Jew. He was no longer the trader, the entrepreneur, the scholar or the financier. He had emerged as a truly formidable fighter. And who will deny that this Maccabean spirit which they had miraculously revived became, in turn, the inspiration of the new generation of Israelis who fought three victorious wars and who brought into being a daring and valiant brand of air-warriors the equivalent in every way of 'The Few' who had saved our own nation from defeat thirty years ago.

For these reasons alone we should not denigrate either Begin or his underground movement. To brand them as merciless terrorists and irresponsible killers is to make a mockery of patriotism, liberty and national honour. One day the audit of history will redress the balance of events and put them into their true perspective. But meanwhile it is the duty of us, who are witnesses of the contemporary scene, to try to keep the record accurate and to counteract public hysteria with the antidote of sober truth.

Fate and circumstances ordained that a gentle, kindly, selfless man should lead a rebellion against stupendous odds and so pave the way for the founding of the Jewish National Home.

Historic irony may decree that the same fighter shall now fulfil the role of Peacemaker and succeed where so many have so signally and consistently failed.

Shortly after Begin became Prime Minister of Israel a wave of pessimism threatened to engulf the various efforts to establish peace in the Middle East. It was widely feared that with a notorious 'hard-liner' in charge of Israel's destiny—plus the collapse of Kissinger's shuttle diplomacy—a new outbreak of hostilities was inevitable. There was, in addition, a notable change of heart in the White House—where Carter, hitherto well disposed towards Israel, appeared to be playing 'footsie' with the Russian bear who was licking his wounds after his Middle East failures. The situation was depressing and as it began to stalemate I decided to chance my arm on a letter to *The Times* with a rather drastic proposal. I boldly suggested that Begin should promptly offer to meet Sadat on Egyptian territory for the express purpose of talking peace! I put words into Begin's mouth. 'Come let us reason together', I had him saying to Sadat, 'are we not semitic brothers, worshipping a common ancestor? Why should we kill each other and waste our substance on guns and armies? Our two nations have given so much to the world. Why don't we combine our talents and make the whole Middle East the mighty power that once it was? We don't need other people to tell us what to do or 'arrange' a peace for us. We can do it ourselves in a man to man talk as equals. Our two nations will rejoice in the desire for peace.'

After this flight of rhetoric I made no bones about the fact that both Egypt and Israel were on the verge of bankruptcy, the one limping along on the bounty of the oil sheiks, the other dependent on the largesse of the Diaspora Jews. Therefore the need for an early peace was paramount.

I showed the letter to an Israeli friend. 'Begin would never buy that', he pronounced. 'You are giving the Palestinian Arabs a rope to hang the Jews with. It's crazy.' Evidently the Editor of *The Times* thought so too. He never published the letter, but he wrote to say it had 'interested' him. Six months later Sadat and Begin were literally dancing the 'Hora' together!

25

Interlude Valedictory

I suppose this is the appropriate plateau in the book where the author looks back on what he has written and, if he is reasonably satisfied he has said all that needs to be said, then he must be ready to sign off.

On a re-reading of the narration it would seem that what I have really done is to interview myself and since from my journalistic days I have been an experienced interviewer, I must assume the job has been sensibly carried out.

But before signing off there are a couple of conceptual points I would like to make. One concerns the portion of the book dealing with Germany's war-guilt. There may be some readers who feel I might have overplayed this a little. Let me therefore say at once that while in my wide experience I have looked upon much that was nightmarish and evil—including witnessing the execution of a murderer—nothing has ever moved me more profoundly than the monstrous obscenity which is now euphemistically called the Holocaust. Even today, over thirty years after the events, I am still unable fully to realise that civilised human beings murdered in cold blood over six million innocent and defenceless men, women and children; that gas chambers and crematoria were specially constructed for that fell purpose; that all the roads of German-occupied Europe once led to the charnel houses; that those well known horrendous photos of striped 'zombies' wandering mindlessly around the concentration camps were really pictures of people who were once exactly like you and me.

Millions like them were rounded up, tortured and then put to ignominious death by uniformed Germans (why sanctify them as soldiers?) all eager and ready to do the slaughtering in the sacred name of the Fuhrer and the Third Reich. This, the foulest and most stupendous crime in all history, was actively carried out by millions of 'cultured' Germans and condoned by the silent inaction of millions more—the entire nation, in fact. Apart from the genocide itself the quiddity must have destroyed the religious faith of millions of people the world over. Where was God in all this? It must have convinced millions more that human life is not sacred as we were led to believe, and that men, in given circumstances, turn quickly back into beasts. It also shattered the idea that there is a divine justice; that there is an inevitable and condign retribution for mass wickedness.

Is it now some sort of macabre cosmic joke that the nation which perpetrated the most loathsome and revolting atrocities in all mankind's bloodstained story should have risen from its depravity within a very short time and become today one of the most prosperous nations on the face of the earth? And isn't it irony gone mad that a vanquished nation can now offer to lend money to its impoverished victors? A few years ago André Malraux said there was a world-wide conspiracy to forget—and forgive—the crimes Germany had committed. There is indeed a school of thought which says the Holocaust is a myth!

But because the Germans (I am unable to differentiate between a Nazi and any typical middle-aged German) made a mockery of our most cherished human values; because they destroyed belief; because they glorified inhumanity; because they substituted hate for love; because their creed regarded mercy as weakness—because of all these things I will never forgive them.

Some fellow publishers—especially in America—think I dislike many *émigré* publishers who set up business here simply because they are Germans. This is not so. I personally rescued a great many Germans fleeing from Hitler. I admire all the Continental refugees who have built up various new businesses from scratch—I actually physically helped an *émigré* publisher (who is now established and well known) to get on his feet when he was almost failing. The ones who I dislike are the many yellow-bellies who rushed back to their 'beloved' Germany when the blood-bath was barely over eager to do business with their erstwhile persecutors. This was a supreme example of the 'arse-licking' which I have so vehemently con-

211

demned in all other spheres of life. I despise 'creeps' of all kinds and races—German, British, American, Jewish, and black, pink or white. God knows the woods are full of them. No doubt a lot of other people despise creeps but (unlike me) they never say so and thus are candidates for the creep label themselves. (See Appendix No. 1).

The other point I would like to make is that in these memoirs I have not been too forthcoming about my personal life. Such information, I know from my peep-hole journalist friends, seems to be a source of perdurable delight to their readers. Well, the reason is simply that—apart from my professional life—I have lived a normal, rather uneventful existence. As a young man in the twenties and thirties I did all the things young men were expected to do in those times—I lived it up; I raced cars at Brooklands; I flew aeroplanes; I skied (I was one of the first 'aquaplaners', the forerunner of water-skiing)—I bought my suits at Kilgour and French; I became a Freemason and a Rotarian; I made trips round the world; I lived in Mayfair most of my life; I possessed four Rolls-Royces (in succession) and I never lacked funds (my own).

I have been wedded to the same woman all my married life; I have two sons, one daughter and two grandsons (with parental pride I think the whole family could hold their own against all-comers for good looks and good style). The sons are in publishing and my daughter has written over twenty children's books. My two brothers are journalists. None of us has ever been 'in trouble' as the saying goes, which may be unremarkable but nevertheless satisfactory—at least so far as Scotland Yard is concerned! So that must suffice for the purely personal and social background of the author—except perhaps for this final observation. I have passed into my middle seventies with perfect health and in full possession of all my faculties. Is there a suitable longevity recipe involved here? Indeed there is. The Talmud supplies it.

> Two things doth prolong thy life;
> A quiet heart and a loving wife.

It so happens that I have been blessed with both!

When in 1939 I bought the very old-established publishing house of W. H. Allen from Wingfields, the auditors and accountants, I did so with my own capital and I never sought or needed what is called 'City Money'.

I nursed it through very difficult times and it climbed consistently and bravely through all the divisions to reach the first league. After about twenty years of profitable trading and steady progress, I turned my thoughts to certain current trends in business which had to do with 'conglomerates', mergers and take-overs and since in those days no 'capital gains tax' plagued the independent proprietor there were obvious attractions in the idea of an 'outright sale'.

Independence in business is a noble aim but it butters no parsnips. Nevertheless, the prospect of sacrificing one's independence after so long a run 'on one's own' was a little scaring. The happy solution would be to sell and yet preserve complete autonomy and continuity of management. Part of my commercial philosophy was that if you are going to join anybody, you may as well pick the biggest—in business 'big is beautiful'.

So I cast around and my choice fell on Doubledays of New York, the biggest trade publisher in the world and a house with whom I already enjoyed a very close association. It therefore wasn't difficult to open *pourparlers* with this fine family concern and I found the principals quite receptive to the idea of buying a well-established British company which would retain complete autonomy in its affairs. Once upon a time they actually owned a British company, the well-known firm of Heinemann, and quite recently they had been in negotiation with another English house but nothing had come of it.

My timing was therefore good and it wasn't long before the preliminaries were disposed of and the stage set for the sealing of a formal offer to purchase. But the scenario for the 'formal offer' couldn't have been more informal. It was actually consummated in the luxurious surroundings of the Four Seasons restaurant on East 52nd Street, a stone's throw from the Doubleday offices. Present at the unusual (in the circumstances) venue were John Sargent, president of Doubleday, Joseph Marks, vice-president, and myself. We were all close friends of long standing. We had a delightful meal in

213

the course of which we 'came to terms'—Doubleday and Co. Inc. of New York would buy W. H. Allen & Co. Ltd of London for £200,000, in the year 1961.

There is a delicious headnote to this memorable transaction. It was actually recorded, dated and signed on the back of a book of matches supplied by the restaurant!

Here, below, is the actual historic 'document' reproduced

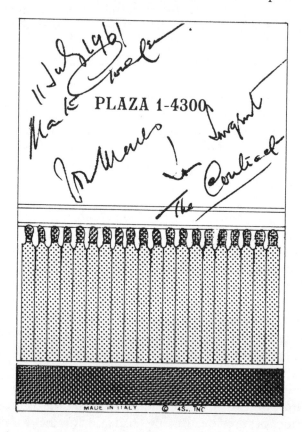

I have heard of a deal being registered on the back of a restaurant menu but I think the 'book-match' background must be unique—certainly it was highly appropriate for a book deal!

The subsequent formalities of the take-over were conducted in London. Acting for me was a very astute young solicitor, name of Eric Levine, who, many years later, was destined to hit the news headlines as a result of his association with his client Sir James Goldsmith.

Levine was then a partner in Paisner & Co., my legal advisers.

Before the sale of the business took place, I had sought legal sanction to split the equity of the company into five equal parts so that the eventual proceeds would be distributed equally as between my wife, my three children and myself. It was my wish that I would like to have the pleasure of seeing my family enjoy the benefits of the business while I was still alive. Too often I had witnessed instances where children waited more or less impatiently for the 'old man' to die to see how much they had been left!

It was a splendid business deal in every way. My company was to be the focal point in Britain for a big expansionist scheme that Doubledays were planning in Europe.

I was seconded to the American side of the business in New York and there I enjoyed the happiest relations with the Doubleday 'top brass' (John Sargent, John O'Donnell, Milton Runyan, Nelson Doubleday and Paul Feffer) and all the editorial people from Ken McCormick, Lee Barker, Sam Vaughan, Maggie Cousins, Bob Banker, Walter Bradbury, Ed Fitzgerald, Irv Goodman, Betty Prashker, right down to the junior editors and editorial assistants. The company's offices in Park Avenue are among the most sumptuous in American publishing.

Doubledays was then—and still is—a very prosperous publishing house. Its share capital being entirely a family holding, the annual profits are private but they are invariably exceedingly substantial.

For eight years the merging of the two companies went along happily and then, as often happens in big business, there was a change of pace in general policy. For some time negotiations had been going on between Doubledays (who owned the prosperous Literary Guild of America) and W. H. Smith & Sons, the world's largest booksellers, concerning the launching of a major book club in Britain under the joint aegis of the two companies. As the scheme was on the verge of completion it occurred to Doubledays that by owning a British publishing house they might run into problems in the development of the new book club. The core and crux of the book club operation is that the organisers buy their material from the various individual publishing houses and it was felt that if one such house was actually owned by a partner in the book club project, the position could become invidious.

It was therefore considered prudent to shed W. H. Allen, but instead of putting the firm on to the open market (as well they might), Doubledays very generously offered to sell the company back to me at a non-profit price.

The transfer duly took place, and back in London in 1971 I at once proceeded to re-structure the financial and corporate substance of the company. I took into partnership with me an old friend, Ralph Yablon, a highly successful industrialist and bibliophile and so once again the venerable publishing company was wholly in British ownership and enjoying complete independence. The reversion—unique in British publishing history—was acclaimed in the press and I personally received congratulatory letters from fellow publishers.

Business seemed to improve dramatically under our own steam and the profit outlook was distinctly encouraging. I had a splendid staff and as a result of my long residence in New York I was *persona grata* with American publishers' agents and authors to such an extent that I had access to much of the best publishing material from New York. It became something of a legend that as a 'talent scout' I had few equals. The facts speak. Of all the books published by the company, eighty per cent were my procurements and a good half of them came from America.

The publishing wind seemed to be set fair when one day I got an urgent person-to-person telephone call from New York. A publisher, whom I knew, had called to ask point blank if W. H. Allen was for sale! The answer was of course 'no' but my friend replied that the offer he had in mind (from a famous conglomerate) might prove to be irresistible. You can't sell a publishing business over the phone, particularly if it isn't even for sale, so I told my caller I would meet him and his connection in New York in two weeks' time on my annual visit. I could then judge just how 'resistible' the offer might be.

I told my co-directors about the transatlantic call and they were less than enthusiastic. The general view was that we should stay as we are.

My New York meeting was an eye-opener. The prospective

buyer was one Walter Reade Jnr, the head of a multi-million combine which, among other things, owned a chain of prime cinema
locations in New York. The Walter Reade Organisation was
unquestionably well regarded and prosperous corporation. I
found Walter extremely likeable and easy to be with even though I
sensed immediately he was the charming super-con-man type which
one so often found at the head of a conglomerate in America. But his
offer was certainly in the 'irresistible' realm. He wanted his company to branch out into England where he already had film interests.
He was being advised by Matt Huttner, a successful New York
publisher whom I knew well, and there seemed to be the makings of a
good merger on extremely attractive terms. One thing was assured if
we joined forces; we would retain our identity and our autonomy.
Walter knew nothing about publishing and he didn't want to. He
relied on his friend, Matt, who in turn had complete confidence in
me and my colleagues.

The subsequent deal was negotiated by Hill Samuel and we were
to sell part of the equity for a substantial cash-down payment with
further annual payments—a sliding scale based on the performance
of the company. If we continued current progress Reade one day
would have to pay out well over a million pounds! The prospect
delighted him. And so another merger marked another milestone in
the history of W. H. Allen.

The new regime was launched with a lavish, well-attended party
at the Savoy and much valuable press publicity resulted. It had really
got off to a good start and no one in the company had any regrets
about the deal we had made. Once again business was buoyant and
we looked forward to the day when we could reap the harvest of the
accrued balance of payments. It was a pleasing prospect to all
concerned.

But later on it became necessary to sever connections with Walter
Reade (who was shortly to perish in a ski accident) and the equity of
W. H. Allen passed into the hands of the British public company
Howard & Wyndham, which held for seventy years an honoured
place in the theatrical profession of Britain.

When in 1976 I relinquished the chairmanship of W. H. Allen I
found pride in the facts that I had built up a fine author-list—always
the strength of any publishing house—and that the 150-year-old

company which I bought and had restarted from scratch in 1939—with a staff of five and a four-roomed office in Essex Street off the Strand—now enjoyed a permanent place among the top ten British publishing houses.

It would be reasonable for the reader—particularly if he is associated with the publishing world—to expect a comment in a book of this kind about the future prospects of our industry—an industry which, if you come to think of it, impinges in some way or other on the life of every literate person in the nation.

It is easy to be dismissive and to simply reiterate the hoary hackneyed commonplace that 'too many books are published'. Of course there are and there always will be, simply because every author and every publisher believes his newest book not only deserves and warrants publication but, since publishing is very much an unpredictable gamble, who is to say that the opus in question may not turn out to be a winner? So one more unit is added to the annual cascade of about thirty thousand new books that compete for places on the attenuated, overcrowded bookshelves in the shops.

But reducing the number of books is not the answer to the trade's major problem. Increasing the number of readers *is*.

This is elementary economics and applies to every product put on the market from margarine to motor-cars. 'Sell more' is the watchword of any commercial enterprise which desires to stay in business, and a principal element in the budget of every successful business—from bananas to banking—is the allocation for 'advertising and promotion'.

When I first went into book publishing such words as merchandising, product, promotion, point of sale, consumer-research, publicity, impulse-buying, eye-appeal, display and similar locutions culled from the trendy vocabulary of selling, were anathema to most of the top practitioners in the 'gentlemen's profession'.

I had, of course, come to these still—not to say stagnant—waters with a background and an expertise gained in the ferociously fought battlegrounds of the 'circulation war' in the newspaper industry. It was perhaps the most competitive and highly-geared promotional activity ever seen in the realm of British commerce. 'Ace' circulation-managers were worth their weight in gold—and were paid accordingly! The cost of adding a single new reader rose steadily to a minimum of ten pounds each (£100 at today's values) and there seemed to be no limits to the inducements—from free sets of Dickens' works to expensive electrical appliances—which were offered to newspaper-readers who might be induced to switch from one journal to another.

The madness to sell more copies which had started in Fleet Street soon extended to the provinces. On one provincial evening paper which I edited we were ingenuous enough to think we could get away with a bare-faced lottery scheme to boost our circulation. We attached a numbering device to our printing presses so that each paper went out bearing an individual number up to the limit of our existing circulation. The scheme was launched with fanfares of publicity and the 'draw' for each day's winning numbers (usually at some factory, office or shop premises) would be made by photogenic young ladies whose pictures would be featured in the published lists of winning numbers. It caught on like a forest-fire and traders of all kinds rushed in to put up additional prizes to be won. The public presentation of the awards caused almost a daily 'riot'. Naturally, circulation rocketed fantastically and the 'small adverts' section (the weakest element in our paper) increased to the point where the adverisement staff simply couldn't cope with the applications. Where once we mustered a forlorn half column, we now filled pages!

The opposition paper was in a panic. It was losing sales and advertisement revenue at a ruinous rate while the whole city was going berserk in the 'numbers racket'. Of course it couldn't last. The rival paper wasn't going to be a helpless spectator of its own doom. So it decided to 'lay an information' before the local magistrates, accusing us of contravening the Lottery Act, and it didn't take the Bench very long to decide that we had perpetrated a game of chance, devoid of any skill, utterly illegal; it must cease at once and we must pay a fine. I am quite sure that had we won our case, the national newspapers would have leapt on to the 'numbers' band-wagon and the circulation insanity would have known no bounds.

But the malady didn't disappear by any means even though the press lords were trembling beneath their coronets at the ever-mounting costs of the endless projects.

Indeed the circulation war was at its height when I arrived in Fleet Street and became a member of the powerful Newspaper Proprietors Association (see Radio Interlude), but within a few years hostilities ceased as a result of sheer economic exhaustion.

As a book publisher I soon put to practical use some of the tricks I had learned and 'the sales philosophy' that I had acquired during my active association with the long, arduous and unrelenting campaign to sell more papers. There were similarities of methodology in both fields but I early realised that the retailers (and wholesalers) handling the publishers' 'products' were considerably less enthusiastic, cooperative and receptive towards their prime suppliers than were the vendors (wholesale and retail) of the wares offered by the newspaper producers.

There was a basic and ineluctable difference in the respective trading terms of newsagents and booksellers. All papers supplied to newsagents were on sale or return—whereas books had to be bought by booksellers on firm sale. I am sure that this has been responsible for the subtle mutual hostility which I have always believed exists between British publishers and British booksellers. The whole structure of the book trade in this country might well have been influenced—to the advantage of all concerned—if we had adopted the American solution of supplying our books on a S.O.R. basis to the bookseller. It has its complications as USA publishers—and authors—know only too well it would have taken the sting out of the bookseller's perpetual grouse that the rapacious publisher has always given him a raw deal.

The consequence is that the British bookseller, with a few notable exceptions, operates under a complete misnomer—a 'seller' of books he certainly is not. A stockist, a distributor, a dispenser he may be, but as a 'seller', in the normal connotation of the word, he doesn't begin to start. There was a time when the bookshop assistant was an informed, knowledgeable person who took a personal pleasure in telling his customers all about what was new and commendable in the literary world.

If it is the fact—and I am convinced it is—that the health of the book trade depends mainly on getting more people to read more books, then obviously the situation cries out for a co-operative effort by all publishers (and booksellers) to create more buyers.

Those who produce the books must propagate—by every means possible—the call to 'read more books', and it must have the back-up of those who retail the books. The thematic idea lends itself to all kinds of effective promotion and if it is really dinned into the minds of the general public that books are good value, that books are an essential part of our cultural heritage, that books will always be unrivalled as pure entertainment, that a good book can be a fascinating companion and so forth and so forth along these lines, then it is a computerised certainty that the sales of books—in every category—will maintain a steady upward curve.

Everything and everybody who can contribute something to advancing the book-buying habit—from the much neglected and under-employed National Book League to the smallest village bookshop—must be encouraged, fostered, assisted and cherished by the book industry as a whole. The flair for publicity which undoubtedly exists in every individual publishing house must be drawn upon to serve and evangelise the corporate effort. The age-long and stupid rivalry among publishers must be defused so all members can participate in a project whose aim is the general welfare of the entire industry and not merely that of the 'big-boys'. There is no other way, if general publishing (except educational) is to survive. The paperback phenomenon, by itself, is not the salvation of the publishing industry any more than North Sea oil is, by itself, the solution to the nation's economic problems. And apropos the paperback book—in the evolution of which I was a pioneer—I might here interject a purely personal and probably disturbing forecast. In a very few years' time there will be no more than five paperback producers in the whole country. The peripheral rest will soldier on until one by one they drop out of the race. Check this prophecy in 1981! I hope to be around. So mark my words!

221

Appendix

Reprinted in the following pages are articles, etc, written by the author and referred to in the text of this book.

The references are keyed to the numbers that accompany the articles.

The index follows the appendix.

1

An article from *Courier*, March 1941

Britannia, Take A Bow!

Let's stop depreciating ourselves; it's not only our policemen who are wonderful. . . .

'The English,' wrote that mordacious critic Carlyle, 'are a dumb people.' He was, of course, writing a hundred years ago so that his use of 'dumb' does not have the same connotation which the Hollywood scriptwriters have since given to it.

Quite plainly he meant that we are a modest people, not given overmuch to talking about ourselves; a people, as he himself amplified it, 'rather stupid in speech'.

Now this legend of the inarticulate, unassuming, self-effacing, unboasting Briton has flourished through the ages and is current in all parts of the globe. It must be conceded too, that we ourselves condone it, and indeed, do our best on all occasions to live up to it. You remember the nickname 'Bumbling Baldwin' that we once bestowed on one of our prize muddlers? It wasn't meant as a symbol of well-merited reproach. It was a term of endearment. The truth is we admire our bumblers, our under-staters, our moderates, because we perceive in them the image of that archetypal Englishman, reserved, restrained, phlegmatic, imperturbable—an enigma to the foreigner and a gift to the cartoonist.

But it isn't a pose. We *are* like that. We were like it when Henry Stanley greeted the lost explorer with his historic laconism, 'Dr Livingstone I presume', and we are like it today when the night-fighter pilot, returning from his rendezvous with death in the starlit skies, casually alludes to his exploit as 'an old gentleman's job'.

This genius for understatement, this studied self-depreciation is more than a trait; it is virtually a creed. We glory in it and extol it. Only the other day I came across this sententious pronouncement on the very subject. 'Our traditional love of self-depreciation must be preserved, for only so can we progress.' The writer, Sir Ernest

Benn, is leader of a quaint body called Individualists (the paradox of 'Individualists' being grouped—and led—is a sticky one), but in this instance his views are by no means individualistic. They are shared, indeed, by vast numbers of Britons, among whom, if we are to judge by his war-time 'understatements', we must number the Prime Minister.

Clearly this blushing-violet mentality has a lot to commend it in a world where the loudspeaker has become a menace, but it can be carried too far, and in my modest and unassuming opinion it has gone too far already.

Understatement is but one jump below under-estimation and the mood that under-rates our own qualities tends to undervalue the motives and intentions of others. It was thus that we grossly under-estimated the Nazi-Fascist peril until it was almost too late.

In a condition of crisis we carry our sense of self-criticism and self-derision to such lengths that it often approaches sheer denigration. Since the war began, for example, we have made bestsellers of books that hold us up to scorn and ridicule (I know, because, God forgive me, I have published such). We have given a ready ear to 'candid friends' from friendly countries who in so many words have called us 'plain mutts'—and worse—and we have even permitted 'friendly aliens' in our midst to shoot off their mouths, quite unabashed (or should it be unbashed!) about our muddle-headedness, our lack of discipline and our pedestrian reaction to imminent perils. In other words we not only delight in running ourselves down; we permit others to rub it in.

All too frankly we have confessed our weakness when we were weak and all too bluntly have we proclaimed our defeats and set-backs when we were taking it on the chin. Metaphorically, we murmured though our bloody and swollen lips, 'Your round, old chap' to brutal opponents utterly devoid of any sporting instinct, because for a long time our self-delusion kidded us into the belief that total war could be fought on Queensberry rules. To vanquished Nazi generals (who ordered our gallant dead to be wired-up as booby-traps) we extended the handshake of the magnanimous victor—together with a nice plate of roast chicken in the desert!

And when success did come our way we tried to soft-pedal it to such an extent that some began to doubt its validity. We have promptly countered any justified cause for rejoicing with the twin bogies: 'beware complacency' and 'dangerous optimism'. Not only do we take our pleasures sadly, as the French say, but we almost apologise for our victories. Truly, as Shakespeare remarked,

> We, which now behold these present days,
> Have eyes to wonder, but lack tongues to praise.

In a nation less inherently virile than the British this enduring indulgence in self-depreciation, this cult of self-disparagement might easily have created a terrific and paralysing inferiority complex.

It is, therefore, nothing short of a miracle that our early reverses in this war, plus our love of undervaluing ourselves, haven't left us incapable of appreciating and seizing the tide of fortune now that it begins to flood for us.

The bread of affliction and woe is poor provender for a victorious people. You can Coué a person into believing his defects are fatal just as surely as you can auto-suggest him into the belief that his will to success is indomitable.

Where, then is the rhyme or reason for persisting in this 'love of self-depreciation'. It is an illusory virtue and I for one refuse to acknowledge it a moment longer. So for the rest of this article I propose to sing the praises of Britain.

Sursum corda.

I will wax lyrical about our astonishing people, our amazing achievements, our prowess, our unconquerable spirit, our abiding humanity, our peerless heroism—yes, even our superb Government.

I constitute myself a hallelujah chorus of one—join in if you feel like it—and every tap on this typewriter shall be a hosanna to our greatness.

Of course, 'it isn't done' but at the risk of giving any Blimp apoplexy who reads it, I propose to do it.

The postulate is that we are the most wonderful nation on earth and in proof of it I will let the record of the past two hundred weeks speak.

Cast your minds back to 1940. In June of that year this nation was virtually out on its feet. Berlin was delirious with joy. 'The greatest battle of all time has ended,' shrieked the Carpet-Chewer. 'Holland and Belgium have surrendered. The British army has been annihilated.'

The civilised world was dumbfounded. Surely this was the end? Make no mistake about it there were heavy hearts, too, in Britain. Rats prepared to leave the ship. I recollect an American (yes, he was an exception), solemnly telling me that he had just had it on the highest authority (he meant Ambassador Joe Kennedy) that the Germans would be here in six weeks and we had nothing to stop them with. So he took a run-out powder and caught the last boat from Southampton. Exit nothing.

But the Germans didn't come.

Then France fell, and—as Mr Churchill has so properly reminded the world in every major speech he has made since then—we stood naked and alone against all our enemies.

But still the Germans didn't come. Oh yes, they tried—and failed. They failed, because though we had only a handful of guns we had a cornucopia of courage and just enough 'self-depreciating' young Englishmen who could fly the finest fighter aircraft (British) in the world. I say 'just enough' advisedly. They were outnumbered fifty to one, but 'just enough' is sufficient when well-armed Britons meet numerically superior Huns.

Kipling, who incidentally can ladle out the 'depreciatory' stuff in describing the English, nevertheless previewed our 'first of the few' when he wrote this:

'God has arranged that a clean-made youth of the British middle-classes shall in the matter of backbone, brains and bowels surpass all other youths. For this reason a child of eighteen will stand up with a tin sword in his hand and joy in his heart until he is dropped. If he dies he dies like a gentleman. . . .'

Well, backbone, brains and bowels—and Spitfires—certainly helped us to repel the would-be invader and, for the second time up to then in this war, he was—to use the resounding Churchillian understatement—'discomfited'.

So the thwarted Boche went berserk and he now tried to blast and burn us out of our island home.

Why 'underestimate' what we went through then? The 'blitz' was hell itself. And why 'underestimate' how we endured it. It was a superb manifestation of human fortitude and mass heroism. Nor need we 'underestimate' what our valour achieved. We saved civilisation. Just that. Pursuing this brief conspectus of events, we find the nation in the months that followed taking more hard knocks—many below the belt—but we didn't squeal and—as witness the survival of America and some others—we didn't surrender. By our example of dauntless courage in the face of unbelievable adversity we inspired and encouraged the rest of the civilised world.

Of course, we muddled and we made mistakes; we were too late and too lax; we tolerated incompetence and exculpated mismanagement. We did all the things which Herrenvolk don't do (or try not to), but we also did all the things which kept us still in the ring, fighting gamely and manifestly unbeatable.

And now today we are on top. We are taking the fight into the enemy's camp; the would-be invader is become the invaded.

But yesterday, we were weak and stumbling; today, we are firm and strong. And we are no longer alone. Those who were preparing to put on mourning for the mighty fallen are now booking seats at our victory banquet!

Consider this metamorphosis. Is there a parallel with it in all mankind's story? Is this not a miracle of national resurgence that would tax the epic skill of Homer himself to narrate? If there be superlatives in the English language that can even begin to appraise this astonishing transmutation, I cannot find them in my dictionary.

Does Britannia deserve to take a bow? If, as Xenophon says, the sweetest sound is praise, we ought to regale her with the minstrelsy of myriads of musicians.

We take too much for granted. Every one of us ought periodically to sit down, take stock of the position and count our many blessings. It is a salutary experience guaranteed to dispel the miasma of self-depreciation and—what is even better—to cure us of a lot of our grumbles and grouses.

We overlook our native genius in so many aspects of this war-effort and we tend—although decreasingly now—to sublimate the virtues of others, not least of all the principal enemy.

Which of us is guiltless of having admired the alleged prowess of runaway Rommel until we had concrete proof that Monty and his 'desert rats' could lick him in everything but sprinting? Which among us has not swallowed and digested the legend of the prodigious efficiency, the fanatical sacrifices of the Germans on their home front, the while we have paid scant attention to the miracles of production and organisation being enacted—albeit unspectacularly—here, before our very eyes.

Suddenly we discover that our erstwhile neglected shipyards have been transfused with new life and they now can turn out ships faster, in proportion to our size, than even America, with its limitless resources, can produce them. Almost imperceptibly we have made the equally neglected 'good earth' of Britain yield abundant food with which to fill our granaries and storehouses, and yet who would think of giving thanks to the farmers and that multitude of humble allotmenteers, the sum of whose combined efforts has made possible this agrarian triumph?

We rightly praise the generosity and altruism of America's Lend-Lease gesture, but let us not overlook our own majestic action in implementing Lord Beaverbrook's wise policy of diverting to Russia vast supplies from our own depleted stocks at a time when we still had to reckon with the threat of invasion. From our little we gave much, which is surely the quintessence of liberality.

By all means let us indulge our inalienable right to excoriate the Government, its administration and all their works, but let us recognise and be thankful for its prescience in so many things which have contributed to our present happy position. They guessed right, for instance, when they plumped for long-range aircraft. We howled for dive-bombers and our fireside strategists and some of our 'air correspondents' advised various other departures, but the higher-ups (itself one of our pet terms of derision) stuck to their production policy of bigger and better bombers, and they have lived to see their perspicacity handsomely rewarded.

True we have been unstinting—if a little belated—in our admiration for Churchill, but it is doubtful if we fully appreciate all his stupendous achievements or stop to think what might have happened had some of his decisions, doubted and criticised by many at the time, been otherwise than they were. In all honesty, do we yet fully realise the emergent wisdom of his grand strategy in 'feeding' the Middle East theatre with what many then thought was unwarranted prodigality, and do we stop to consider the concatenation of decisive events that has flowed from the initial 'gamble' of going into Greece? It would take several books to tell the story of all this, but the point here, is that we ought occasionally to 'appreciate the situation' and by keeping it in perspective trace the miraculous, the almost divinely inspired course which the man at the helm has steered towards the landfall of victory.

Some people are still 'surprised' when a sudden smashing success of our armies is baldly announced. Perhaps 'incredulous' is the proper word. 'Let us not rejoice' they whisper to themselves, mentally. 'You never know. The enemy is still strong, etc. etc.' Always give the enemy that gratuitous boost! And here let me interpolate that our 'military critics' and 'expert correspondents' are the worst offenders in this incessant building-up of the foe. So unsure of themselves are these quill-pen paladins that they always alibi their prognostications with a saving bet on the 'ability of the enemy to hit back'.

Did you ever read an 'expert commentary' on some allied success that didn't 'urge caution' in assessing the results or solemnly warn that 'we must expect the enemy to make a powerful counter-move? Incredulity, caution, doubt—all these things are legacies from our years of 'self-depreciation' and 'under-statement' and the joke is they are invariably unnecessary and unwarranted. Isn't it time we caught the rhythm of success and began to talk and act like the victors we have proved ourselves to be? And we should not only act as victors, we must *think* victoriously, every one of us, because there is a force in mass-thought that may be more potent and more far-reaching than some of us realise. This doesn't imply the assuming of a swaggering, nauseating, bombast. We are so dreadfully afraid of appearing self-satisfied prigs that we cling desperately to our 'cautious approach' and behave like the author, who on the first night of his play anticipates a 'flop' and is bewildered to find he has made a hit success.

The simple truth is that we have achieved more than we think we have, but we hand ourselves cabbage leaves instead of laurels!

Take that cynicism about us being a nation of shopkeepers; we have accepted that insult with dumb resignation. Yet we can glory in the fact that a 'shopkeeper' in our midst arose at a moment of crisis

231

and with no Teutonic ruthlessness, quietly and calmly rationed the nation's larder to such good purpose that our war-time nosebags have always been satisfyingly full. To Lord Woolton we should give praise for achieving the miracle of egalitarianism in our food distribution. Not even the super-methodical Germans have done that much.

And another hoary fiction blown sky-high by the facts of war is that the only great scientists are foreigners with unpronounceable names, and the only real inventors are American technologists. Well, in both these fields—believe it or not—Britain leads the world. The full story of radio-location, degaussing, and a host of other inventions at present 'hush-hush' will make the name of many a British scientist and inventor live for ever; while in the art of healing and war-time surgery our doctors and researchists have performed wonders that posterity will acclaim.

My anxiety is to hand them bouquets while they can still smell them. And that goes too for the mechanics, the unproclaimed stakhanovites of our munition factories, the blitz-fighters, the seamen, the women workers—in a word the whole P.B.P., which, of course, includes the warriors, male and female, of all services. They make up a nation which has risen phoenix-like through the flames of war, a nation whose deeds have given the lie direct to the traducers who once called us 'a decadent people'.

And there is something else of which we have every right to be proud and which in our anxiety to be 'self-effacing' we too often take for granted. In these last thousand days and more, we have done battle with the foulest thing on earth's uneasy surface, and yet, we have managed to keep our hands and hearts clean. We have shot no hostages; we have built us no Dachaus or Oranienburgs; there is no Lidice to shame our future generations; we have sullied ourselves with no pogrom; no slave labour has produced our weapons of war; and the while we have acquiesced in a measure of regimentation we have rededicated our faith in the democratic ideal. We have upheld the rule of law in our own midst without shooting profiteers or black-marketeers. And to signify our condemnation of military bullies of all kinds, we have jailed a couple of our own soldiers who went 'Prussian' in a prison camp.

These are considerable things on which we dwell insufficiently in our secret hearts, and not by underestimating them, but by contemplating them, shall we draw new strength and new pride in our efforts.

They are glorious things, rendered possible only by the most wonderful people on earth and if in gratefully acknowledging them and lauding them I invite the scoffer to mutter 'Chauvinism' then I am proud to consider myself such a Chauvinist.

I liked writing this article; it's good to think that all our fine deeds didn't happen in Elizabethan days and in any case it was high time we made it plain, to our foreign friends at least, that it's not only our policemen who are wonderful.

If perchance, I have not made it quite clear that this piece was in praise of Britain I will sign off by paraphrasing Dr Boteler:

'Doubtless God could have made a better nation, but doubtless he never did.'

2

Reprinted from *The Bookseller*

The Frankfurt Book Fair

Publishers, authors, agents and booksellers from all parts of the world have now returned to their homes after attending the annual literary jamboree which is known officially—and to some of us a little jarringly—as the Frankfurt Buchmesse.

Over the years the Germans have spent a fortune on building up this international get-together. Hospitality is reputedly devastating in its lavishness, and the parties at the Frankfurter Hof are by now legendary.

What the Germans have set out to do is to make Frankfurt 'the cultural and intellectual centre of the civilised world'—a vaulting ambition, the impudence of which is matched only by the success it seems to have achieved. Surely it must be the supreme irony of our day and age that Germany—of all countries—should have become the Mecca of an annual pilgrimage by the literati of the world. Surely it is a monstrous reversal of all logic, as well as a tragic betrayal of cultural and ethical values.

Should we forget that Germany—which today attracts the writers, the thinkers, the producers and the sellers of literature—is the one country that tried to extinguish the intellectual and literary light of the world? It was Germany that committed the greatest single act of vandalism against the human intellect ever recorded—the official burning of books.

But perhaps the crowning infamy of the German book-burners was the plunder and destruction of the famous Institute of Dr Magnus Hirshfeld. Not only was the lovely building gutted but the irreplaceable life's work of the great scientist wiped out in less than an hour. Reporting the foul deed at the time it occurred, the *Frankfurter Zeitung* (which presumably reported the shenanigans of the visiting publishers in 1960), hailed this outrage as the nation's 'protest' against the 'un-German spirit'.

The literary pilgrims who journeyed to Frankfurt last month were promised by their hosts—some six hundred German publishers—that the 'Buchmesse' would be launched with what is described as 'traditional celebrations'. Taken literally, that might have been a trifle ominous in the light of the foregoing facts!

Let it not be thought that the German publishers and booksellers were entirely innocent during the book-burning period. On the contrary, the lists of forbidden books were printed regularly in the *Boersenblatt fuer den Deutschen Buchhandel* the trade's official organ.

The leading publishers indeed played a leading and ignoble part in the official onslaught against knowledge and learning. I wonder just how many of them glad-handed the visitors to Frankfurt a few weeks ago?

I may perhaps be the only publisher in the Western world who, on principle, stays away from the Frankfurt Book Fair. I have never bought a manuscript from Germany, nor have I ever sold one of my books there.

On 10 May 1933, in the presence of cabinet ministers, university professors and publishers, assembled in the Opernplatz in Berlin, thousands upon thousands of books—the intellectual masterpieces of two centuries—were cast into the flames of a vast public bonfire. It was a 'symbolic act to cleanse the minds of the German people'! Simultaneously in Dresden, Munich and Breslau similar pyres consumed the works of the world's most illustrious writers.

And it was in Frankfurt itself—the town which the Germans now claim to be the 'cultural centre of the world'—where the biggest *auto-da-fé* of all took place. It blazed on the famous Roemerberg in front of the Town Hall, and this act of desecration was led by a very eminent Frankfurter indeed—Dr Fricke, the university chaplain, no less. This cultured incendiary urged the students to hurl into the devouring flames the works of Henri Barbusse, Thomas Mann, Ernst Toller, Lion Feuchtwanger, Stefan Zweig, Freud and scores of other world-renowned authors and philosophers. As the fire was fed with the brain-children of these noble minds, the multitude of ordinary citizens who had come to watch, signified their approval by a mighty chorus of the Horst Wessel song. 'And from these ashes,' proclaimed the evil Goebbels, 'will arise, victoriously, the phoenix of the new spirit.'

I gather that Germany today is the 'best book market in Europe', and my travellers say they could pick up orders worth thousands a year if I permitted them to work this territory. The *émigrés* can have it!

Personally, I am not prepared to take the risk of doing business with someone who may be an ex-book-burner or, worse still, an ex-Nazi. Indeed, when one recalls that it is only a few short years ago that the Germans were behaving like blood-lusting barbarians, is it not typical Teutonic effrontery to boost Frankfurt today as being 'the cultural and literary centre of the world'. And what mass aberration on the part of publishers and authors has encouraged this fraudulent claim? Have Paris, Rome or London nothing to offer culturally or intellectually?

The mighty burden of guilt which Germany carries is sufficient reason for the Bonn Government to pour out money on book fairs and 'culture' propaganda. Her literary status is abysmally low and it is clear that the profession of letters declined in Germany from the day she 'burned the books' and destroyed the writers. Germany, now so avid for the books of other nations, has not produced a single important book or one great new writer since the war. Some seven hundred authors, artists and composers fled from Germany and few ever returned. So Germany, bereft of any literary distinction of its own, now lures the world's writers and publishers to the shrine of culture in Frankfurt. It is rather like holding a wedding feast in a graveyard!

One can understand the politicians, military 'top-brass' and professional do-gooders falling so easily for the ingratiating, carefully contrived subtleties of the repentant and re-constituted Germans, but that the intelligentsia of the world could so readily be deceived and seduced by this Frankfurt caper is almost beyond belief.

3

An article from the *Courier*, March 1944

The 'Good German' Myth

Common sense and a little simple arithmetic explode a fantastic piece of sophistry about the barbarians. . . .

About the time these words appear in print the calendar will be reminding us that the season of 'Peace on earth and goodwill towards men' is at hand. Well, of course, there is today no peace on earth, and precious little goodwill is to be discovered; yet it is appropriate at this traditional period, which enshrines the fellowship of man, to give some thought to a problem that is due for settlement ere another Yuletide comes round. Briefly expressed, the problem is: how are we going to deal with the defeated Germans? Clearly, it is the biggest issue which the world has to face. On its solution depends the answer to the question whether this war is to be but the prelude to another and even vaster holocaust.

The intrinsic difficulties of this formidable problem have now been added to and rendered more complex by the maze of theories, opinions, factions and controversies with which it has been hedged about by writers, spokesmen and politicians of all shades of opinion, from ultra-altruism to para-cannibalism. The very crux and core of the matter is the degree of culpability that shall be apportioned to the German people *as a whole*, and on this topic our rival theorists will quote history, science, Euclid, economics, biology, psychology and even Deuteronomy in support of their arguments. It splits Trades Union Congresses to the chine, it turns simple citizens with names like Jones and Smith into Vansittartites and anti-Vansittartites, and, among other things, it is responsible for the incessant and irrelevant misquotation of one of Burke's more ponderous periods.

And what it all boils down to is just this: are there 'good Germans' apart from Nazis, and if so, how many? It needs no dialectics or polemics to arrive at the answer. Like the whole issue, it calls only for some plain common sense and simple arithmetic. The facts speak. Here is the accountancy of the matter. There were sixty-three million Germans in the republican Reich of 1932. In that year a rabble-rouser called Hitler had the temerity to put up as a candidate for the Presidency against Marshal von Hindenburg. More than thirteen million Germans voted for the upstart. Less than twelve months later the same Hitler was voted into supreme power by the German nation in an election based on universal adult suffrage. In other words, a known political gangster and his trigger-men were deliberately chosen by the German people to rule the country.

That is an ineluctable historical fact. But there is something else. In making their choice the Germans knew precisely, down to the minutest detail, just what they were committing themselves to, and, further, the methods by which the gangster's programme was to be achieved. It was all written down for them. They got the gospel along with the apostles. Perhaps for the only time in his life, Hitler deceived nobody, for not only did he blue-print the destiny of the Dritte Reich but he saw to it that every literate in the realm should read, mark and inwardly digest it. So for six whole years the Germans conditioned their lives on this credo:

'We shall breed a new race, trained to hardness, cruelty, violence; supermen leading masses. On them we shall found a new Reich that will last for a thousand years.' And when the hour struck—on 3 September 1939—to implement this historic mission—not a soul in the Grossdeutsches Reich (now eighty million strong) raised a voice in protest, not even the courageous prelates who had denounced the Nazis' pogroms.

How can it be pleaded, then, that the 'good Germans' have acted in 'ignorance of the law'? They knew every clause by heart.

Now let us apply the same commonsense approach to the fiction about a majority of 'good Germans' being held in thraldom by a minority of Nazi fanatics. According to the experts—the first and last out of Berlin included—there are one million members of the Gestapo and SS legions, that is, one million real three-star vintage Nazis. It is permissible to add at least another 500,000 who make up the civilian-clad Sicherheitsdienst, and of ten million Germans in the armed services not less than fifty per cent must be regarded as unequivocal Nazis, taking the known attitude of prisoners captured as the criterion. Thus, leaving aside the Partei-men in the war industries and the female of the species (some thirty million, by the way) we arrive at a grand total of sixty million Nazi adherents. Who, then, is holding down whom?

But to clinch the matter, let us halve the figure, or better still, water it down to an indisputable two million dyed-in-the-wool hundred-per-cent Hitlerites. Now who are these two million fanatics, ready to commit homicide, fratricide and even matricide in the name of the Fuehrer? Were they imported into Germany from some other planet? Not so. They are Germans born and bred. Ten years ago, before the world knew the name Nazi, these men were the typical Fritzes, Hans, Karls and Wilhelms of pre-Hitlerite Germany, polite to the tourist, happy in their beer-gardens, addicted to nothing worse than carving up masses of liver-sausage. By what legerdemain have they suddenly become killers, sadists and barbarians? And by what process of logic do we assume that these two million, a mighty cross-section of the whole nation, can be essentially different from the millions of their own relatives, kinsfolk and even next-door neighbours? Common sense dictates there can be no difference; things which equal the same thing equal one another. The alleged existence of 'good Germans' and 'bad Germans' is a myth; no such dichotomy is known to ethnologists. Do we divide England up into 'good' and 'bad' Britons? And do not the Germans themselves boast of being 'Ein Volk' within 'Ein Reich'?

But, the still-unconvinced might plead, but what of the German womenfolk? Well, it seems that because there is no feminine gender of Nazi we are apt to assume thirty million German women have no part in Hitler's Reich other than the 'sacred duty' of producing more Nazis. It is a facile assumption. Only a few weeks back Lord Derby, with a lofty sense of the humanities, exclaimed, 'A mother is still a mother, even in Germany'. But is she? Or just a Hitler-Maedchen?

Bill Shirer's little vignette of typical 'Mutterliebe' (mother-love) supplies the effective answer to his lordship. A German mother was in mourning for her airman son, missing, believed killed. One day, friends who had listened-in to the British radio told her that her son was safe and a prisoner in England. Did the mother weep for joy on the necks of her friends? No, this 'good German mother' promptly reported her friends to the Gestapo for listening-in to 'verboten' British broadcasts. Assuredly, the kind-hearted Lord Derby shares the error which so many less-informed Britons make in assessing the German character—the fallacy that the average German is very much the same, under the skin, as the average Englishmen. That is an illusion, or sophistry.

Anyone who has lived in close association with Germans knows that fundamentally the two peoples are poles apart. There is not a single trait, characteristic or quality, either mental or physical, common to both and until that irrefragable truth penetrates the skulls of our national leaders we shall never solve our European problem. It is our misfortune that so many of our diplomats and statesmen have never realised this. Conglomerate masses like British Trade Unionists, reared in the traditions of freedom, fair dealing, the sanctity of the pledged word, and regard for human decencies, lightly assume that similar conglomerate masses in Germany are similarly heritaged. It is a grievous miscalculation.

In the sympathy campaign which the defeated Germans will organise after the Armistice—the vanguard is already at work—they will make great play with this fallacy that the British and Germans are very much akin. They discovered once they were almost blood-brothers of the Russians, and at the moment they are at least 'cousins' of the unspeakable Japs. Not for nothing is the chameleon classified as a reptile! Could there be a greater insult to any nation, at

239

this time, than to link it spiritually or physically with crime-soaked Germany?

When you try to survey—to apprehend fully is declared impossible—the crimes committed by the Germans in the last ten years you feel that not only has the name of Germany been shamed beyond recall but that the very name of Man has been sullied. The supreme question surely, is not so much *who* among the Germans shall be punished but rather *what amount* of punishment could possibly be commensurate with the immensity of the crime. Is there a solitary mitigating circumstance in Germany's record? Even in this, the fifth year of the war, after Germans have filled the cup of infamy to its brim, you might expect some diminution of their brutality, if only from sheer exhaustion. But no, in the penultimate hour of their doom they are unrepentant, nay, readier than ever to murder and to plunder. Rome must be looted; Naples must have its blood bath; the last remaining handful of Jews in Nazified Europe must be pogrommed. And in the case of the Danish Jews, just to show they have not lost their exquisite sense of timing in the art of massacre, the Nazis choose the Jewish New Year as the date for the latest *auto-da-fé*. Have the 'good Germans' raised an eyebrow over this? To their eternal glory and honour the good Swedes have shown that even 'threatened minorities' can cry 'shame'—if they feel like it.

If anybody is entitled to plead for clemency for the vanquished Germans surely it should be the peoples who have suffered most. One has yet to read a defence of the 'good Germans' by a Russian who has had his family butchered and his home razed by the German invader. If Lidice was in Surrey or Yorkshire instead of Czechoslovakia I doubt if we should permit our 'humanitarians' to busy themselves with schemes for 're-educating the misguided Germans'. Had the bodies of burgesses dangled from balconies in Birmingham or Liverpool, as they have in Kharkov and other places, it is doubtful whether we should be inclined, in 1943, to let exiled Germans hold cultural meetings in the Holborn Hall!

Of all the cold-blooded atrocities committed by the Germans there is probably nothing more horrifying than those 'deportations' which they have systematically carried out all over Europe. Deportation is a bland word. It disguises the most monstrous of all cruelties. Whole families uprooted, children literally torn from their parents' arms, and, like cattle, countless human beings herded into trucks and dumped into the tundras of Eastern Europe. Yet comfortable hack-writers in this country (who would be outraged if told to move their homes intact even into the next street) can find it in their hearts to plead not for the victims of these foul inhumanities but for the very perpetrators of such soul-sickening crimes. Truly, he jests at scars who never felt a wound. Could all the waters of the world ever wash away the bloodstains from German hands? One archbishop says the 'mind is staggered and quite unable to apprehend the enormity of German brutalities'. That is nonsense. The mind can apprehend it all—if it cares to face the facts.

I have before me a photograph taken from the body of a dead German soldier. It shows a line of Russian peasants—women and children among them—kneeling beside an open grave and a line of German soldiers taking careful aim at them. It is a mass execution (another glib term), one of hundreds to the credit of the German merchants of death. I invite you to visualise this picture (it is absolutely authentic) and to ask yourself who and what kind of men these soldiers are who can kill, in cold blood, a row of defenceless human beings. And what of the photographer who looked on and snapped the ghastly scene? Did no twinge of pity disturb their trigger-fingers? Did the cries of the frightened children, the wails of the distracted parents, affect them? Did the preliminaries of digging the grave and arranging the victims neatly along the edge tear at their very heart-strings?

Are they a race of sub-men devoid of all human feeling? Not at all. They are young German men, Hans, Fritz, Karl and Wilhelm, etc., who hope one day to return to the bosom of their families in the Fatherland. And remember, there are millions of them. Their trail of blood and rapine stretches from the Pyrenees to the Volga. It must be grand consolation to a Tommy defying death on beaches like Salerno to reflect that what he is enduring is all part of a great and wise plan to 're-educate the misguided Germans'. Fortunately our fighting men are realists. They coined an axiom about the 'only good German' in the last war. It still stands.

When the war ends our first consideration must be for those who have suffered—the victims of the war, not the perpetrators of it. The freshet of sympathy that is welling up in the hearts of 'good Britons' must be directed to the homeless and the persecuted.

Salvation for the Germans must come from within. They must 're-educate' themselves, but the prerequisites, the logical steps in the procedure, must be punishment, repentance and reformation. That is the method adopted in Dartmoor, Sing-Sing and Alcatraz with some success. Why should it be otherwise with German criminals? Unless 'war' is to be accounted an alibi for all wrong-doing, and gangsterism, when it is on the international plane, is it to be regarded as above the law.

The main purpose of this article was to state the case for condign punishment of the guilty nation rather than to suggest the penalty. I know not what retribution the Allied leaders have in mind. If the 'be-kind-to-the-Hun' school have their say, there will, of course, be no real expiation. But to me it makes no difference. I for one will neither forgive nor forget. Retribution is something which rests with me, an individual, who, archbishops notwithstanding, has managed fully to apprehend the enormity of Germany's barbarities. And I have devised my own plan. This is it: I have vowed that for a period of ten years after the war I will have no personal contact with any German who was in Germany during the war years, except he can prove to have been in a concentration camp. The 'good Germans', in my eyes, are guilty of condoning the felonies of their brethren. I will not set foot on German soil during this period of quarantine. Above all, no business dealings. How would I know that the hand offered to me in commercial friendship is not the hand of the poised killer in the left foreground of that massacre picture?

No, as a people the Germans have outlawed themselves. They are beyond the pale for at least a decade. Ten years is little enough time for them to do penance and try to purge their souls—which doubtless they will not. Of course, I realise this is harsh. I realise the economists will call it a 'boycott' and denounce it as such. I realise too that if millions of other ordinary folk, who are particular about the company they keep, were to think and act along my lines, there would be little hope of the 'speedy rehabilitation of beaten Germany so that she might again take her place in the comity of nations'. And realising all that, I rejoice at the prospect.

4

Article in *The New York Times*, 1959

Appraising Germany
British and American Attitudes
On Her Recent Past Contrasted

On my frequent and always amiable visits to your hospitable shores I usually try to appraise the current trend of thought on some major topic and then equate it with the climate of opinion in my own country on the same subject. This can be a very rewarding experience, particularly when there happens to be a vigorous and healthy dissimilarity in our respective thinking.

But never before have I found so wide a divergence of Anglo-American views on a common problem as that which appears to exist on the important and urgent question of Germany—in all its aspects.

The astonishing thing about it is that apparently there is no German problem at all so far as America is concerned. Nowhere do I find any evidence of overt anti-German feeling such as there is in some quarters of England. I get the impression of a general and unquestioning acceptance of accomplished fact that Germany is now your firmly established and estimable ally.

CRIMES FORGOTTEN

So far as I can gather, the awful past is now utterly forgotten by the average American and the memories of Germany's unspeakable crimes have been consigned to the limbo of historical monstrosities, as remote as the Spanish Inquisition.

This negative attitude I find wholly inexplicable, and in the particular case of New York City (with its vast Jewish population) the inarticulate disinterestedness is illogical as well as ironical.

It may surprise your readers to know that in England, where we are notoriously forgiving and forgetful, the issue is viewed rather differently. Although an officially inspired 'don't-be-beastlyto-the-German' campaign is in full swing, there is no overwhelming anxiety on the part of the masses to forget that Germany was responsible, primarily, for two world wars and responsible, exclusively, for the most atrocious massacre in all recorded human history.

Perhaps it is because we in England are a little nearer than you are to the scene and the actualities of the European tragedy that we have not been avid to accept the thesis that piacular Germany—contrite, repentant, chastened and redeemed—has now 'worked its passage home' to the family of nations.

There are many in England who share my own firm resolve never to have any business or social contacts with post-war Germany until there is irrefutable proof that the poison which entered the German soul when it came nazified is now completely and irrevocably eliminated. I, for one, do not believe that by some legerdemain the millions who (by their actions) supported Hitler's infamy or the millions who (by their silence) condoned it, have now entirely disappeared into thin air.

It is less than fifteen years since the renowned German genius for method and industry was painstakingly engaged in the odious business of putting six million human beings to shameful and lingering death. The sheer numerical enormity of this crime is beyond the mind's comprehension, even if one tries to visualise it in terms of a solid unbroken phalanx of doomed men, women and children marching thirty abreast along a Fifth Avenue which stretches for over a hundred miles!

Is fifteen years enough to obliterate all memory of such an abomination? By all civilised juridical standards it takes longer than that for a reprieved murderer to expiate his single crime. What then is the time-span of atonement for six million murders?

It is deplorable but, I think undeniable, that many of those who are so ardent about forgiving and forgetting are by no means motivated by any desire to re-educate or democratise the hitherto misguided Germans. The hatchet buriers are mostly the business men (with an incredibly high percentage of Jewish merchants and ex-refugees) who lead the mad scramble to muscle in on Germany's present astonishing prosperity.

244

5

Article in the *Hull Evening News*

Cheeky Face

(by our Special Reporter)

He was a sturdy little chap but not very big for his twelve years. Indeed his bright alert eyes only just managed to clear the top of the 'defendant's rail' behind which he stood as he stared at the three forbidding lay-magistrates in the juvenile court.

His hair was tousled; he was the possessor of what is called a 'Cheeky Face' and to judge from his firm—almost defiant—stance he didn't seem unduly awed by the oppressive, ecclesiastical ambience of the courtroom.

But his mother was. A typical middle-aged working woman, she cowered, in obvious distress, against the side of the public bench, listening but trying not to hear, what the constable in the witness-box was telling the court about her errant son's 'previous record'.

It was a formidable 'past' as the officer told it, wilful damage to property; pilfering from the penny arcade; persistent truancy and now the larceny of a bottle of Sarsaparilla from an open stall!

As the diapason of his misdemeanours slowly subsided in the echoing courtroom the flicker of a wry smile seemed to wrinkle the cheeky face. But it faded instantly when, in ponderous tones, the Chairman addressed him.

'What made you steal this bottle?' was the slightly fatuous question that travelled the vast distance from Bench to boy. And hardly less fatuous was the answer—'Becos' I wuz thursty'—that winged its way back to the dais of jus-

tice, borne on a ripple of suppressed 'laughter in court'.

Three magisterial craniums converged. There was much muttering, and nodding of heads and then an ominous silence seemed to descend on the proceedings. It was rudely splintered by the Chairman's cold, cultured and concise words: . . . 'an absence of parental control . . . the boy's own best interests . . . probation officer has tried . . . and will therefore be committed for two years to a REFORMATORY'.

That was the one and only word Cheeky Face heard distinctly and it smote him like a blow between the eyes. His little frame shuddered and his wild gaze searched the Courtroom frantically seeking the maternal refuge towards which he always scurried (tough though he was) whenever he was in real trouble.

To normal ears the word 'reformatory' with its overtones of sixteenth-century Protestant zeal may have an impressive sonority but to the bad boys of the back doubles in provincial industrial towns—and to their mothers—it is the very metonym of Doom itself. It conjures up the image of some remote Devil's Island to which wicked little boys are sent by the 'Beaks', there to endure unimaginable punishments and the agony of age-long sunderance from home, parents and companions.

It can strike terror into the heart of the toughest miscreant—or his mother—as now indeed it did to the bewildered youngster and the sobbing woman who both stood on the threshold of the most soul-searing experience of all human emotions—the dread moment of parting. In every parting, says a proverb, there is an image of death.

Fear and panic suddenly gave wings to the limbs of the condemned lawbreaker. The tiny figure scrambled under the rail, leapt across the solicitor's benches and literally flew into the outstretched arms of his mother. For an instant, a trembling little boy, tearful, fearful but no longer tough, had found sanctuary from the pursuing ogre of the Law. But it was a fleeting respite. Inexorable is the pace of retribution.

The mother looked up at the impassive magistrates, 'Don't send him away,' she whispered, 'he's all I've got.'

Uniformed arms gently but firmly unclasped the clutching embrace of mother and son.

'Git 'im below,' barked the case-hardened dock-sergeant.

Then the Court rose. Three wise and learned men went off to their lunch; the policemen made a bee-line for the canteen and a lonely mother shuffled wearily from the tribunal where she had witnessed the administration of Justice. As her oblation to the might and majesty of the Law she had left a wayward little boy whom she had reared so indifferently but yet loved so dearly.

And as this reporter closed his notebook on a routine morning's work he recalled a line from the Merchant:

'Earthly power doth
then show likest God's
when mercy seasons justice.'

6

To the editor of the *Spectator*

British Arrogance

Sir,
As a British subject and one who is immensely and unashamedly proud of his country's history and traditions, I take the strongest possible exception to the gratuitous denigration which informs the article from your correspondent in Bonn. She says we are 'arrogant and crude'; that we must change 'our self-righteousness and arrogance' and that our colonial record does not 'entitle us to feel superior to other Europeans'. And, if these three swift kicks in our imperial pants are not enough to make us wince, she weighs in with this

246

wallop below the belt: 'they (the Europeans) know that they are our equals and in some ways our betters'.

The syndrome of the superman dies hard and your Bonn reporter seems to have been mixing with the germ-carriers in the German capital. Does she seriously suggest that the people who, within living memory, created special death camps wherein millions of innocent human beings (including 950,000 children under the age of thirteen) were shovelled like vermin into incinerators and gas chambers—does she suggest that these are 'our betters'? Or is it those 'superior' Europeans who, a few years ago, capitulated so ignominiously to their enemies leaving the ('inferior') Britons to stand alone in the fight for freedom? Is it these whom we must now regard as 'our betters'? What bloody nonsense!

Your pro-European correspondent then proceeds peevishly to complain that she finds nothing but rudeness when she travels along our country roads in her German car bearing German number plates. It could well be that the appearance of such Teutonic symbols may remind some of our citizens of those other German machines that once appeared over our fair and pleasant land not so very long ago. The latter were certainly our 'superiors' for a while, but inevitably and arrogantly we bashed the daylights out of them—as always—and so made our highways safe and secure for Fräulein Gainham to tootle along in her Mercedes a few years later.

MARK GOULDEN
12 Charles Street, W.1

(Mr Goulden's letter would seem to be a perfect example of the kind of arrogance Miss Gainham was writing about.—Editor, *Spectator*)

7

To the editor of the *Spectator*

Dylan Thomas

SIR,

The number of people who climb on the band-wagon of a celebrity—dead or live—always seem to be in inverse ratio to the number who 'gave him his start'. One would assume from some of the tributes currently being paid to the memory of Dylan Thomas that his work was acclaimed from the very outset of his career. The facts are quite to the contrary, and there appears to be a good deal of misconception about his debut on the literary scene.

It goes back to the time in 1934, when, as editor of the *Sunday Referee*, I had the temerity to initiate a feature called 'Poets' Corner', the purpose of which was to encourage and publish the work of hitherto 'unknown' versifiers. Many a 'knowing' eyebrow was lifted at this curious innovation in a national newspaper, but nevertheless the response, both quantitatively and qualitatively, was quite remarkable. Among the very first entries were some verses from a Welsh reader named Dylan Thomas. Both I and Victor Neuberg (who conducted the feature for me) were so impressed by the outstanding excellence of these pieces that we invited the writer to come to London, and in due course he presented himself at my office looking as unlike a poet as even a poet might imagine. His surprise that his efforts should have merited our interest was only matched by our astonishment that this rather 'bucolic' young man, apparently innocent of any 'literary' background, could have produced such elegant, subtle and intricate versification.

I awarded him one of the modest prizes we were offering and when, later, we published the collection of his poems in volume form, we sent out a number of copies for review, in the hope that our 'discovery' would receive the applause he so richly deserved. But, so far as I can remember, not a solitary critic noticed the book.

Regretfully, it must be recorded, a similar fate befell the other prize-winning volumes which we published and, in due course, I decided to drop the Poets' Corner feature from the paper. It may, however, have served its purpose in some small measure, even though its genesis now seems to have become a trifle snarled up in some of the biographical eulogies that are being paid to Dylan Thomas.

Thus, John Arlott's remark that Thomas's first volume of poems was 'sold outright to a publisher for a few shillings in 1934' is a little patronising as well as slightly inaccurate. Might I remind him, in parenthesis, that if James Thomson had not sold his first poem outright to a publisher for three guineas in 1726, our poetic literature might well have been the poorer for *The Seasons*.

Yours faithfully
MARK GOULDEN

To the editor of the *New Statesman*

SIR,
Just for the sake of the record, may I correct Miss Pamela Hansford Johnson's proffered answer to Miss Kathleen Raine's recent reference to the unidentified 'editor of more than usual discrimination' who first published the poems of Dylan Thomas.

I happened to be the editor of the *Sunday Referee* at the time, and it was I who initiated the feature called 'Poets' Corner' wherein we published the work of unestablished but aspiring poets. I engaged Victor Neuberg to conduct the feature, sort out the entries and provide a critical commentary on the contributions, all of which he did superbly. But the final choice of the prize-winners was my prerogative, and it was my pleasure to select Dylan Thomas for an award. Incidentally, it was also my pleasure to select Miss Pamela Hansford Johnson herself for an award!

I defrayed the costs of the subsequent publication in volume form of Thomas's *Eighteen Poems*, and Miss Johnson's *Symphony For Full Orchestra*, and (as an editor who later became a publisher) I have always liked to think of these 'firsts' as being also my 'firsts' in the field of publishing.

Yours faithfully
MARK GOULDEN

8

To the editor of the *Spectator*

Shining the Ball

SIR,

There must be a great many cricket spectators besides me who would like to know just why a bowler chooses his groin, of all places, as the appropriate spot for rubbing a shine on the ball before delivering it. Surely there must be a less, shall we say, erogenous zone in the human anatomy which could be used quite as effectively for the purpose of imparting lustre to the leather.

The TV cameramen tend to dwell on the zoom frontal shot of each bowler indulging in this vigorous inguinal exercise and watchers of the England–Australia series on television have been treated to endless close-ups of one fast bowler polishing furiously—with both hands—while leisurely walking the forty paces to his starting mark.

To any spectator, unaware that a player was actually holding a cricket ball in his hands, the burnishing performance might be alarmingly misconstrued!

Would not the laws of cricket permit the bowler to use a special cloth for this ball-buffing ritual and so eliminate gestures that are embarrassing, monotonous and—to some people—inexplicable?

An American visitor watching these antics enigmatically asked me if the phrase Test Play wasn't some sort of abbreviation!

MARK GOULDEN

Index

251